The Wordsworth

Book of Dinosaurs

—

David Lambert

Wordsworth Reference

First published in 1983 by William Collins & Son.

This edition published 1998 by Wordsworth Editions Ltd.
Cumberland House, Crib Street, Ware, Hertfordshire SG12 9ET.

Copyright © Diagram Visual Information Ltd 1998.

Wordsworth® is the registered trademark
of Wordsworth Editions Ltd.

ISBN 1-85326-754-6

Printed and bound in Great Britain by Mackays of Chatham PLC.

The Diagram Group

Editors: Ruth Midgley, Elizabeth Pring, Elizabeth Wilhide
Indexer: Mary Ling

Art director: Mark Evans

Artists: Joe Robinson, Graham Rosewarne, Sean Gilbert,
Ashley Haddock, Brian Hewson,
Richard Hummerstone, Janos Marffy, Eitetsu Nozawa,
Max Rutherford, Jerry Watkiss

Art assistant: Neil Coplestone

Book of Dinosaurs

Author	David Lambert

General consultants	**Dr Angela Milner** Department of Palaeontology, British Museum (Natural History), London, England
	Dr Ralph E. Molnar Queensland Museum, Queensland, Australia

Other advisers	**Dr David S. Berman** Carnegie Museum of Natural History, Pittsburgh, Pennsylvania, USA

Professor José F. Bonaparte Museo Argentino de Ciencias Naturales, Buenos Aires, Argentina
Dr Alan Charig Department of Palaeontology, British Museum (Natural History), London, England
Professor Peter M. Galton University of Bridgeport, Bridgeport, Connecticut, USA
Professor Sohan L. Jain Geological Studies Unit, Indian Statistical Institute, Calcutta, India
Dr John S. McIntosh Wesleyan University, Middletown, Connecticut, USA
Dr David Norman Department of Zoology, University of Oxford, England
George Olshevsky San Diego, California, USA
Dr Halszka Osmólska Paleobiology Department, Polish Academy of Sciences, Warsaw, Poland
Professor John H. Ostrom Peabody Museum of Natural History, Yale University, New Haven, Connecticut, USA
Dr Pamela Robinson University College, London, England
Dr Dale A. Russell National Museum of Natural Sciences, Ottawa, Canada
Masahiro Tanimoto Osaka, Japan
Dr Philippe Taquet Institut de Paléontologie, Paris, France
Dr Dong Zhi-ming Institute of Vertebrate Paleontology and Paleoanthropology, Academia Sinica, Peking, China

Members of Staff, Department of Library Services, British Museum (Natural History), London, England

Acknowledgment

The author wishes to thank the following museums for providing details of their collections:

American Museum of Natural History, New York City, New York, USA

British Museum (Natural History), London, England

Buffalo Museum of Science, Buffalo, New York, USA

Carnegie Museum of Natural History, Pittsburgh, Pennsylvania, USA

Denver Museum of Natural History, Denver, Colorado, USA

Dinosaur National Monument, Jensen, Utah, USA

Dorchester Museum, Dorchester, Dorset, England

Field Museum of Natural History, Chicago, Illinois, USA

Geology Museum, Indian Statistical Institute, Calcutta, India

Institut Royal des Sciences Naturelles de Belgique, Brussels, Belgium

Institut und Museum für Geologie und Paläontologie, Universität Tübingen, Tübingen, West Germany

Ipswich Museum, Ipswich, Suffolk, England

Los Angeles County Museum of Natural History, Los Angeles, California, USA

Maidstone Museum, Maidstone, Kent, England

Museum für Naturkunde der Humboldt-Universität, Berlin, East Germany

Muséum National d'Histoire Naturelle, Paris, France

National Museum of Natural History, Smithsonian Institution, Washington, DC, USA

National Museum of Natural Sciences, Ottawa, Ontario, Canada

Natur-Museum Senckenberg, Frankfurt am Main, West Germany

New Walk Museum, Leicester, England

Peabody Museum of Natural History, Yale University, New Haven, Connecticut, USA

Peking Museum (Natural History), Peking, China

Provincial Museum of Alberta, Edmonton, Alberta, Canada

Queensland Museum, Fortitude Valley, Queensland, Australia

Royal Ontario Museum, Toronto, Ontario, Canada

South African Museum, Cape Town, South Africa

Staatliches Museum für Naturkunde der Humboldt-Universität, Stuttgart, West Germany

University Museum, Oxford, England

Utah Museum of Natural History, Salt Lake City, Utah, USA

FOREWORD

This book is a concise, up-to-date key to the dinosaurs – their physical characteristics, behavior, evolution, extinction, fossilization, discovery, and display. Above all it describes all currently known dinosaur genera, one in five of which has been named since 1970.

The author uses simple words, explains scientific names, and shows how these scientific names arose (see page 33). Everyone – from the eleven-year-old to the professional scientist – will find this a useful guide to the most successful group of backboned animals that have ever lived on land.

Dinosaur illustrations are based on reconstructions of skeletons in museums and scientific publications. In addition to labeled illustrations, "field guide" silhouettes, diagrams, family trees, and maps help the reader to pick out at a glance important facts about dinosaur groups and their members.

There are six chapters. Each has a brief explanatory introduction, followed by topics arranged under bold headings.

Chapter 1 (What were the dinosaurs?) tells briefly how dinosaurs were built, how their bodies may have worked, and what kinds of lives they led.

Chapter 2 (Dinosaurs in the making) explains how and when dinosaurs evolved from early reptiles. This chapter goes on to survey the two great dinosaur orders and their subdivisions.

Chapter 3 (Dinosaurs identified) is the core of the book. Its six sections describe all main dinosaur subgroups, their more than fifty families, and their more than 340 genera.

Chapter 4 (Their changing world) briefly describes how lands, climates, plants, and animals changed through the Age of Dinosaurs, and ends with the mysterious disappearance of these animals.

Chapter 5 (Discovering dinosaurs) reveals how dinosaurs' bones became preserved in rocks, and when and where fossil hunters in six continents have unearthed dinosaur remains.

Chapter 6 (Dinosaurs displayed) shows how museums clean and rebuild fossil dinosaurs, and tells the reader where to go to see most of the world's best, and many lesser, dinosaur displays.

The book ends with a list of books for further reading and an index.

The author is answerable for the facts in this Guide, but he gratefully thanks the many experts whose generous advice made the project possible.

CONTENTS

CHAPTER 1   WHAT WERE THE DINOSAURS?

CHAPTER 2   DINOSAURS IN THE MAKING

CHAPTER 3   DINOSAURS IDENTIFIED

CHAPTER 4   THEIR CHANGING WORLD

CHAPTER 5   DISCOVERING DINOSAURS

CHAPTER 6   DINOSAURS DISPLAYED

CHAPTER 3
DINOSAURS IDENTIFIED

These two pages give fuller details of this chapter's sections than those given in the main contents list

Section 1
COELUROSAURS

Section 2
CARNOSAURS

Section 3
PROSAUROPODS

Section 4
SAUROPODS

Section 5
ORNITHOPODS

Section 6
FOUR-LEGGED ORNITHISCHIANS

Explanation of symbols

Here and elsewhere in this book, symbols are used to provide immediate information about different groups of dinosaurs.
In each instance the first symbol indicates the order to which a dinosaur belongs. (For an explanation of how dinosaurs are classified, see pages 32-33.)
Symbols for the two dinosaur orders are:
A Saurischian dinosaurs
B Ornithischian dinosaurs

A second symbol indicates a suborder, an infraorder, or a group of closely related infraorders:
a Coelurosaurs
b Carnosaurs
c Prosauropods
d Sauropods
e Ornithopods
f Scelidosaurs
g Stegosaurs
h Ankylosaurs
i Ceratopsians

CHAPTER 1

WHAT WERE THE DINOSAURS?

People have been uncovering dinosaur bones for hundreds of years. Some of these bones were so large they gave rise to legends of giants stalking the Earth. Later, scientists were able to date and identify the bones more accurately, although it was only in the 1820s that dinosaurs – "terrible lizards" – were properly described for the first time. This chapter looks first at the dinosaurs' great variety. It then studies how these animals were built, how they moved, what they ate, how they dealt with enemies, and how they reproduced.

This illustration of *Iguanodon* bones appeared a century ago in Sir Richard Owen's *A History of British Fossil Reptiles*. Although this British scientist coined the name dinosaurs, his understanding of these beasts was based on scanty finds of their remains. Since Owen's time thousands of dinosaur discoveries have added greatly to our knowledge.

12

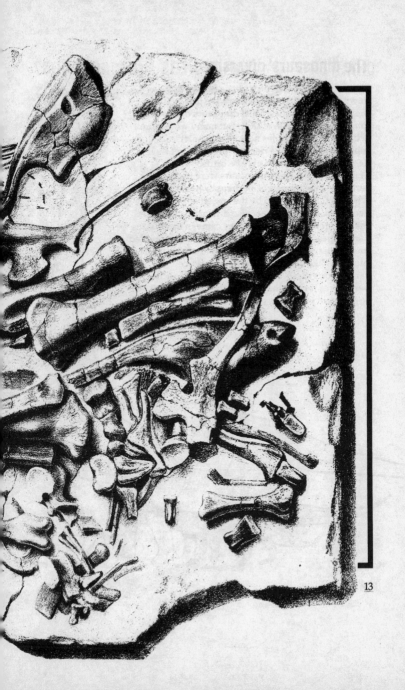

13

The dinosaurs' diversity

Since about 1970, scientists have turned upside-down old ideas that dinosaurs were just pea-brained giant reptiles. Most dinosaurs did have a tough, reptilian type of skin; but many were more active than any reptiles now alive. Their close reptile ancestors gave rise to crocodiles, yet their nearest living relatives may be birds.

Many people imagine dinosaurs were huge. Some certainly were monsters, perhaps as heavy as a blue whale, once thought to be the largest animal that ever lived. Yet there were also dinosaurs no bigger than a chicken. In between they came in many sizes and shapes, as the illustrations show. Some plodded on all fours, while others walked and ran on their hind legs like ostriches. There were fierce carnivorous (flesh-eating) dinosaurs and docile herbivores (beasts that only browsed on plants). All in all, there were dinosaurs to fit the roles played by

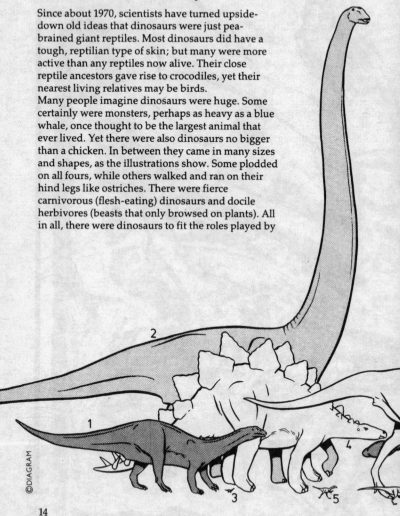

©DIAGRAM

every type of mammal living today, except maybe those that burrow, climb, fly, or live in water. The earliest dinosaurs appeared over 205 million years ago. The last died out about 65 million years ago – over 60 million years before man first appeared on Earth. People often think dinosaurs must have been stupid and badly built because they all became extinct. In fact, no other group of backboned animals that ever lived on land has been so successful. Dinosaurs flourished for more than 140 million years. Evolving at a time when all the continents were joined, they spread around the world. Flourishing for more than 30 times as long as man has lived on Earth, they produced hundreds of genera at least as different from one another as lions are from bears, and cows from horses. By the 1980s, scientists had found remains of about 340 genera, but no doubt many more await discovery.

Dinosaur parade
Here are 14 of the more than 340 known genera of dinosaurs described in this book.
Compare them with the man for size. Different genera lived at different times in the Mesozoic Era (about 225–65 million years ago).
1 *Plateosaurus*
2 *Barosaurus*
3 *Mussaurus* (juvenile)
4 *Stegosaurus*
5 *Compsognathus*
6 *Ornitholestes*
7 *Deinonychus*
8 *Daspletosaurus*
9 *Hypsilophodon*
10 *Lambeosaurus*
11 *Spinosaurus*
12 *Ankylosaurus*
13 *Torosaurus*
14 *Dromiceiomimus*
15 Man

15

Their bony framework

Fossil bones are almost all we have to tell us what the long-dead dinosaurs were like. (For how their bones were fossilized, see Chapter 5.)

As with most backboned animals, dinosaurs depended on internal bony scaffolding to bear their weight, to anchor muscles, and to protect such vital organs as the brain. Small, speedy dinosaurs tended to have lightweight, hollow bones. Creatures as big as elephants needed thick-walled limb bones to support them – yet many had deep hollows in their spinal bones and holes in the sides of their skulls to reduce weight.

Hip, thigh, and ankle bones tell us much about what made these creatures special. Above all, straight thigh bones with a sharply inturned top that slotted in a hole between the hip bones suggest that dinosaurs walked erect like horses; they did not sprawl. High ankles and long foot bones prove they walked on their toes. Long shin bones imply that ostrich dinosaurs could sprint. Stiff ankle joints suggest that all dinosaurs only moved easily over level ground and probably none could climb a tree.

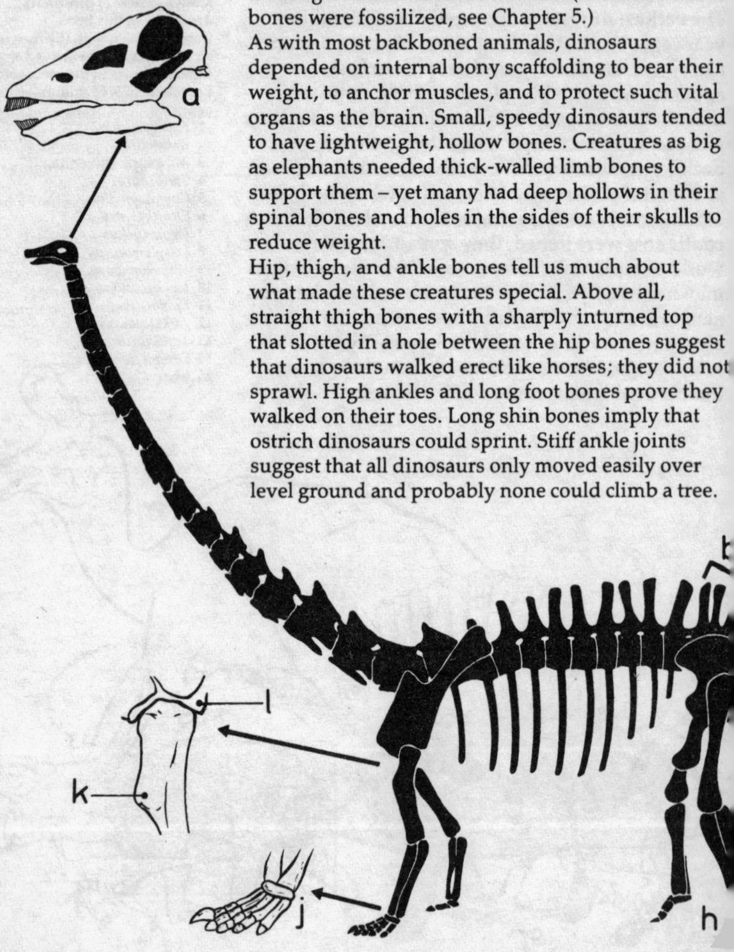

a

l

k

j

b

h

Ancient tracks bear out this evidence. Narrow tracks prove that most dinosaurs indeed walked erect. The long strides of some small flesh-eating dinosaurs show they could run faster than a man can sprint. Other tracks indicate that dinosaurs could swim.

Bumps, grooves, and scars on bones show where muscles were attached; in this way, body shapes can be guessed by studying skeletons. The forms of jaws and teeth betray whether a dinosaur ate plants or meat. Sizes and positions of holes in the skull reveal sizes of the brain, ears, eyes, and nostrils. This tells us that a few dinosaurs were brainier than living reptiles, and many had keen sight, hearing, or sense of smell. Many could breathe while eating and some may have had a long, prehensile tongue. A single bone may be enough to show an expert that its owner was a dinosaur – even which kind of dinosaur it was. But badly worn bones or bones of certain types can prove so baffling that experts argue about just what they represent.

Dinosaur features

Many of these features also occur in close relatives of the dinosaurs.

a Skull with "windows" (closed in some dinosaurs), notably one in front of each eye
b From two to 11 (fused) sacral vertebrae joining spine to:
c hip girdle with a hole (not found in other reptiles) – its strong upper rim helped this socket to take the:
d inturned top of the (fairly straight) thigh bone
e Flange to anchor muscles aiding backswing of the leg
f Ridge aiding knee extension
g High, stiff, simple ankle
h Dinosaurs walked on tiptoe
i From three to five clawed or hoofed toes
j From two to five clawed or hoofed fingers
k Crest on upper arm bone aiding backswing of the forelimb
l Shoulder socket angled to restrict forelimb movements to to-and-fro
m Skin smooth or scaly, sometimes with bony armor

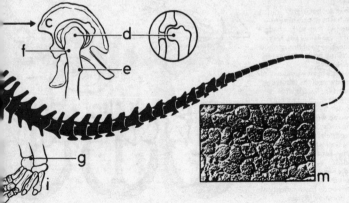

©DIAGRAM

17

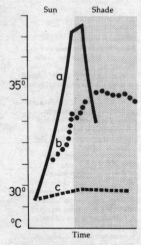

Sun   Shade

35°

a

b

30°

c

°C

Time

Were dinosaurs warm-blooded?

All scientists used to think that dinosaurs were "cold-blooded" reptiles just like crocodiles or lizards. Some still think this, but many experts now believe that at least some dinosaurs were warm-blooded, as birds and mammals are.

If dinosaurs were warm-blooded this would help to explain why they became so plentiful and ruled the land for so long. Cold-blooded animals like lizards cannot control their body temperature: they warm up or cool down with their surroundings. Lizards bask in sunshine to get warm enough to use the energy they need for moving actively. Once warmed up, they must seek shade or die from overheating. Even a warm lizard cannot run far: its heart cannot pump enough oxygen-rich blood to the muscles to keep them working. Warm-blooded animals like birds and mammals work differently. A rich blood supply helps them "burn" food to produce body heat, and a natural thermostat helps to stop them overheating. They always have the energy to chase prey or escape attack and their

Sun and shade (above)
Small, cold-blooded beasts warm up and cool down faster than big ones. Lines show the rise and fall of body temperature for a small alligator (**a**), medium-sized alligator (**b**), and large dinosaur if it were cold blooded (**c**).

Warm but not hot (right)
A lizard basks in sunshine to warm up (**A**), then seeks shade to avoid overheating (**B**). Maybe dinosaurs also used this method of controlling body temperature.

Types of heart
A dinosaur's heart would have resembled one of the following:
1 the hearts of lizards, snakes, and turtles, which pump out oxygen-rich blood from the lungs mixed with spent blood from the body;
2 a crocodile's heart, which has a central wall with a valve that sometimes separates both kinds of blood;
3 a bird's heart, which always separates the two kinds of blood and feeds body tissues plenty of energy-boosting oxygen.

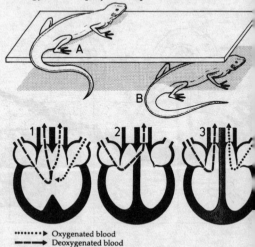

•••••••▷ Oxygenated blood
━ ━ ▶ Deoxygenated blood
▪▪▪▪▪▪▷ Mixed blood

efficient hearts keep them active longer than a reptile.

Dinosaurs resembled birds and mammals in several ways. Straight legs held their bodies high off the ground. Long-necked dinosaurs must have had efficient hearts to pump blood up to their brains. A few dinosaurs were at least as intelligent as birds. Some had a type of bone found in many living mammals. Some seem to have needed as much food for their size as mammals do. At least a few seem to have had feathers, and some cared for their young. None of this proves that dinosaurs controlled body temperature just as birds and mammals do. All big dinosaurs, whether warm- or cold-blooded, would have kept warm because their bodies would have lost heat slowly after dark, and cold winters were unknown. Then, too, some dinosaurs had plates, frills, spikes, or nasal cavities that could have served as heat exchangers, helping to warm or cool their bodies.

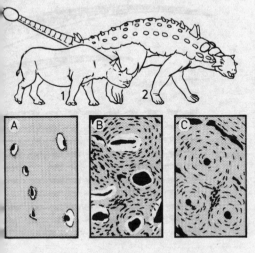

Gait and posture
How creatures stand may hint at their type of blood supply.
1 The black rhinoceros walks with legs straight down below its body. Of living backboned animals only birds and most mammals stand and walk in just that way.
2 *Euoplocephalus* and most other dinosaurs also had upright gait and posture. This may mean they were warm blooded as birds and mammals are.

A bony riddle
These are much enlarged sections of bone from a lizard (A), dinosaur (B), mammal (C). The last two show central tubes containing blood vessels and surrounded by rings of bony tissue (known as Haversian systems). Some experts have said that such systems occur only in warm-blooded creatures. But other studies suggest that dinosaurs also had a type of bone that is found in cold-blooded animals.

©DIAGRAM

19

Food and feeding

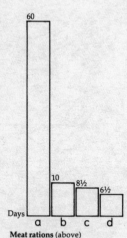

Meat rations (above)
The diagram shows how long different carnivorous beasts take to eat their own weight in food. All but the lizard (a) are warm-blooded.
a Komodo dragon
b Cheetah
c Lion
d Wild dog
If they were cold-blooded, flesh-eating dinosaurs had an appetite like **a**, if warm-blooded, like **b**, **c**, or **d**.

Prey and predators (right)
Shown are percentages of herbivorous and carnivorous dinosaurs, as discovered in Alberta. Because finds of bones depend on chance this may not give us a true picture. Perhaps flesh-eating dinosaurs were more plentiful than this. If warm-blooded, though, a few needed many plant-eaters to provide their food supply.

Like any group of animals, dinosaurs had to eat to stay alive. All depended in the end upon the nourishment in plants to fuel and build their bodies. Weight-for-weight, leaves hold less nourishment than meat, so the plant-eaters probably spent hours each day just browsing. Creatures like the horned and duckbilled dinosaurs had teeth designed for chewing large amounts of vegetation. Sauropods – the biggest herbivores of all – were much less well equipped. Yet a big sauropod would have had to eat perhaps 300lb of food a day if cold-blooded – or a ton a day if warm-blooded.

Sharp fangs and claws helped flesh-eating dinosaurs prey upon the herbivores (whose main defense was a quick getaway or armor plating). Some scientists think that flesh-eating dinosaurs were warm-blooded, and would have had to eat their own weight in meat just over once a week, like lions do. If so, these dinosaurs needed perhaps 10

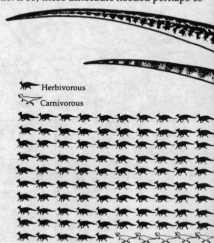

Herbivorous
Carnivorous

times the meat that satisfies other types of reptile, and herbivores would have had to be much more numerous than the carnivores that preyed upon them. It seems they were: of every 100 dinosaurs found in certain rocks of southwest Canada, only three to five were carnivores. Different dinosaurs living in the same area at the same time formed part of a food web whose strands joined many kinds of animals eating or eaten by each other.

Flesh-eating and plant-eating dinosaurs would have been colored and patterned in ways that camouflaged them from their enemies. Some woodland species may have been mottled green, brown, and yellow. Dwellers in the open countryside may have had patterns of black and white that helped to hide their body shape. Young dinosaurs probably sported brighter colors than adults. Big sauropods, however, were probably as drably colored as elephants.

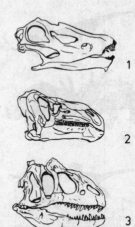

Teeth for special needs (above)
Dinosaurs had teeth designed to help them eat the kinds of food they lived on.
1 *Diplodocus*'s peg-like teeth cropped vegetation.
2 Sharpened cheek teeth helped *Iguanodon* to munch tough twigs and leaves.
3 Flesh-eating carnosaurs had saw-edged, blade-like fangs to slice through meat.

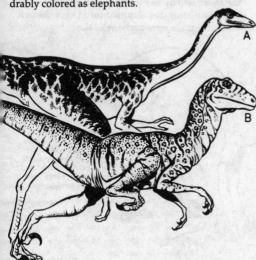

Camouflage (left)
Dinosaurs were probably patterned and colored like modern mammals and reptiles living similar ways of life in similar types of countryside.
A *Struthiomimus* lived in open countryside. A black and white pattern may have helped conceal its body outline.
B Agile predators like *Deinonychus* may have had a camouflage of "leopard's" spots.

© DIAGRAM

21

Family life

People once believed that the family life of
dinosaurs was as simple as that of most living
reptiles. But fossil nests, eggs, and young found
from the 1970s on tell us differently. We now think
that at least some dinosaurs produced and raised
their young in complex, fascinating ways.

When mating time drew near, rival males most
likely fought for females, and perhaps to decide
who should rule a herd. Certain males may have
merely threatened one another. Others banged
heads, locked horns, or slashed with clawed feet.
Like sparring deer or antelopes, probably they
seldom caused real injury. Male duckbills with
showy crests and loud voices would have used
these to attract their mates.

After mating, female dinosaurs laid eggs (a few just
possibly bore live young). Surprisingly, the biggest
sauropod eggs discovered were slightly smaller
than those laid by one of the largest known
prehistoric birds (the elephant bird), even though
adult sauropods were perhaps 20 times bigger than

Male rivalry (above)
Male dinosaurs probably fought
over females at mating time.
1 Male pachycephalosaurids
probably banged heads.
2 *Styracosaurus* males may have
locked horns like this.
3 Sparring *Deinonychus* could
have delivered vicious kicks.

The nursery (left)
Maiasaura and maybe other
dinosaurs laid eggs in
hollowed-out mud mounds.
Some mothers brought food to
their hatchlings until these
could safely forage on their own.

these birds. If eggs had been much larger they probably would not have hatched, for too little life-giving oxygen from the surrounding air would have filtered through the shells to reach the growing embryos inside. Some females may have covered their eggs with sand and left them to hatch in the sun. But certain duckbills built nests with raised mud rims, and they may have brooded eggs as chickens do. They evidently brought their nestlings food. Certain dinosaurs even bred in hillside colonies, where adults shared the task of guarding nurseries.

Young dinosaurs probably grew fast. Small, vulnerable young sauropods may have traveled in the middle of herds of adults; flesh-eaters would have killed any young that straggled – and also any sick or wounded adults. Many a fossil dinosaur has old bone damage showing where the beast had survived attack, disease, or accident. With luck, a few individuals may have lived 100 years or more.

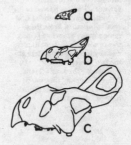

Growing up (above)
Skulls of hatchling (**a**), juvenile (**b**), and adult (**c**) *Protoceratops* show the neck frill getting larger in relation to the rest of the skull. Bodily proportions changed as dinosaurs grew up.

Egg into dinosaur (left)
Protoceratops young are shown hatching from eggs. All dinosaurs probably came from eggs, warmed by the sun, the mother's body, or a mound of rotting leaves.

Family parties (below)
Sauropods were among dinosaurs that roamed in herds. Young may have walked in the middle of such herds for safety.

©DIAGRAM

23

CHAPTER 2

DINOSAURS IN THE MAKING

This chapter starts by tracing the origin of dinosaurs, from the beginning of life to the rise of the reptiles. More than 200 million years ago, small, sprinting reptiles related to the crocodiles gave rise to the first small dinosaurs. From these came a many branched family tree of dinosaurs. The chapter ends by looking separately at the two great groups of dinosaurs – the saurischians ("lizard-hipped" dinosaurs) and the ornithischians ("bird-hipped" dinosaurs).

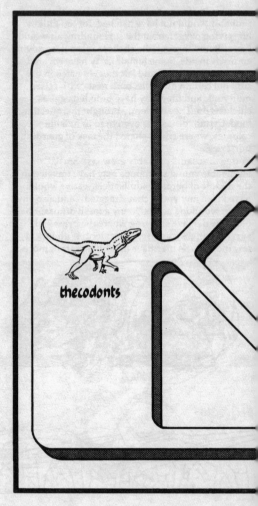

thecodonts

This simplified family tree shows that both main groups of dinosaurs evolved from the now long-extinct reptiles known as thecodonts. Crocodilians and pterosaurs emerged as "cousins" of the dinosaurs, and birds are dinosaurs' probable descendants.

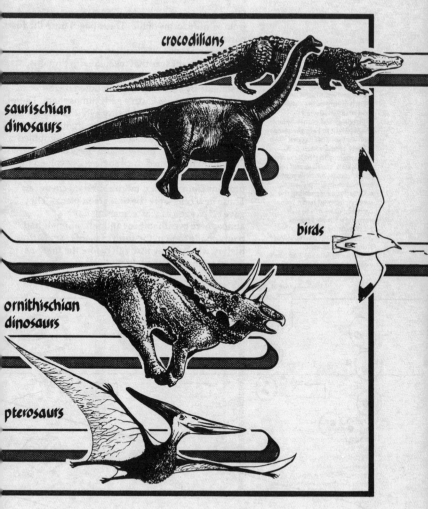

crocodilians

saurischian
dinosaurs

birds

ornithischian
dinosaurs

pterosaurs

25

How backboned animals evolved

Dinosaurs and their backboned ancestors evolved from minute forms of life. These pages trace the first parts of that story.

Life began at least 3500 million years ago, most likely in ancient seas that teemed with proteins. Proteins are complex chemicals that were perhaps first made by sunshine beating down on the poisonous gases of Earth's early atmosphere. These proteins provided food for tiny jelly-like blobs – the first living cells. Food helped these living cells grow and then divide in two. Multiplying cells gobbled up the ready-made proteins and these disappeared. Starvation threatened until some cells evolved the knack of using energy from sunlight to manufacture proteins from simpler, more abundant chemicals. These new cells were the first green plants. They gave off oxygen as waste, making Earth's atmosphere breathable for animals; animals had ready-made food in the form of plants. Yet Earth's history was halfway through before the first one-celled animals evolved. From them came larger

From sea to land
Arrows trace some of the step-by-step changes by which sea organisms led to land animals.
a Early living cells – these found food ready made.
b Single-celled plants – plants use sunlight to help them make food and give off oxygen.
c Early animals included protozoans and simple worms.
d Jellyfish, starfish, and other backboneless animals probably evolved from simple worms.
e Creatures resembling the modern lancelet had a spinal cord and gave rise to fish – animals with backbones.
f Lobe-finned fish breathed atmospheric air and could use stumpy fins as legs.
g Early amphibians had limbs evolved from fins.

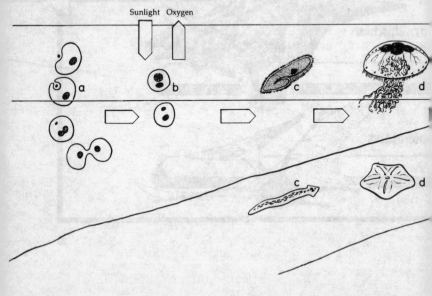

Sunlight   Oxygen

animals, built of many cells that remained together
after dividing. Animals gained different types of
cell performing different tasks like feeding, moving,
and reproduction.

Six hundred million years ago began what
geologists call the Paleozoic Era or "Age of Ancient
Life." Worms, jellyfish, and other backboneless
animals were now living in the seas. Some sea
creatures began using lime to build shells for
protection and support. Then came the first fish –
animals with a skeleton *inside*. Unlike crabs, fish
need not shed their skeletons to grow, and they can
move around more freely. Later came fish with
lungs and lobe-like fins that served as props. Young
lobe-finned fish may have skipped ashore to snap
up snails and insects eating the plants that now
fringed pools and rivers. From the lobefins' stumpy
fins 350 million years ago evolved the sprawling
limbs of early salamander-like amphibians. These
could breathe and move on land, but had to lay their
unprotected eggs in water.

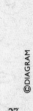

27

Reptiles colonize the land

The reptile egg
A section through a reptile egg shows a liquid cradle that nourishes and protects the growing embryo inside.
a Shell, protecting the embryo and curbing loss of liquid
b Chorion, a membrane that lets oxygen in, waste gas out
c Albumin, a food supply
d Amnion, a liquid-enclosing membrane – a shock absorber buffering the embryo
e Yolk, a food supply
f Allantois, where body wastes collect.

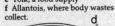

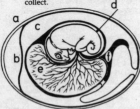

About 290 million years ago amphibians gave rise to the first backboned animals designed to live entirely on dry land. These ancestors of the mammals, birds, and dinosaurs were *reptiles* – cold-blooded beasts with scaly, waterproof skin. Their eggs were fertilized inside the female's body and had shells or tough skin that stopped them drying out once laid. All this freed reptiles from the waterside, and many colonized the higher, drier ground between the river valleys.

As the Paleozoic Era gave way to the Mesozoic Era or "Age of Middle Life," 225 million years ago, several major groups of reptiles were evolving. Their names come from the number of holes behind the eyes on each side of the skull: holes that left room for the jaw muscles to contract. *Anapsids,* with no such holes, include the tortoises and turtles still living today. *Synapsids,* with a single opening low down in the cheek, made up a group of mammal-like reptiles. These mammal-like reptiles ruled the

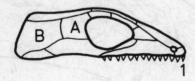

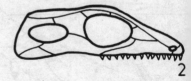

lands for 70 million years and gave rise to the true mammals before becoming extinct.

The largest, and for us the most important, reptile group was that of the *diapsids*: reptiles with two openings behind each eye. Diapsids produced two main subgroups. One contains the snakes and lizards. But it was the other group – the *archosaurs* or "ruling reptiles" – in which the dinosaurs appeared. Archosaurs differed from other diapsids in having an extra hole, or rather a bony basin, in each side of the head. This may have held a salt gland for ridding the body of excess salt – a help for animals in deserts where blood can get too salty.

The dinosaurs' direct ancestors came from that great group of early archosaurs called *thecodonts* or "socket toothed." Most thecodonts were big, heavy, four-legged reptiles that ate flesh. They competed so successfully for food with the mammal-like reptiles that all these died out during the Triassic Period, the first part of the Mesozoic Era.

Four types of reptile
The skulls of four main types of reptile are illustrated here above an example of each.
1 Anapsids, including those early reptiles cotylosaurs, show no hole between the skull's postorbital (**A**) and squamosal (**B**) bones. The example illustrated is *Hypsognathus*, a cotylosaur.
2 Synapsids such as the extinct mammal-like reptiles show one hole between and below those bones. *Cynognathus*, a mammal-like reptile, is given as an example.
3 Euryapsids such as the extinct plesiosaurs show one hole between and above those bones. *Elasmosaurus*, a plesiosaur, is illustrated.
4 Diapsids such as archosaurs, which include dinosaurs and their thecodont ancestors, show two holes between those bones – one hole above the other. The example illustrated is *Proterosuchus*, a thecodont.

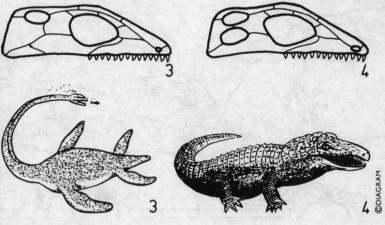

3   4

3   4

©DIAGRAM

29

From thecodonts to dinosaurs

Dinosaurs evolved from one of the four main groups of those socket-toothed reptiles the thecodonts, which first appeared about 225 million years ago. Early thecodonts were sprawling, crocodile-like beasts called proterosuchians ("earlier crocodiles"). From these came the three other groups.

Many thecodonts had bodies that equipped them for a hunting life spent largely in the water. They swam by waggling their long, deep tails. But the powerful thrust that got them started came from their hind limbs which were longer and stronger than the forelimbs. This thrust also acted from the hips, not from the knees, as with their sprawling ancestors. Such thecodonts that took to living on the land could thrust their whole limbs down and back, giving them a longer stride than other reptiles of their size. Most could not walk as upright as a dog, but raised their bodies off the ground like trotting crocodiles. *Pseudosuchian* ("sham crocodile") thecodonts like little *Euparkeria* walked on all fours. Short front legs made running difficult, but they

Dinosaurs evolving (below) Shown here are possible ancestors of dinosaurs, and one very early dinosaur.
1 Lizard-like *Millerosaurus*
2 *Proterosuchus*, a thecodont
3 The thecodont *Euparkeria* running (a), walking (b)
4 *Lagosuchus* (a thecodont?)
5 *Ornithosuchus*, probably a thecodont
6 *Staurikosaurus*, one of the first undoubted dinosaurs

Evolution and gait (bottom)
A Early thecodonts had a sprawling gait with knees and elbows stuck out from the body.
B Later thecodonts had a semi-improved gait.
C Dinosaurs and possibly some later thecodonts had a fully improved gait with legs held straight down below the body.

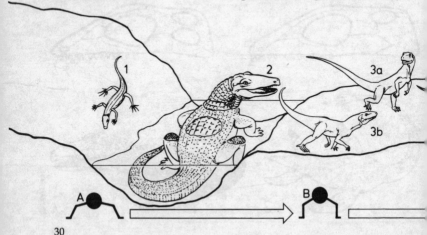

could sprint by rearing on their long hind legs and balancing with their long, strong tail.

In time, there were many sizes of flesh-eating pseudosuchians – from little "rabbit thecodonts" like long-legged *Lagosuchus* ("hare crocodile") to larger beasts like *Avalonianus*, *Zatomus*, and *Ornithosuchus* ("bird crocodile"), a hunter 9ft 10in (3m) long. Superior speed may have helped the thecodonts to multiply at the expense of the mammal-like reptiles.

By 205 million years ago, pseudosuchians had given rise to the first flesh-eating dinosaurs. Indeed some of the animals just named may have been early dinosaurs. A fully upright gait helped small dinosaurs like *Staurikosaurus* to outrun both prey and rivals. This made the early dinosaurs more dangerous than many thecodonts. Soon there were large and small dinosaurs, including some with teeth designed for eating leaves, not meat. By the end of the Triassic Period, 193 million years ago, flesh-eating dinosaurs had replaced thecodonts, and nearly all big herbivores were dinosaurs.

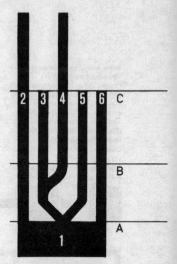

Archosaur family tree (above)
1 Thecodonts; **2** Crocodilians;
3 Saurischian dinosaurs;
4 Birds; **5** Ornithischian
dinosaurs; **6** Pterosaurs. Most
groups lived in the Mesozoic
Era's Triassic (**A**), Jurassic (**B**),
and Cretaceous (**C**) periods.

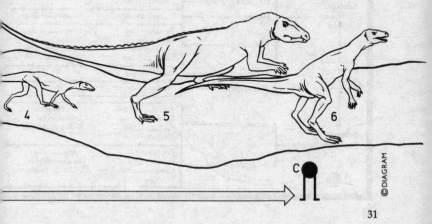

©DIAGRAM

31

How dinosaurs are classified

From kingdom to order (below)
The kingdom Animalia
(animals) has many phyla. The
phylum Chordata has many
classes. The class Reptilia
(reptiles) includes the subclass
Diapsida. Its superorder
Archosauria includes both
orders of dinosaurs.

These pages set out the main relationships within
both orders of dinosaurs, and show how such
relationships fit into a scheme worked out for all
animals. The following four pages briefly describe
important differences between the two dinosaur
orders and between their main subgroups, and
show when these appeared and flourished.

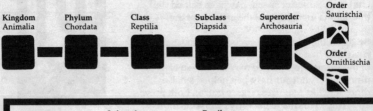

Kingdom	Phylum	Class	Subclass	Superorder	Order
Animalia	Chordata	Reptilia	Diapsida	Archosauria	Saurischia
					Order Ornithischia

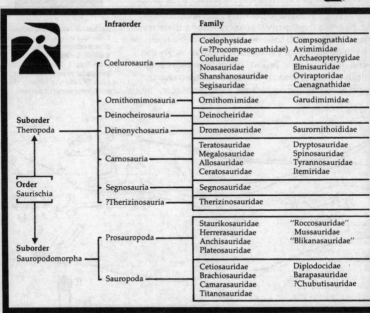

	Infraorder	Family	
Suborder Theropoda	Coelurosauria	Coelophysidae (=?Procompsognathidae)	Compsognathidae Avimimidae
		Coeluridae	Archaeopterygidae
		Noasauridae	Elmisauridae
		Shanshanosauridae	Oviraptoridae
		Segisauridae	Caenagnathidae
	Ornithomimosauria	Ornithomimidae	Garudimimidae
	Deinocheirosauria	Deinocheiridae	
	Deinonychosauria	Dromaeosauridae	Saurornithoididae
	Carnosauria	Teratosauridae	Dryptosauridae
		Megalosauridae	Spinosauridae
		Allosauridae	Tyrannosauridae
		Ceratosauridae	Itemiridae
Order Saurischia	Segnosauria	Segnosauridae	
	?Therizinosauria	Therizinosauridae	
Suborder Sauropodomorpha	Prosauropoda	Staurikosauridae	"Roccosauridae"
		Herrerasauridae	Mussauridae
		Anchisauridae	"Blikanasauridae"
		Plateosauridae	
	Sauropoda	Cetiosauridae	Diplodocidae
		Brachiosauridae	Barapasauridae
		Camarasauridae	?Chubutisauridae
		Titanosauridae	

Each scientific name used here and elsewhere in the book comes at least partly from a dead language: Greek or Latin. Scientists the world over use the same scientific name for the same kind of animal or plant. This helps to avoid confusion when two experts speaking different languages get together to discuss dinosaurs.

From order to species (below) The dinosaur order Ornithischia has suborders including the Ceratopsia (horned dinosaurs). Among its families is the Ceratopsidae with many genera. The genus *Triceratops* includes the species *Triceratops horridus*.

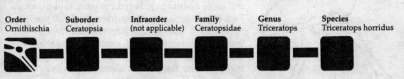

Order	Suborder	Infraorder	Family	Genus	Species
Ornithischia	Ceratopsia	(not applicable)	Ceratopsidae	Triceratops	Triceratops horridus

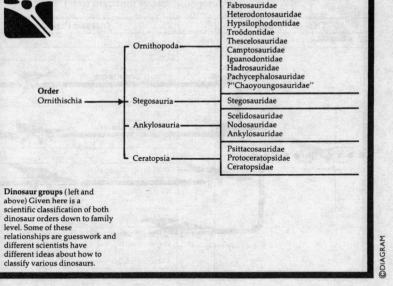

	Suborder	Family
		Fabrosauridae
		Heterodontosauridae
		Hypsilophodontidae
		Troödontidae
		Thescelosauridae
	Ornithopoda	Camptosauridae
		Iguanodontidae
		Hadrosauridae
		Pachycephalosauridae
		?"Chaoyoungosauridae"
Order Ornithischia	Stegosauria	Stegosauridae
	Ankylosauria	Scelidosauridae
		Nodosauridae
		Ankylosauridae
	Ceratopsia	Psittacosauridae
		Protoceratopsidae
		Ceratopsidae

Dinosaur groups (left and above) Given here is a scientific classification of both dinosaur orders down to family level. Some of these relationships are guesswork and different scientists have different ideas about how to classify various dinosaurs.

©DIAGRAM

Saurischian dinosaurs

From one or more pseudosuchian thecodonts evolved two great orders of dinosaurs. First came the saurischians or "lizard-hipped" dinosaurs – so named for a hip girdle with three main bones arranged like those of most reptiles: the pubis (the front bone) pointed forward in most but not all saurischians. Teeth occupied the rims of the jaws and large openings reduced the weight of the skull. Two main saurischian suborders evolved: the two-legged, flesh-eating theropods or "beast feet," and the four-legged, mostly plant-eating sauropodomorphs ("lizard-feet forms"). Each of these, in turn, had subdivisions. Big, heavily built theropods form the infraorder of carnosaurs ("flesh lizards"). Smaller, lightly built theropods are often grouped as coelurosaurs or "hollow-tailed lizards." The early sauropodomorphs were prosauropods ("before the lizard feet"). They

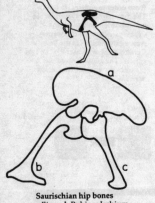

Saurischian hip bones
a Ilium; b Pubis; c Ischium.

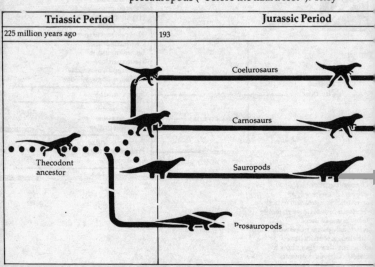

Triassic Period	Jurassic Period
225 million years ago	193

Coelurosaurs

Carnosaurs

Thecodont ancestor

Sauropods

Prosauropods

included the first plant-eating dinosaurs, and most lived before the much larger, herbivorous sauropods ("lizard feet"). Sauropodomorphs may have had the same largely two-legged thecodont ancestor as theropods, or have come from a four-footed thecodont like *Ticinosuchus* ("Ticino crocodile"). Each infraorder held different families made up of genera divided into species.

As time passed, new families and genera replaced earlier kinds, which were perhaps less well equipped for killing prey, or eating and digesting plants.

Saurischians thrived from the Late Triassic Period all through the Jurassic and Cretaceous periods – the three parts of the Mesozoic Era. But as the Age of Dinosaurs was ending, saurischians were outnumbered by the second major group of dinosaurs: the ornithischians.

Saurischian time lines
Saurischian dinosaurs evolved and diversified in the Triassic Period. Of sauropodomorphs, the prosauropods died out relatively early, but the huge plant-eating sauropods persisted all through the Jurassic and Cretaceous Periods. Similarly persistent were small and large theropods (flesh-eating dinosaurs), grouped here respectively as coelurosaurs and carnosaurs. As time passed, old kinds became extinct, but new ones took their place.

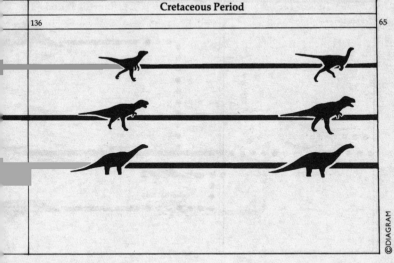

Cretaceous Period

136

65

©DIAGRAM

Ornithischian dinosaurs

Ornithischian ("bird-hipped") dinosaurs – the second dinosaur order – had hip bones arranged like those of birds, with a pubis pointing back instead of forward. They also had an extra bone forming the tip of the lower jaw. Many had a horny, toothless beak, powerful grinding teeth, cheek pouches, and a lattice of bony tendons reinforcing the spine.

Ornithischians were so unlike saurischians that some say both had separate thecodont ancestors. This would mean that dinosaurs were not a single group. Yet the joints of both ornithischians and saurischians show similarities. This persuades some paleontologists – scientists who study ancient prehistoric life – that saurischians gave rise to

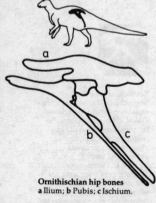

Ornithischian hip bones
a Ilium; b Pubis; c Ischium.

Triassic Period	Jurassic Period
225 million years ago	193

Thecodont ancestor

Scelidosaurids

ornithischians. In 1974 the Americans Robert Bakker and Peter Galton even argued that these two, with birds, formed three subclasses in the class Dinosauria. That would make dinosaurs equal to and different from the class Reptilia (reptiles). We may never know for certain if dinosaurs were reptiles or which ancestor gave rise to ornithischians.

Ornithischians had several suborders (or orders, if ornithischians were a subclass not an order). They were the two-legged ornithopods ("bird feet") and the four-legged plated, horned, and armored dinosaurs. As time passed, ornithischians outnumbered plant-eating saurischians, partly because the saurischians had less efficient teeth.

Ornithischian time lines
Indicated are the four great groups of ornithischians and when each of them lived. Scelidosaurs may have made a fifth group, and some experts divide ornithopods into several major groups. As time passed, old genera became extinct, but new ones took their place.

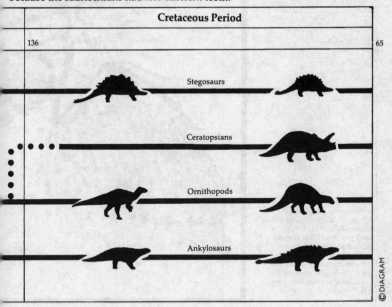

Cretaceous Period

136

65

Stegosaurs

Ceratopsians

Ornithopods

Ankylosaurs

©DIAGRAM

CHAPTER 3   DINOSAURS IDENTIFIED

This chapter – divided into six sections – describes all known dinosaur families and their genera. Each family name appears as a heading ending in -*ids* (scientists use -*idae*). Then follow names of the family's genera, boldly printed and in alphabetical order. Generic names in quotation marks have still to be officially described and named. Many genera are poorly known, so restorations of their bodies are largely guesswork. Maps show where genera were found.
(For a family tree of all main groups of dinosaurs, see pages 32–33.)

Archaeopteryx, the "bird dinosaur," is often thought of as the world's first bird. Yet it could just as well have been a small, flesh-eating dinosaur with feathers.
Illustration after G. Steinmann and L. Döderlein, appearing in *Evolution of the Vertebrates* by E.H. Colbert (John Wiley & Sons).

Section 1 COELUROSAURS

Included here in the first section of our guide to dinosaur identification are the coelurosaurs or "hollow-tailed lizards." This term embraces 16 families of small, lightly built members of that great flesh-eating group of saurischian dinosaurs known as theropods or "beast feet." Many experts think coelurosaurs should be divided into half a dozen so-called infraorders; some would even place archaeopterygids and their bird descendants in a special subclass.

Coelurosaur family tree
This family tree of small flesh-eating dinosaurs is largely guesswork. No-one can be sure how closely some families were related.

a Coelophysids (here taken to include the procompsognathids)
b Segisaurids
c Compsognathids
d Archaeopterygids
e Avimimids
f Coelurids
g Noasaurids
h Shanshanosaurids
i Dromaeosaurids
j Saurornithoidids
k Oviraptorids
l Caenagnathids
m Elmisaurids
n Ornithomimids
o Garudimimids
p Deinocheirids

About coelurosaurs

Coelurosaurs ("hollow-tailed lizards") were mostly small, speedy dinosaurs with thin-walled, fragile bones, long legs, and fairly long arms. They had sharp claws on toes and fingers, and many must have used their hands for grasping prey or bringing food to their long, narrow jaws.

Some of these lightly built, two-legged dinosaurs grew no larger than a chicken, others were bigger than an ostrich. Coelurosaurs probably ate insects, lizards, eggs, and baby dinosaurs, and tore flesh from carcasses of any size. So they fitted the roles played today by animals as different as hyenas, jackals, roadrunners, and ostriches.

Many of the later kinds were larger, with fewer toes and fingers and a toothless beak instead of sharp-toothed jaws. Some coelurosaurs were probably the speediest and brainiest of all dinosaurs – at least as brainy as birds, which may be their descendants.

Triassic	Jurassic			Cretaceous	
Late	Early	Middle	Late	Early	Late

Coelophysids 1

Coelophysids ("hollow forms") had hollow bones like other coelurosaurs. Their light, wedge-shaped heads were armed with sharp, narrow teeth set quite far apart. Coelophysids had a long, flexible neck, balanced by a long tail that could be held up off the ground. Most had long forearms, large clawed hands, long legs, and long, bird-like feet. This family of early coelurosaurs lived in Late Triassic times in lands as far apart as North America, Europe, and Africa, and possibly South America and Asia. Some grew no larger than a chicken, others as long as a man (but less than half as heavy), a few twice as long as that. Probably roaming dry areas, these hunters were quick enough to catch big, low-flying insects, lizards, and even their own agile babies. In 1981 one expert decided that *Coelophysis, Halticosaurus,* and *Procompsognathus* deserved to be placed in their own family, the procompsognathids.

Coelophysid features
Here the largest and smallest coelophysids are shown with a man to give an idea of their sizes. Letters mark some of the coelophysids' features.
a Light, wedge-shaped head
b Long, flexible neck
c Large, clawed hands
d Long forearms
e Long, bird-like feet
f Long, agile legs with long shins
g Long tail

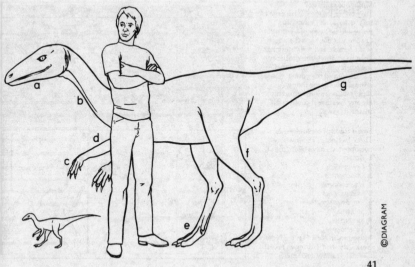

©DIAGRAM

41

Coelophysids 2

1 **Avipes** ("bird foot") was a very early coelophysid. It is known only from fused bird-like foot bones from Thuringia, East Germany. Length: perhaps 4ft (1.2m). Time: Late Triassic.

2 **Coelophysis** ("hollow form") is known from many skeletons of beasts that may have lived and died together, perhaps smothered by a sandstorm. *Coelophysis* had a long, low, narrow skull armed with many small, sharp, saw-edged teeth. The neck was long and snaky, the tail very long. It had fewer useful fingers than some early coelurosaurs (only three per hand), but had a strengthened joint to anchor hips to spine. Length: up to 10ft (3m). Weight: up to 65lb (29.5kg). Time: Late Triassic. Place: southwest and eastern USA.

3 **Dolichosuchus** ("long crocodile") had a shin bone like *Halticosaurus*'s, so perhaps was also rather large. Time: Late Triassic. Place: southwestern West Germany.

Mother or monster?
Tiny bones inside the rib cage of this fossil adult *Coelophysis* proved to be those of a young *Coelophysis*. Perhaps the adult was a female and the young her unborn infant. More probably the adult was a cannibal that had devoured the young animal. Like some living reptiles, *Coelophysis* probably ate any creature it could cram inside its jaws.

Fossil finds of coelophysids
These two maps show where coelophysids have been found.
1 *Avipes*
2 *Coelophysis*
3 *Dolichosuchus*
4 *Halticosaurus*
5 *Lukousaurus*
6 *Procompsognathus*
7 *Saltopus*
8 *Syntarsus*
9 *Velocipes*
Museums in New Haven, New York City, and Tübingen (West Germany) show specimens.

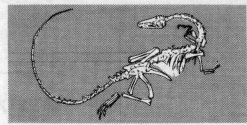

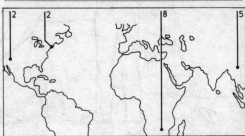

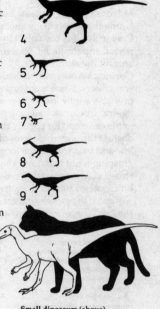

4 **Halticosaurus** ("nimble lizard") from Late Triassic southern Germany was big with a large head, very short arms, and five-fingered hands. Length: 18ft (5.5m).

5 **Lukousaurus** ("Lu-kou lizard") from Late Triassic (some say Early Jurassic) southern China had tiny brow horns. Length: 6ft 6in (2m).

6 **Procompsognathus** ("before *Compsognathus*") from Late Triassic southern West Germany had a head like *Coelophysis*. Two of the five fingers on each hand were short, as was the first toe, which pointed backward. Length: 4ft (1.2m).

7 **Saltopus** ("leaping foot") from Late Triassic northeast Scotland had five-fingered hands (the fourth and fifth fingers were tiny). Length: 2ft (60cm). Weight: 2lb (900g).

8 **Syntarsus** ("fused tarsus" – a bone in the foot) from Late Triassic Zimbabwe resembled *Coelophysis* and had fused foot bones. Some experts think it had feathery scales. Length: up to 10ft (3m).

9 **Velocipes** ("quick foot") was named from a Late Triassic shin bone found in Germany.

Small dinosaurs (above)
Picturing *Saltopus* next to a house cat helps to stress the small size of many early dinosaurs (but *Saltopus* just may have been a thecodont).
Plumed dinosaurs? (left)
Perhaps *Syntarsus* and some other coelurosaurus had feathers which they raised to lose body heat and lowered to trap it. (Illustration after Bakker.)

©DIAGRAM

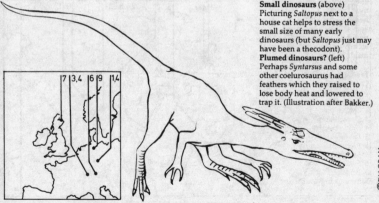

Coelurids 1

Millions of years separate known members of this family from their likely ancestors, the coelophysids. Coelurids ("hollow tails") lived in the Late Jurassic period and through Cretaceous times. They spread around the world.

Coelurids were small to medium-sized hunter-scavengers. Some were turkey-sized; most were probably a little longer than a man, although much lighter. Coelurids had long hind legs with ankle joints designed for speedy running. They probably dashed through undergrowth, neck and head held low and balanced by the long, slim tail. Each large, grasping hand had three long fingers with curved, strong claws, for seizing unsuspecting lizards, small birds, pterosaurs, or mammals. Perhaps coelurids were also the jackals of their day – tearing flesh from the carcasses of big herbivores killed by the great carnosaurs.

Fossil finds of coelurids
Numbered dots on the map show locations of coelurid finds.
1 *Aristosuchus*
2 *Coeluroides*
3 *Coelurus*
4 *Compsosuchus*

5 *Inosaurus*
6 *Jubbulpuria*
7 *Kakuru*
8 *Laevisuchus*
9 *Microvenator*
10 *Ornitholestes*
11 *Ornithomimoides*

12 *Sinocoelurus*
13 *Teinurosaurus*
New York City's American Museum of Natural History is one of few with good coelurid fossils.

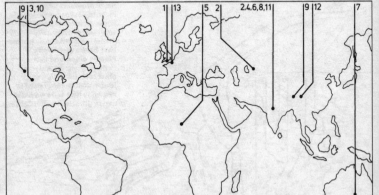

©DIAGRAM

1 **Aristosuchus** ("best crocodile") was an Early Cretaceous coelurid, probably resembling *Coelurus*. Length: perhaps 6ft 6in (2m). Place: Isle of Wight, southern England.

2 **Coeluroides** ("Coelurus form") is a poorly known Late Cretaceous coelurid larger than *Jubbulpuria*. Length: perhaps 7ft (2.1m). Place: central India and Kazakhstan.

3 **Coelurus** ("hollow tail") seemingly had a head slightly smaller than a man's hand; mostly small teeth; and long, but rather weak, hands. Length: about 6ft 6in (2m). Time: Late Jurassic. Place: Wyoming, USA.

4 **Compsosuchus** ("pretty crocodile") is another poorly known coelurid from Late Cretaceous central India. Length: perhaps similar to other coelurids: about 6ft 6in (2m).

Coelurid features (left)
Most coelurids probably shared these features.
a Small, low skull
b Small, sharp teeth
c Light, hollow bones
d Long neck
e Tail longer than neck
f Long legs with long shins
g Ankle joint designed for running
h Three main toes
i Long arms
j Long, weak but grasping hand with three fingers – digits 4 and 5 tiny or absent
k Strong, curved claws on hands

Skull size (below)
A *Coelurus* skull and a man's hand are here compared for size.

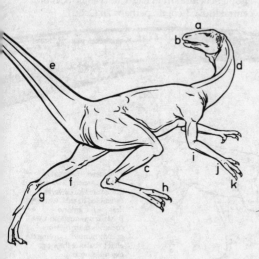

Coelurids 2

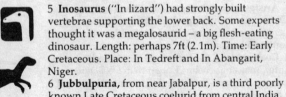

5 **Inosaurus** ("In lizard") had strongly built vertebrae supporting the lower back. Some experts thought it was a megalosaurid – a big flesh-eating dinosaur. Length: perhaps 7ft (2.1m). Time: Early Cretaceous. Place: In Tedreft and In Abangarit, Niger.

6 **Jubbulpuria,** from near Jabalpur, is a third poorly known Late Cretaceous coelurid from central India, described from bits of backbone. Length: perhaps about 4ft (1.2m).

7 **Kakuru** ("rainbow serpent") is the first coelurid (or kin of that family) found in Australia. It was described in 1980 from a shin bone longer than *Coelurus*'s and which had largely turned to opal, a semiprecious stone. Length: perhaps 8ft (2.4m). Time: Early Cretaceous. Place: central South Australia.

8 **Laevisuchus** ("lucky – or left – crocodile") is another coelurid from Late Cretaceous rocks of central India. Length: perhaps 7ft (2.1m).

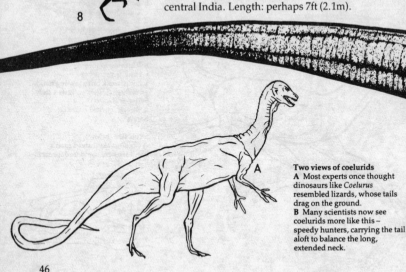

Two views of coelurids
A Most experts once thought dinosaurs like *Coelurus* resembled lizards, whose tails drag on the ground.
B Many scientists now see coelurids more like this – speedy hunters, carrying the tail aloft to balance the long, extended neck.

9 **Microvenator** ("small hunter") was a delicately built, turkey-sized hunter found in Montana, USA and also in Tibet. Time: Early Cretaceous.

10 **Ornitholestes** ("bird robber") was named for its supposed bird-catching habits. Some experts have thought it and *Coelurus* were the same creature. Length: about 6ft 6in (2m). Time: Late Jurassic. Place: Wyoming, USA, where scientists found an almost complete skeleton.

11 **Ornithomimoides** ("bird-mimic form") is a fifth coelurid from Late Cretaceous central India. Length: perhaps 7ft (2.1m).

12 **Sinocoelurus** ("Chinese hollow tail") lived in Late Jurassic south-central China. It was named from four scattered teeth.

13 **Teinurosaurus** ("extended lizard") was named from a tail bone, now lost. Time: Late Jurassic. Place: Boulogne, France.

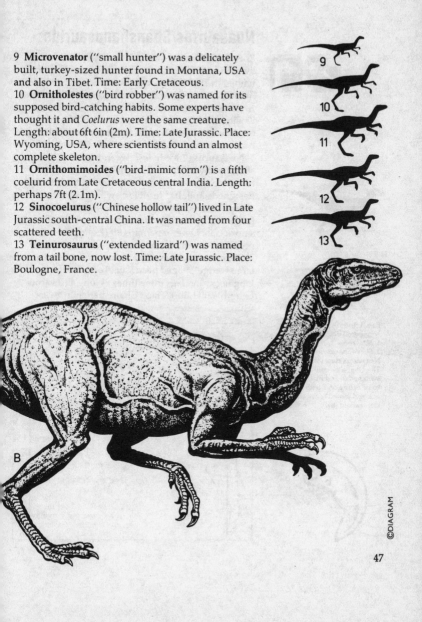

B

©DIAGRAM

Noasaurids/Shanshanosaurids

Both these families of small, flesh-eating dinosaurs lived in Late Cretaceous times. Noasaurids were named in 1980 from bones found in South America. Shanshanosaurids were described in 1977 from finds in eastern Central Asia. Noasaurids had a terrible "switchblade" claw on the second toe, like the dromaeosaurids. Shanshanosaurids were light, agile hunters with a large head like that of *Deinonychus*.

1 **Noasaurus** ("northwest Argentina lizard") was a slim, lightly built, medium-sized hunter. It resembled the dromaeosaurids but had a differently designed skull. Its "terrible claw" was also more sharply curved than *Deinonychus*'s and switched farther to and fro. *Noasaurus* could have killed young sauropods. Length: perhaps 8ft (2.4m). Place: Salta province, northwest Argentina.

2 **Shanshanosaurus** ("Shan-shan lizard") had a large wedge-shaped head, small eyes, sharp teeth, long neck, and legs three times as long as its arms. Length: 6ft (1.8m). Place: Shan-shan, northwest China.

Fossil finds (right)
Numbered dots locate finds.
1 *Noasaurus*
2 *Shanshanosaurus*
Noasaurus claw (below)
The great claw could be switched to and fro by muscles, some acting on a tendon (**a**) with one end joined to the claw in the slot marked (**b**).

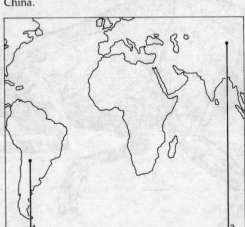

Compsognathids

Compsognathids ("pretty jaws") were among the smallest dinosaurs, yet in some ways they were built like carnosaurs – predatory dinosaurs that mostly weighed a ton or more. It is possible that they did grow larger than the few whose bones have been discovered. Compsognathids were swift hunters of small game, darting fast enough through undergrowth to catch and kill small lizards. Only one Late Jurassic genus has been found.

Compsognathus ("pretty jaw") was chicken-sized and built much like *Archaeopteryx*, the "bird-dinosaur." It had a long neck and very long tail, with three-toed feet on legs that were twice as long as its arms. There were maybe only two clawed fingers on each hand, as in the huge *Tyrannosaurus*. Length: 2ft (60cm). Weight: 6lb 8oz (3kg). Place: southern West Germany and southeast France.

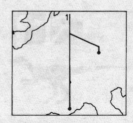

Fossil finds (above)
The map shows fossil finds of *Compsognathus*. Bones from southeast France seemed to come from a specimen with flippers for arms but close study proved that this idea was mistaken. The German fossil is now in a Munich museum.

1 🦕

Size and speed (below)
A *Compsognathus* and a cockerel are here compared for size. The *Compsognathus* is shown chasing a lizard. We know it caught such agile, speedy prey because lizard bones were found inside a *Compsognathus* rib cage.

© DIAGRAM

49

Segisaurids

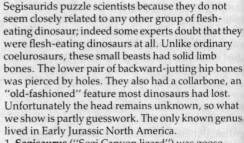

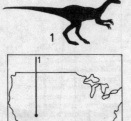

Segisaurids puzzle scientists because they do not seem closely related to any other group of flesh-eating dinosaur; indeed some experts doubt that they were flesh-eating dinosaurs at all. Unlike ordinary coelurosaurs, these small beasts had solid limb bones. The lower pair of backward-jutting hip bones was pierced by holes. They also had a collarbone, an "old-fashioned" feature most dinosaurs had lost. Unfortunately the head remains unknown, so what we show is partly guesswork. The only known genus lived in Early Jurassic North America.

1 **Segisaurus** ("Segi Canyon lizard") was goose-sized but slim, with long shin bones and strong upper arm bones. Its bird-like foot had a short first toe and a tiny fifth toe. Segisaurus was found in north-central Arizona, USA.

Fossil finds (above)
The map indicates where *Segisaurus* has been found.
Foot comparisons (right)
a Bones of the right foot of *Segisaurus*
b Bones of the right foot of *Procompsognathus*
c Arm bones of *Segisaurus* (to a different scale)
In 1981 Professor John Ostrom showed that *Segisaurus* and *Procompsognathus* possessed similar feet, with short toe bones compared to metatarsal bones (bones above the toes). He also showed that the pubic bones (part of the hip girdle) of these beasts were similar. Yet he still thought *Segisaurus* different enough to have belonged in its own family.

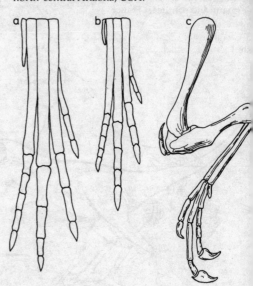

Avimimids

Described in 1981, this family of small "bird mimics" looked surprisingly like birds. They almost certainly had feathered wings. In fact, the Russian scientist who found the first avimimid fossil listed nearly two dozen bird-like features – even more than those in *Archaeopteryx*, often supposed to be the first bird. Avimimids lived later than *Archaeopteryx*, so they could not have given rise to birds. Their wings were also probably too weak to keep them airborne, but they could run fast. They probably ranged open plains, fluttering briefly off the ground to snap up flying insects, or to escape an enemy, in the same way that chickens do today.

1 **Avimimus** ("bird mimic") was a small, fast-running dinosaur with long, slim thighs and shins, long bird-like feet, and a long neck and tail. It probably had broad, short wings, which it could fold against its body. Eyes and brain were large. Length: 3–5ft (about 1–1.5m). Time: Late Cretaceous. Place: southern Mongolia.

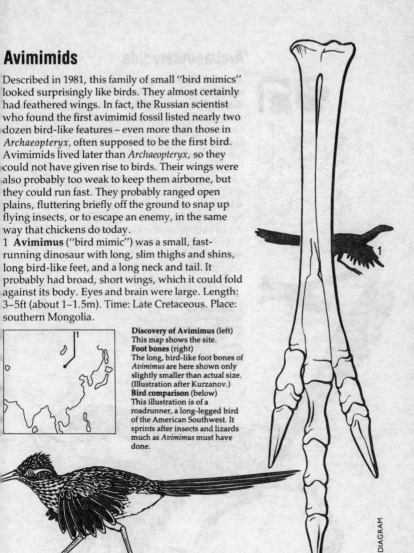

Discovery of Avimimus (left)
This map shows the site.
Foot bones (right)
The long, bird-like foot bones of *Avimimus* are here shown only slightly smaller than actual size. (Illustration after Kurzanov.)
Bird comparison (below)
This illustration is of a roadrunner, a long-legged bird of the American Southwest. It sprints after insects and lizards much as *Avimimus* must have done.

©DIAGRAM

51

Archaeopterygids

Where they lived
Shown are *Archaeopteryx* (**1**) and
Laopteryx (**2**) finds.

Most people think of these crow-sized "ancient
feathers" as the world's first birds. Like modern birds
they had feathered wings, but the collarbone, and
some hip and foot bones resembled those both of
birds and some dinosaurs. They also shared with
coelurosaur dinosaurs some features unknown in
modern birds. For instance, small teeth rimmed the
long, slim jaws; three clawed fingers sprouted from
each wing or "feathered arm"; the tail had a long,
thin, bony core. Such comparisons make most
scientists think that birds evolved from coelurosaurs.
Some argue that birds *are* dinosaurs – continuing to
thrive over 60 million years after all the rest died out.

1 **Archaeopteryx** ("ancient feather") may have
seemed like a feathered form of *Compsognathus*.
Length: 3ft (about 1m). Time: Late Jurassic. Place:
Bavaria, southern West Germany.

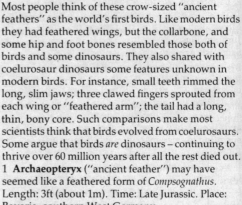

Winged sprinter
Archaeopteryx possibly ran fast
enough to catch airborne
insects. But this "bird dinosaur"
probably could only rise weakly
off the ground or flutter down
from trees.

2 **Laopteryx** ("woodland feather") was described in 1881 by the American paleontologist Othniel Charles Marsh. It may have been a pterosaur. Time: Jurassic. Place: Wyoming, USA.

Scientists agree that archaeopterygids were not as good at flapping flight as modern birds like pigeons. Some think they may have used the claws on their fingers to help them climb up trees from which they just fluttered or glided down. Others suppose they took off from the ground. Like avimimids, they were probably swift runners, sprinting to seize insects or avoid enemies. Running fast into a headwind they could have flapped their wings and taken off.

Of course, before birds could fly they needed feathered wings. Feathers probably evolved as "frayed" scales that trapped body heat. Small warm-blooded creatures like birds need some such body covering to keep their body temperature steady. *Archaeopteryx* had merely evolved feathers that were also shaped and grouped for flight. Its wishbone and the way bones in its shoulder girdle were angled helped this strange "bird dinosaur" to get aloft and wing its way through air.

Birds and dinosaurs (below)
Archaeopteryx (a) shared many features with coelurosaurs like *Microvenator* (b). These include: a short body; a thin, flexible neck; very long legs; stiff ankle joints; and long fingers with claws for seizing prey. (Illustrations after Bakker and Galton.)

Birds old and new (left)
A modern flying bird (A), unlike *Archaeopteryx* (B), has a big, flat sternum or breastbone (shaded here) for anchoring wing muscles.
Evolving feathers
Feathers may have evolved from faulty scales that split as they grew (1–4). (Diagram after Regal.)

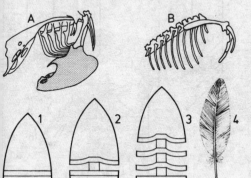

Ornithomimids (ostrich dinosaurs)

These tall, keen-eyed, toothless "bird mimics" are so unlike most coelurosaurs that some scientists put them in their own infraorder, the ornithomimosaurs. Ornithomimids were the emus and ostriches of the dinosaur world. Like those big birds they could sprint swiftly on their very long, slim legs. Each foot had three effective toes. The long, thin arms ended in "hands," each hand having three, long, spindly fingers tipped with claws. The long, slender, mobile neck supported a small head. Fragile skull bones and a toothless beak made the head light. When they walked or ran, ornithomimids balanced head and neck by holding the long tail out stiffly, level with the back. Some roamed fairly open country; others ranged mainly through forests. The earliest may have lived in Late Jurassic Africa, but most kinds have been found in Late Cretaceous rocks of northern continents.

Where they lived
This map shows the known homes of the ornithomimids.
1 *Archaeornithomimus*
2 *Betasuchus*
3 *Dromiceiomimus*
4 *Elaphrosaurus*
5 *Gallimimus*
6 *Ornithomimus*
7 *Struthiomimus*
8 *Tugulusaurus*

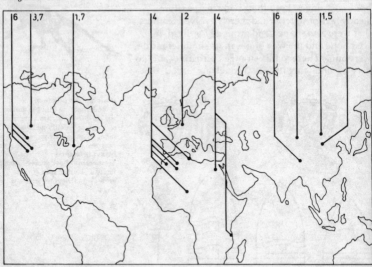

Except for their long tails, arms, and bare skin, the "ostrich" dinosaurs looked so much like ostriches that it is tempting to suppose they lived much like these big, flightless birds. Like ostriches they may have searched low-growing plants for leaves, fruits, and seeds, also snapping up insects, lizards, and small mammals. Some people more fancifully suppose that they lived largely on shellfish or even on the eggs of other dinosaurs. Certainly their long fingers would have made useful shovels for removing the sand hiding a buried clutch of big eggs. Ostrich dinosaurs lacked weapons to fight off more powerful dinosaurs, but their keen eyes soon glimpsed any coming danger. Their best defense was a fast getaway; no known dinosaur could catch an ornithomimid at full speed. Some of these ostrich dinosaurs may have run faster than a horse can gallop, though they could not dodge quickly.

Built for sprinting
Dromiceiomimus was possibly the fastest dinosaur of all. It ran faster than a horse can gallop, thanks to a body built to reduce weight and increase speed.
a Light, toothless head
b Slim neck
c Thin arms with grasping hands
d Slender tail held level to maintain balance
e Long, powerful legs
f Shins longer than thighs (**g**)
h Long foot bones

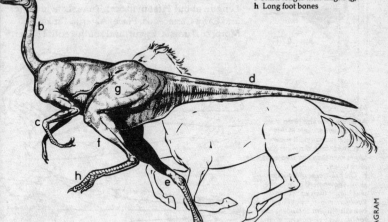

©DIAGRAM

55

Ornithomimids (ostrich dinosaurs)

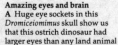

1 **Archaeornithomimus** ("ancient bird mimic") was rather primitive but had straight claws on the fingers and curved claws on the toes, like *Ornithomimus*. Length: about 11ft 6in (3.5m). Time: early Late Cretaceous. Place: northern China and eastern North America.

2 **Betasuchus** ("B crocodile") is the only ostrich dinosaur so far found in Europe. Length: maybe 11ft 6in (3.5m). Time: Late Cretaceous. Place: southeast Netherlands.

3 **Dromiceiomimus** ("emu mimic") had weak hands but longer shins than other ornithomimids. It could probably run faster than an ostrich does today. Its big brain controlled the limbs, and huge eyes may have helped it feed at dusk. Length: 11ft 6in (3.5m). Weight: 220lb (100kg). Time: Late Cretaceous. Place: southern Alberta, Canada.

4 **Elaphrosaurus** ("light lizard") had rather shorter legs and arms and ran more slowly than the later ostrich dinosaurs. It may have been their ancestor. Length: about 11ft 6in (3.5m). Time: Late Jurassic and Early Cretaceous. Place: Algeria, Tanzania, Morocco, Tunisia, Egypt, and south-central Niger.

Amazing eyes and brain
A Huge eye sockets in this *Dromiceiomimus* skull show us that this ostrich dinosaur had larger eyes than any land animal alive today.
B The brain case of the same skull, shown here from above, was bigger than an ostrich's. *Dromiceiomimus* would have been intelligent enough to care for its own free-ranging young; indeed bones of an adult and two young were found together.

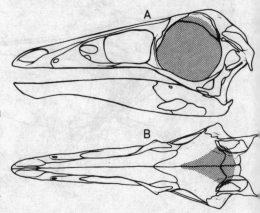

5 **Gallimimus** ("fowl mimic") may have been the largest ostrich dinosaur. Its hands seem poorly made for grasping. The long snout had a broad, flat end. Length: 13ft (4m). Time: Late Cretaceous. Place: southern Mongolia.

6 **Ornithomimus** ("bird mimic") had thinner arms than *Struthiomimus* (yet some people think that these two and *Dromiceiomimus* were all in the same genus). More than half its length was tail. It lived in gloomy swamps and forests. Length: about 11ft 6in (3.5m). Time: Late Cretaceous. Place: western North America and Tibet.

7 **Struthiomimus** ("ostrich mimic") appears to have had stronger arms and hands than most other ostrich dinosaurs. There were powerful curved claws on the fingers, not weak, straight ones. It evidently lived on open river banks. Length: 11ft 6in (3.5m). Time: Late Cretaceous. Place: southern Alberta, Canada and New Jersey, USA.

8 **Tugulusaurus** ("Tugulo lizard") was an Early Cretaceous ostrich dinosaur of Sinkiang, northwest China. Length: perhaps 11ft 6in (3m).

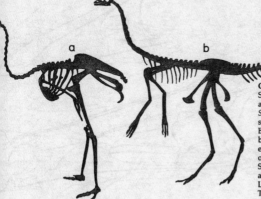

Ostrich and ostrich mimic
Skeletons of a living ostrich (**a**) and the "ostrich mimic" *Struthiomimus* (**b**) show striking similarities of size and shape. But *Struthiomimus* had a long, bony tail and its arm bones ended in clawed hands instead of bearing feathered wings. Skeletons of ostrich dinosaurs are in museums in East Berlin, London, New York, Ottawa, and Toronto.

©DIAGRAM

57

Garudimimids

Garudimimids ("Garuda mimics") were a family of toothless dinosaurs first described in 1981 by the Mongolian scientist Rinchen Barsbold. He named the only known fossil for the Garuda, a bird in Indian mythology. Skull and foot bones show that in some ways *Garudimimus* resembled ostrich dinosaurs (ornithomimids). In other ways it seemed quite different – so different that Barsbold felt the animal must have been a member of another family, until that time unknown to science.

1 **Garudimimus** ("Garuda mimic") had a long, light, narrow head, with large eyes, much like the ornithomimids. Yet the beak tip seems more rounded, and a low bony crest rises from the skull roof above the front of the eyes. *Garudimimus* also seems to have had shorter toes than ostrich dinosaurs. Length: perhaps 11ft 6in (3.5m). Time: Late Cretaceous. Place: southeast Mongolia.

The never-never "bird"
Named for a mythical bird of India, *Garudimimus* had an unusual kind of skull.
a This socket was designed to hold a very large eye.
b This bony ridge may have supported a head crest.
c The tip of the beak's upper mandible was deeper and more rounded than that of an ostrich dinosaur (d). (Large illustration after Barsbold.)

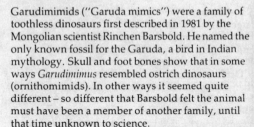

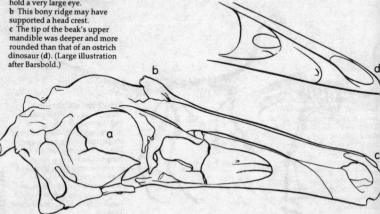

Deinocheirids

Among the strangest and most mystifying of all families of dinosaurs, the "terrible hands" are known only from a pair of immensely long arms and hands discovered in a Mongolian desert. Of all known beasts alive or dead, only the flesh-eating therizinosaurids had arms approaching these in size. In both groups, three-fingered hands bore gigantic claws, yet deinocheirid arms were much slimmer and less powerful than the therizinosaurids'. Deinocheirids might have resembled gigantic ornithomimid or dromaeosaurid dinosaurs, or the rest of their body might have been much smaller than the arms suggest. Either way, these hands could have served as horrifying weapons for attacking dinosaurs of almost any size.

Where they lived
Both *Deinocheirus* (**a**) and *Garudimimus* (**b**) lived in Mongolia, as this map shows.

1 **Deinocheirus** ("terrible hand") had rather slim arms, each measuring an unbelievable 8ft 6in (2.6m). The three fingers on each hand bore long, curved, powerful-looking claws capable of ripping open a sauropod's soft underbelly. Time: Late Cretaceous. Place: southern Mongolia.

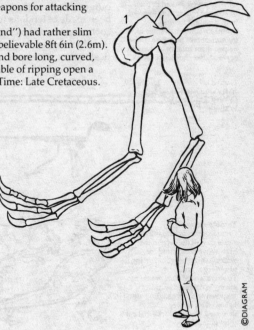

1

Mysterious arms (right)
Deinocheirus's enormous arm bones are arranged here as if hung from the shoulder bones. The arms dwarf a human figure shown beside them. Some scientists think their owner must have been a giant, lightweight ostrich dinosaur; yet the huge, powerful, sharply curved claws seem very different from the straighter, weaker claws of most ostrich dinosaurs.

©DIAGRAM

59

Dromaeosaurids 1

In 1969 the first full description of these "running lizards" did much to upset old notions that dinosaurs had been merely sluggish, stupid reptiles. These small to medium-sized flesh-eaters proved to have been among the fastest, fiercest, most agile hunters of any age. Their special features lead many scientists to group them in their own infraorder, deinonychosaurs, separate from their coelurosaur ancestors.

Dromaeosaurids had a huge claw on the second toe, and long arms with three-fingered hands that were designed for grasping and equipped with claws. The tail was specially stiffened with slim, bony rods, outgrowths from the tail bones, once thought to have been made of tendons turned to bone. Like most coelurosaurs, dromaeosaurids had sharp teeth, but their brains were big compared with those of most flesh-eating dinosaurs.

Stiff tails
From about the tenth tail bone (**a**) on toward the tail tip (**b**), each bone sprouted long, slim bony rods. These overlapped other tail bones, so locking them together. Some of *Deinonychus*'s tail bones were locked in place by 40 bony rods jutting forward from vertebrae behind. Dromaeosaurids had some of the stiffest tails in nature. These helped them balance as they ran or stood upon one leg to attack.

Terrible claws (right)
Dromaeosaurids held the big, sickle claw of the second toe high above the ground for walking; but they could swing it to and fro at will.
To attack a rival male or other enemy, a dromaeosaurid grappled with its gangling arms, balanced on one leg, and delivered slashing kicks that cut through hide.

Dromaeosaurids may have used claws, tail, and brain to kill their prey in a uniquely terrifying way. They may have hidden in ambush, or ranged the countryside in packs, running down poorly defended small or medium-sized plant-eating dinosaurs. Leaping on its victim, a dromaeosaurid could have grasped the creature with its hands, digging in the claws to keep its enemy at arm's length as it delivered slashing kicks. The great claw on its second toe may have ripped through the victim's side, disemboweling it. An attacking dromaeosaurid could carry out an attack while standing on one leg, for its big brain automatically controlled posture so that the stiffened tail helped it keep its balance. These savage hunters must have been among the most feared carnivores of northern continents during the Cretaceous Period.

Where dromaeosaurids lived
This map shows the homelands of all six known kinds of dromaeosaurid described on the next two pages.
1 *Adasaurus*
2 *Deinonychus*
3 *Dromaeosaurus*
4 *Phaedrolosaurus*
5 *Saurornitholestes*
6 *Velociraptor*

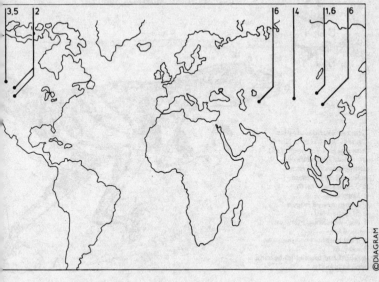

©DIAGRAM

61

Dromaeosaurids 2

1 **Adasaurus** – named but not yet described – had hip bones arranged more like those of ornithischians than saurischians – the great group of dinosaurs to which dromaeosaurids belonged. Length: perhaps 7ft (2m). Time: Late Cretaceous. Place: southern Mongolia.

2 **Deinonychus** ("terrible claw") was one of the largest dromaeosaurids. Like the others it had a short, clawed, first ("big") toe turned back. The second toe bore a sickle-shaped claw 5in (12.7cm) long. Its weight rested on the long third and fourth toes of each foot. The tail was stiffened by up to 40 bony rods around each vertebra. Length: 8–13ft (2.4-4m). Time: Early Cretaceous. Place: western USA.

3 **Dromaeosaurus** ("running lizard") was an agile, man-sized predator – like *Deinonychus* but smaller. Length: 6ft (1.8m). Time: Late Cretaceous. Place: southern Alberta, Canada.

Dromaeosaurid body plan
Deinonychus (**A**) from North America and *Velociraptor* (**B**) from Asia shared these dromaeosaurid features.
a Relatively big brain
b Small, sharp teeth
c Long arms
d Long, clawed fingers
e Stiffened tail
f Big, switchblade claw on second toe
g First toe short and pointing backward
h Third and fourth toes bearing weight of body

Phaedrolosaurus ("gleaming whole lizard") resembled *Deinonychus* and may have been its ancestor. Time: Early Cretaceous. Place: Sinkiang, northwest China.

Saurornitholestes ("lizard-bird robber") was a small, lightly built dromaeosaurid or perhaps a saurornithoidid, described in 1978. Its skull shape suggests that it might have had a bigger brain than *Dromaeosaurus*, but a poorer sense of smell. Its small, sharp, saw-edged teeth also differed from that dinosaur's. The hands were well designed for powerful grasping and bore small but strong, sharp, curved claws. Length: about 6ft (1.8m). Time: Late Cretaceous. Place: southern Alberta, Canada.

Velociraptor ("swift plunderer") had a long, low head and depressed muzzle. Scientists found one that had died fighting a *Protoceratops*. Length: 6ft (1.8m). Time: Late Cretaceous. Place: Mongolia, China, and Kazakhstan.

Grappling hooks (right)
Bones and curved claws of a *Saurornitholestes* hand appear here actual size. At least some dromaeosaurids could turn claws toward each other to grip prey.

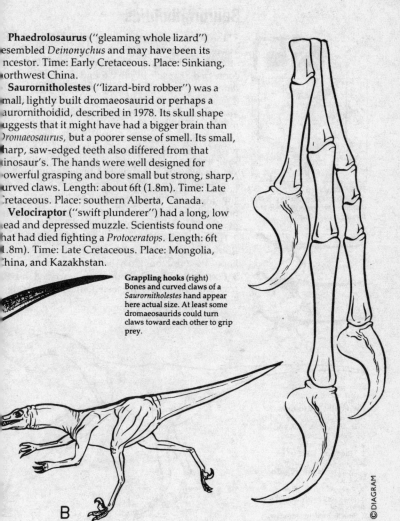

B

©DIAGRAM

63

Saurornithoidids

These "bird-like lizards" were lightweight predators as long as a man. They shared some features found in other small theropods. Their long, light skulls contained a capsule like that found in ostrich dinosaurs, but also bore sharp teeth. Like dromaeosaurids, they had a stiffened tail, long arms, and a second toe sprouting a "terrible claw"; but this toe was relatively weak and the claw was rather small. What made saurornithoidids most remarkable was a surprisingly big brain and enormous, wide-set eyes. These beasts probably stalked and seized small mammals at dusk. They lived in northern lands in Late Cretaceous times.

1 **Bradycneme** ("heavy leg") is known only from a broken limb bone, once thought to be a giant owl's. It lived in Translyvanian Romania.

2 **Heptasteornis** ("seven town bird") is another Romanian saurornithoidid known from just one bone, also once thought to be an owl's.

3 **Pectinodon** ("comb tooth") was described in 1982 from *Saurornithoides*-like teeth found in Wyoming.

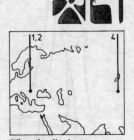

Where they lived
Bradycneme (1), *Heptasteornis* (2), and *Saurornithoides* (4) finds are located on this map.

Saurornithoidid features
Saurornithoidids were slighter than dromaeosaurids, and had the following features.
a Even larger brain
b Huge eyes, wide set for judging distance easily
c Small teeth, saw-edged only at the back
d A capsule in the skull
e More tooth sockets in the lower jaw
f Smaller switchblade claw

© DIAGRAM

64

4 Saurornithoides ("bird-like lizard") had a long, ~~nar~~row head, depressed muzzle, and sharp teeth. Bulk-~~f~~or-bulk *Saurornithoides* had a brain six times larger ~~t~~han a crocodile's and must have lived less by instinct ~~t~~han ordinary reptiles. Both eyes could focus on one ~~o~~bject, which helped it to judge distances just as we ~~d~~o. *Saurornithoides* probably used its long arms and ~~g~~rasping hands to seize small mammals and feed ~~t~~hem to its mouth. Length: 6ft 6in (2m). Place: ~~M~~ongolia.

5 Stenonychosaurus ("narrow claw lizard") was an ~~a~~gile, rapid runner with a brain bigger than an emu's. ~~I~~t closely resembled *Saurornithoides*. Length: 6ft 6in ~~(~~2m). Weight: 60–100lb (27–45kg). Place: southern ~~A~~lberta, Canada.

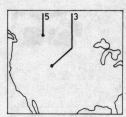

Where they lived
Finds of *Pectinodon* (3) and *Stenonychosaurus* (5) are shown on this map of North America.

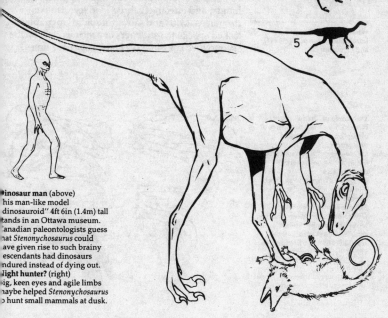

Dinosaur man (above)
~~T~~his man-like model ~~"~~dinosauroid" 4ft 6in (1.4m) tall ~~s~~tands in an Ottawa museum. ~~C~~anadian paleontologists guess ~~t~~hat *Stenonychosaurus* could ~~h~~ave given rise to such brainy ~~d~~escendants had dinosaurs ~~e~~ndured instead of dying out.
Night hunter? (right)
~~B~~ig, keen eyes and agile limbs ~~m~~aybe helped *Stenonychosaurus* ~~t~~o hunt small mammals at dusk.

65

Oviraptorids

Oviraptorids ("egg thieves") was the name given in 1976 to a group of small theropod dinosaurs discovered in the deserts of Mongolia. Besides ostrich dinosaurs, oviraptorids and caenagnathids are the best-known toothless saurischians, with jaws ending in a bird-like beak. Even more surprising is that an oviraptorid's beak was short and deep, like its head; quite different from the long, narrow head and beak of ostrich dinosaurs. Despite their lack of teeth, oviraptorids could bite with a powerful, crushing action. They could obviously crunch up harder foods than the dinosaur eggs that fossil finds suggest they enjoyed. Some oviraptorids had an unusual nasal crest. The rest of the body probably resembled a coelurid's. There were three-fingered grasping hands, and effectively three-toed feet. Unlike dromaeosaurids and saurornithoidids, oviraptorids lacked special tail stiffeners or a vicious claw on the second toe. They lived in Late Cretaceous times.

Where they lived
Located are finds of *Ingenia* (**1**)
and *Oviraptor* (**2**).

Two kinds of "hand" (right)
Finger bones from two kinds of oviraptorid show marked differences.
a *Oviraptor*'s fingers had long bones and strong, sharply curved claws.
b *Ingenia*'s fingers were short and stubby and the claws less strongly curved.
Strange skull (far right)
Oviraptor's short, deep skull (**A**) looks like no other known dinosaur's, yet surprisingly resembles that of a flamingo (**B**).

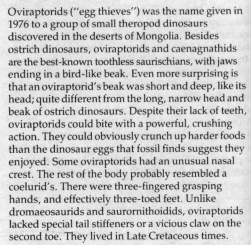

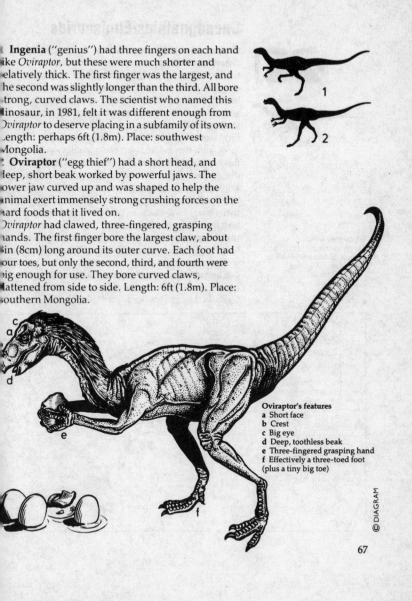

1 Ingenia ("genius") had three fingers on each hand like *Oviraptor*, but these were much shorter and relatively thick. The first finger was the largest, and the second was slightly longer than the third. All bore strong, curved claws. The scientist who named this dinosaur, in 1981, felt it was different enough from *Oviraptor* to deserve placing in a subfamily of its own. Length: perhaps 6ft (1.8m). Place: southwest Mongolia.

2 Oviraptor ("egg thief") had a short head, and deep, short beak worked by powerful jaws. The lower jaw curved up and was shaped to help the animal exert immensely strong crushing forces on the hard foods that it lived on.

Oviraptor had clawed, three-fingered, grasping hands. The first finger bore the largest claw, about 3in (8cm) long around its outer curve. Each foot had four toes, but only the second, third, and fourth were big enough for use. They bore curved claws, flattened from side to side. Length: 6ft (1.8m). Place: southern Mongolia.

Oviraptor's features
a Short face
b Crest
c Big eye
d Deep, toothless beak
e Three-fingered grasping hand
f Effectively a three-toed foot
(plus a tiny big toe)

© DIAGRAM

67

Caenagnathids/Elmisaurids

Caenagnathids ("recent jawless") and elmisaurids ("foot lizards") are strange families of Late Cretaceous theropods from northern lands. Some scientists have argued that caenagnathids were really toothless birds. Others think they were oviraptorids – man-sized dinosaurs with short, deep heads, and strong, toothless jaws.

First described in 1981, elmisaurids probably had long, slim heads like most other small to medium flesh-eating dinosaurs, but their skulls remain to be discovered. These slim-limbed hunters are best known from their hand and foot bones. They had three slender fingers on each hand, and effectively three long, bird-like toes per foot. Some foot bones had fused together in a way that scientists used to think happened only in birds. In fact the elmisaurids' foot design strengthens the idea that birds evolved from dinosaurs.

1 **Caenagnathus** ("recent jawless") was described from two toothless lower jaws found in Alberta, Canada. Length: perhaps 7ft (2m).

Where they lived
Known caenagnathids lived in Canada. Elmisaurids lived in Canada and Mongolia.
1 *Caenagnathus*
2 *Chirostenotes*
3 *Elmisaurus*
4 *Macrophalangia*

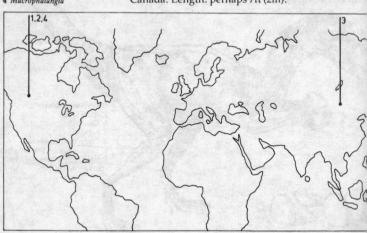

2 **Chirostenotes** ("slender hands") may have resembled a dromaeosaurid like *Stenonychosaurus* but had longer, less sharply curved claws. Its long fingers had narrower claws than *Elmisaurus*'s. It may have been the same as *Macrophalangia*. Length: perhaps 7ft (2m). Place: Alberta, Canada.

3 **Elmisaurus** ("foot lizard") was a lightly built, medium-sized flesh-eater with a thinner hand than coelurids or dromaeosaurids. It had a bird-like foot with three long toes and a short first ("big") toe, which might have been turned back. The second finger and the third toe were its longest digits. Length: maybe 7ft (2m). Place: southern Mongolia.

4 **Macrophalangia** ("big phalanges" – end bones of toes or fingers) is known from a right foot with relatively longer toes (especially the first toe) than *Elmisaurus*. It may have been the same as *Chirostenotes*. Length: perhaps 7ft (2m). Place: Alberta, Canada.

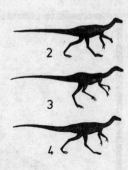

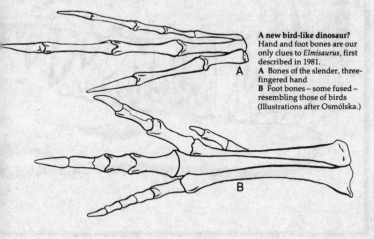

A new bird-like dinosaur?
Hand and foot bones are our only clues to *Elmisaurus*, first described in 1981.
A Bones of the slender, three-fingered hand
B Foot bones – some fused – resembling those of birds
(Illustrations after Osmólska.)

© DIAGRAM

69

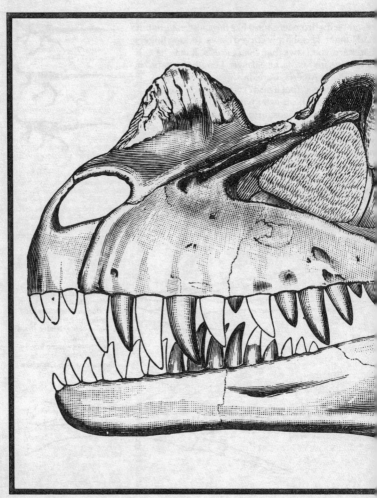

Section 2 CARNOSAURS

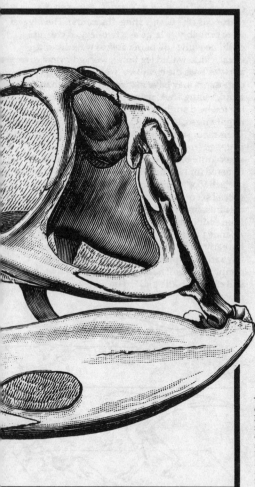

Carnosaurs ("flesh lizards") were big, heavy, powerful animals belonging to the great group of flesh-eating saurischian dinosaurs called theropods or "beast feet."

In this section the term carnosaur is used loosely to cover members of the infraorder carnosauria and other big theropods.

Carnosaurs may have evolved from those smaller theropods the coelurosaurs, or even from prosauropods.

Or perhaps different carnosaurs had different ancestors and did not form one related group of families. This section describes 10 families of carnosaurs, and some theropods whose families remain unknown. Most of the latter left so few remains that it is impossible to say just what they came from.

(For general information about this section, see the chapter introduction on page 38.)

This old illustration of a *Ceratosaurus* skull reveals its large size, powerful jaws, and formidable fangs. No beasts that ever lived on land had such savage teeth and claws as the big flesh-eating dinosaurs. Illustration after O.C. Marsh, appearing in *Dinosaurs* by W.E. Swinton (British Museum, Natural History).

About carnosaurs

Carnosaurs or "flesh lizards" included all the larger theropods (the flesh-eating dinosaurs). The biggest were probably as large as a two-legged creature could be while still being able to walk around. Great, thick-walled leg bones worked by massive muscles bore the creatures' weight. The largest carnosaurs may have managed no more than a rapid, rolling walk, using powerful muscles to keep the tail held stiffly off the ground, so balancing the mighty torso, short, thick neck, and big, deep head. Their main weapons were big, sharp, curved teeth, flattened from side to side and saw edged like a steak-knife blade; strong, sharp claws on three-fingered (or two-fingered) hands; and great talons on each foot's three big, forward-pointing toes. A special set of extra ribs, found also in the coelurosaurs, may have helped protect the belly from sudden lunges made by victims.

As time passed, larger kinds of carnosaur replaced the early types. The smaller, more active ones could have attacked plant-eaters at least as big as camptosaurids. The largest were probably too slow and clumsy to kill, and fed on corpses – behaving more like jackals than like lions.

Ogres or trash collectors?
1 The carnosaur *Albertosaurus* chases a fleet-footed ostrich dinosaur. Perhaps carnosaurs were active hunters – but most big ones would have been too slow to catch small sprinters.
2 The carnosaur *Rapator* drives pterosaurs from the corpse of a dinosaur that has died of old age. Maybe big carnosaurs were scavengers, not hunters.

72

Carnosaur family tree
This family tree shows the 10
carnosaur families described in
this chapter. Relationships and
origins are largely guesswork.
a Teratosaurids
b Therizinosaurids
c Ceratosaurids
d Spinosaurids
e Allosaurids
f Megalosaurids
g Dryptosaurids
h Tyrannosaurids
i Itemirids
j Segnosaurids
A Triassic Period
B Jurassic Period
C Cretaceous Period

Man and monster
Skeletons of a man (**A**) and a
Tyrannosaurus (**B**) reveal the
huge size reached by the largest
kinds of carnosaur.

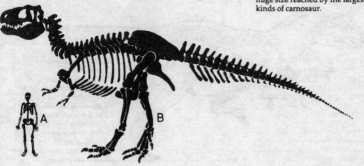

©DIAGRAM

73

Teratosaurids

These "monster lizards" may have been the first of several families of big, flesh-eating dinosaurs called carnosaurs. Their remains are scanty and some scientists think they were not dinosaurs. Some weighed as much as a racehorse. The large head, short, strong neck, and short body were probably balanced by a long, stiff tail, and borne on long, powerful hind legs. Their weapons were blade-like fangs, and claws on toes and fingers. Most have been discovered in West European rocks of Late Triassic Age – perhaps 200 million years ago.

1 **Basutodon** ("Basuto tooth") was named from a Late Triassic tooth found in Basutoland (Lesotho).

2 **Picrodon** ("sharp tooth") was named from a pointed tooth found in Somerset, England.

3 **Teratosaurus** ("monster lizard") had strong arms. Each ended in three fingers tipped with claws for slashing or seizing prey. Length: 20ft (6m). Weight: up to ¾ US ton (0.7 tonne). Place: West Germany and maybe Africa.

4 **Zanclodon** ("sickle tooth") is named from a piece of jaw. Place: West Germany.

Teratosaurid finds
Locations are marked by dots.
1 *Basutodon*
2 *Picrodon*
3 *Teratosaurus*
4 *Zanclodon*

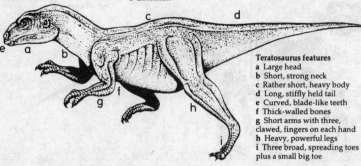

Teratosaurus features
a Large head
b Short, strong neck
c Rather short, heavy body
d Long, stiffly held tail
e Curved, blade-like teeth
f Thick-walled bones
g Short arms with three, clawed, fingers on each hand
h Heavy, powerful legs
i Three broad, spreading toes plus a small big toe

Megalosaurids 1

Megalosaurids or "great lizards" made up the largest family of big, flesh-eating dinosaurs. Like teratosaurids, which may have been their ancestors, most were heavy-bodied and ambled on huge hind legs. Each leg was armed with three powerfully clawed toes. There may have been a small "big" toe turned backward. A hunting megalosaurid may have used its fairly long and strongly muscled arms to strike out at big, undefended browsing dinosaurs, ripping victims with claws on the three long outer fingers of each hand. (The inner two were tiny.) Gripping with its hands and feet, it would have bent its short, powerful neck to sink its saw-edged, blade-like fangs into the victim's body, slicing flesh and crunching bone as it closed the mighty jaws hinged in its big, high, narrow head.

Early Jurassic megalosaurids seem to have been relatively small and lightly built, but their remains are poorly known. Bigger, burlier beasts lived later – some were as heavy as an elephant. Megalosaurids reached all regions of the globe.

Megalosaurid finds
This map shows many places where megalosaurid fossils have been found.

  1 *Bahariasaurus*
  2 *Carcharodontosaurus*
  3 *Chingkankousaurus*
  4 *Dilophosaurus*
  5 *Embasaurus*
  6 *Erectopus*
  7 *Eustreptospondylus*
  8 *Kelmayisaurus*
  9 *Macrodontophion*
 10 *Majungasaurus*
 11 *Megalosaurus*
 12 *Orthogoniosaurus*
 13 *Poekilopleuron*
 14 *Proceratosaurus*
 15 *Sarcosaurus*
 16 *Szechuanosaurus*
 17 *Torvosaurus*
Berkeley, Los Angeles, Washington, DC, and Oxford (England) have museums with megalosaurid remains.

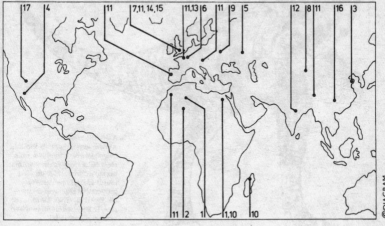

©DIAGRAM

75

Megalosaurids 2

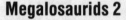

1 **Bahariasaurus** ("Baharije lizard") is known from bones found in northern Egypt and Algeria. It was a Late Cretaceous dinosaur.

2 **Carcharodontosaurus** ("*Carcharodon* lizard") is named for *Carcharodon*, the great white shark. It had a big skull, high back vertebrae, short arms, large claws and murderously sharp, straight teeth. It lived where the Sahara Desert is today. Time: Early Cretaceous. Length about 26ft (8m).

3 **Chingkankousaurus** ("Ch'ing-kang-kou lizard") was probably like *Allosaurus* but smaller. It roamed Late Cretaceous China.

4 **Dilophosaurus** ("two ridged lizard") had two wafer-thin, fragile, bony ridges along the top of its head. Only males might have grown these. *Dilophosaurus* lived in Early Jurassic Arizona. Length: over 20ft (6m).

5 **Embasaurus** ("Emba lizard") is known from pieces of backbone from near the Emba River in Soviet Central Asia. Time: Early Cretaceous.

A double crest
At first some scientists thought *Dilophosaurus*'s fragile double crest came from another animal because crests and skull were found apart. Later discovery proved that skull and crests belonged together. Despite its size, *Dilophosaurus* might have been a coelurosaur.

6 **Erectopus** ("upright foot") is named from the shape of leg and foot bones found in Early Cretaceous rocks of northeast France.

7 **Eustreptospondylus** ("well-twisted vertebra") may have had a head like *Allosaurus*'s. It lived in Middle Jurassic England. Length: 23ft (7m).

8 **Kelmayisaurus** ("Kelmayi lizard") was an Early Cretaceous megalosaurid from Sinkiang in Chinese Central Asia.

9 **Macrodontophion** ("large tooth snake") lived in Jurassic south European Russia. We know it only from a round-topped tooth. This was shorter from front to back than most megalosaurid teeth.

10 **Majungasaurus** ("Majunga lizard") comes from Late Cretaceous rocks of Majunga in northwest Madagascar, and maybe Egypt. Scientists have found teeth, and pieces of skeleton.

5

6

7

8

9

10

Bony clues to a killer
1 A *Eustreptospondylus* skeleton found near Oxford, in southern central England, is the best preserved of any European theropod. Thick-walled leg bones helped bear the creature's bulky body, which was some four times longer than a man's.
2 Large openings in the big skull helped to reduce its weight.

77

Megalosaurids 3

11 **Megalosaurus** ("great lizard") was a big, heavy-bodied carnosaur with curved, saw-edged teeth flattened from side to side, and strong curved claws on toes and fingers. Scores of bones, teeth, or footprints thought to be from this dinosaur have been found in Europe, South America, Africa, and Asia. Time: perhaps Early Jurassic to Early Cretaceous. Length: 30ft (9m). Weight: 1 US ton (900kg).

12 **Orthogoniosaurus** ("straight angle lizard") is a megalosaurid known only from a small tooth of odd form from Late Cretaceous rocks in India.

13 **Poekilopleuron** ("varying side") had powerful arms and may have looked like *Torvosaurus*. It roamed Mid Jurassic northern France. Length: probably up to 30ft (9m).

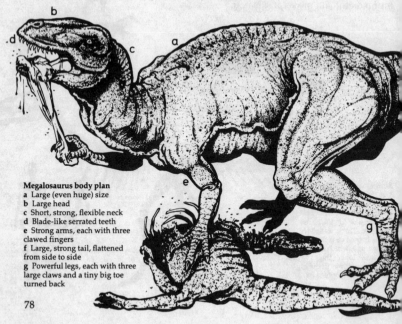

Megalosaurus body plan
a Large (even huge) size
b Large head
c Short, strong, flexible neck
d Blade-like serrated teeth
e Strong arms, each with three clawed fingers
f Large, strong tail, flattened from side to side
g Powerful legs, each with three large claws and a tiny big toe turned back

14 Proceratosaurus ("before the horned lizard") from Mid Jurassic England was rather small, with a horn over its nose. It might have been a ceratosaurid ancestor of *Ceratosaurus*.

15 Sarcosaurus ("flesh lizard") was small and lightly built, and lived in Early Jurassic England. Length: 11ft 6in (3.5m).

16 Szechuanosaurus ("Szechuan lizard") from Szechuan, China, looked somewhat like the much larger *Allosaurus*. Time: Late Jurassic. Length: about 26ft (8m).

17 Torvosaurus ("savage lizard") was as long as *Allosaurus* and more massive, with short but powerful arms and frightful claws. Despite these features, it might have been just a harmless scavenger. Length: 33ft (10m). Weight: up to 6 US tons (5.4 tonnes). Time: Late Jurassic. Place western North America.

©DIAGRAM

A megalosaurid oddity (below) *Proceratosaurus*'s skull shows a small horn sprouted from the snout. Some experts think this unusual megalosaurid was really a ceratosaurid.

Four legs or two? (left) In 1854 a British paleontologist pictured *Megalosaurus* as four legged. The first to realize that such dinosaurs stood on their hind limbs were paleontologists in the United States. Fossil tracks give clues to how these bulky bipeds actually walked. One trackway in the south of England shows that the toes pointed inward. Maybe megalosaurids waddled like giant ducks, the tail swinging from side to side each time they took a step.

79

Allosaurids

Allosaurus features
a Huge size (compare it with this family car)
b Massive head with unusual bumps and nasal crest
c Vast jaws, with more saber-like teeth than *Megalosaurus*
d Short, strong neck
e Deep, narrow body
f Strong arms
g Three-fingers per "hand"
h Long, stiffly held tail
i Great legs
j Three-toed feet

Allosaurids have been called the tigers of their age. They were flesh-eaters as long as a bus – larger and maybe more agile than most megalosaurids. Over half their length was tail, held up to balance the short, heavy body, thick, flexible neck, and massive head. Allosaurids' huge jaws gaped wide enough to bolt great chunks of meat torn from victims with sharp, curved fangs. Some scientists think allosaurids ate only carrion because they were too big and clumsy to hunt. Others believe they ran fast and swam well. Packs of allosaurids might have killed huge sauropods. They probably thrived from Early Jurassic to Late Cretaceous times and most have been found in North America, where one quarry yielded 40 specimens. Allosaurids lived in every continent, however.

1 **Allosaurus** ("other lizard") was much like *Megalosaurus* but was even larger. It also had more teeth in its front upper jaw, and an extra pair of openings in the sides of its skull. There were two bony bumps above and just ahead of the eyes, two smaller bumps behind them, and a low, narrow,

bony ridge that ran from eyes to snout. Many grew to 36ft (11m) and most weighed 1–2 US tons (around 1–2 tonnes). One is supposed to have measured 42ft (12.8m) long and 16ft (4.9m) high. *Allosaurus* lived in Late Jurassic North America, Africa, Australia, and maybe Asia.

2 **Indosaurus** ("Indian lizard") had a remarkably thick, massive braincase. Time: Late Cretaceous. Place: central India.

3 **Piatnitzkysaurus** ("Piatnitzky's lizard") from Late Jurassic southern Argentina was like *Allosaurus* but more "old-fashioned" and its upper arm was relatively longer.

4 **Piveteausaurus** ("Piveteau's lizard") had a longer braincase and lower bumps above the eyes than *Allosaurus*. It lived in northern France in Mid Jurassic times. Length: perhaps up to 36ft (11m). Weight: up to 2 US tons (1.8 tonnes).

5 **Yangchuanosaurus** ("Yang-ch'uan lizard") had a flexible neck and tail. It lived in early Late Jurassic China. Length: up to 33ft (10m).

Where they lived
Allosaurid homelands are shown on the map.
1 *Allosaurus*
2 *Indosaurus*
3 *Piatnitzkysaurus*
4 *Piveteausaurus*
5 *Yangchuanosaurus*
Many museums show allosaurid fossil bones or casts.

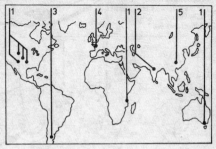

©DIAGRAM

Ceratosaurids

Ceratosaurids seem to have been an unusual family of big flesh-eating dinosaurs with a horn above the nose. Rival males may have butted one another with their horns – but were unlikely to do real damage. Ceratosaurids lived at the same time as *Allosaurus* but were half the size and probably hunted more actively. Discoveries of groups of fossil footprints suggest they roamed in packs to hunt beasts like *Camptosaurus*.

1 **Ceratosaurus** ("horned lizard") had a short horn core on its nose and bumps above the eyes. A row of small bony plates ran down the middle of its back. Its arms were short but strong. There were four clawed fingers on each hand and three clawed toes per foot. Some foot bones were fused. *Ceratosaurus* lived in North America and East Africa. Length: 15–20ft (4.6–6m).

2 **Chienkosaurus** ("Chien-ko lizard") from China is known from just four teeth. Some experts think they came from a prehistoric crocodile.

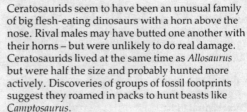

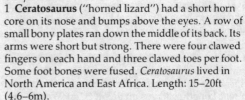

Ceratosaurid finds
The map shows sites of finds.
1 *Ceratosaurus*
2 *Chienkosaurus*

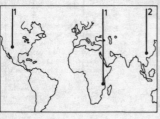

Clues to ceratosaurids
A, B Two views of the skull of a *Ceratosaurus*. Its light "lacy" build is like that of the allosaurids and megalosaurids. But the low bony bump on the snout may have been sheathed by a tall, sharp spike or horn.
C Of *Chienkosaurus* only teeth like this survive. Chinese experts now suspect that they were a crocodile's.

Dryptosaurids

This family of "wounding lizards" lived in North America and Asia in Late Cretaceous times. Yet the fossil finds are so few that no-one has been able to come up with a convincing full description of what made the family distinctive. Some scientists think that dryptosaurids were really tyrannosaurids. But if their family indeed existed it may have had three, not two, members: a powerful arm found in Mongolia may have been a dryptosaurid's.

1 Dryptosauroides ("*Dryptosaurus* form") was the name given to six big spinal bones found in central India in rocks laid down in Late Cretaceous times. Length: probably more than 20ft (6m).

2 Dryptosaurus ("wounding lizard") had short but powerful arms and great muscular legs. The curved teeth and claws were like a megalosaurid's, but the top of the thigh bone more resembled *Iguanodon*'s. *Dryptosaurus* lived in North America (New Jersey, Maryland, Colorado, Montana, and perhaps Wyoming). Length: well over 20ft (6m).

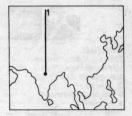

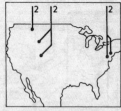

Fossil finds
Dryptosaurid fossil finds are located on these maps of Asia and North America.

©DIAGRAM

"Laelaps" the leaper
Dryptosaurus's discoverer, in 1866, believed it had used its huge hind limbs to leap kangaroo-like on prey, as it struck with its eagle-clawed feet. He named it *Laelaps* for a hunting dog which, in an old Greek myth, was turned to stone while leaping.

83

Spinosaurids

One group of huge, flesh-eating dinosaurs developed long spines jutting up from the back. Each spine was an overgrown part of a vertebra, one of the bones making up the backbone. Ordinary vertebrae have jutting spines that serve to anchor muscles and in *Acrocanthosaurus* this might have been their only purpose. (Perhaps *Acrocanthosaurus* was just an unusual megalosaurid, and not a spinosaurid.) But in dinosaurs like *Spinosaurus*, the spines must have supported a skin "sail." Rival males may have shown off their sails to threaten each other, or the sails might have been heat exchangers. At dawn the beasts may have stood sideways to the sun to warm up quickly. If they were cold-blooded, this may have helped the spinosaurids to grow active earlier than most other dinosaurs; they could start hunting while their prey were too cold and slow to escape. At midday, an overheated spinosaurid would have turned its back to the sun to shed unwanted heat.

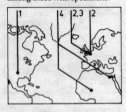

Fossil finds
This map shows the sites of spinosaurid fossil finds.
1 *Acrocanthosaurus*
2 *Altispinax*
3 *Metriacanthosaurus*
4 *Spinosaurus*
Museums of the universities of Oklahoma and Oxford are among those with specimens.

Sails as battle flags?
Rival male spinosaurids may have displayed their skin sails to threaten one another, perhaps rearing to exaggerate their height. Because their sails were very vulnerable to damage, actual fighting would have been unlikely.

Sails as radiators
Blood from *Spinosaurus*'s body coursed through its sail (shown in these diagrams from above) and back again.
A If a *Spinosaurus* stood sideways to the sun, many solar rays hit the sail, warming blood in sail and body.
B If a *Spinosaurus* stood with its back to the sun, fewer rays hit the sail. This shed body heat, so helping to stop *Spinosaurus* overheating.

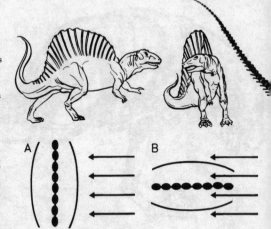

1 **Acrocanthosaurus** ("very spiny lizard") had spines up to 12in (30cm) long jutting from its backbone and probably embedded in a ridge of muscle. The head was relatively small. Length: 40ft (12m). Time: Early Cretaceous. Place: Oklahoma, USA.

2 **Altispinax** ("high thorn") had spines four times longer than the vertebrae they grew from. Spines may have held up a skin sail that rose above its shoulders. Length: 26ft (8m). Time: Early Cretaceous. Place: northwest Europe.

3 **Metriacanthosaurus** ("moderately spined lizard") had spines up to twice as long as the vertebrae they grew from. This Early Jurassic spinosaurid from England may have given rise to *Spinosaurus*. Length: about 26ft (8m).

4 **Spinosaurus** ("thorn lizard") had a skin sail on its back taller than a man, supported by blade-like spines up to 6ft (1.8m) long. Its teeth were straight, not curved like most carnosaurs'. It lived in Late Cretaceous Niger and Egypt. Length: 40ft (12m). Weight: up to 7 US tons (6.4 tonnes).

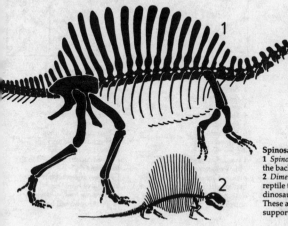

©DIAGRAM

Spinosaurus and Dimetrodon
1 *Spinosaurus*'s skeleton shows the backbone's tall spines.
2 *Dimetrodon* – a flesh-eating reptile that lived before the dinosaurs – had tall spines too. These also served as masts supporting a skin sail.

85

Tyrannosaurids 1

Tyrannosaurids ("tyrant lizards") included some of the biggest flesh-eating land animals of all time. Some weighed as much as a large elephant. They had a massive head, body, and legs, huge fangs, and enormous claws on the toes. The arms were small and each "hand" had only two fingers. Resting tyrannosaurids may have used these to stop their bodies sliding forward when they rose. Some scientists think tyrannosaurids were the most savage hunters that ever lived on land. They may have fought and killed horned and armored dinosaurs. Other experts claim tyrannosaurids were too big and clumsy to do more than waddle slowly and eat beasts they found already dead. Most lived in Asia or North America in Late Cretaceous times.

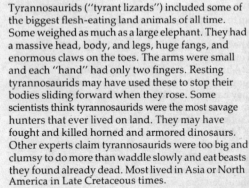

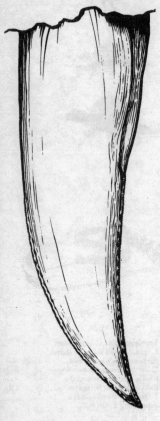

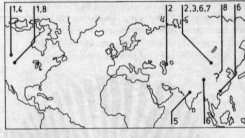

Where they lived (above)
Tyrannosaurid finds are shown.
1 *Albertosaurus*
2 *Alectrosaurus*
3 *Alioramus*
4 *Daspletosaurus*
5 *Indosuchus*
6 *Prodeinodon*
7 *Tarbosaurus*
8 *Tyrannosaurus*
Tyrannosaurus fang (left)
This *Tyrannosaurus* tooth is pictured actual size. Such huge blades with zigzag edges were designed to slice through hide and flesh.

Daspletosaurus (right)
The main features are shown.
a Huge size
b Enormous head
c Short, deep jaws
d Dagger-like teeth
e Short arms
f Two-fingered hands
g Short, flexible neck
h Short trunk (body)
i Broad hip girdle fused to the backbone
j Heavy, muscular tail
k Massive hind legs
l Three big toes
m First toe turned back

1 **Albertosaurus** ("Alberta lizard") was much like *Tyrannosaurus* but smaller and more lightly built, with puny arms but more teeth. Place: Alberta, Canada and Montana, USA. Length: 26ft (8m). Weight: 2 US tons (1.8 tonnes).

2 **Alectrosaurus** ("unmarried lizard") is known from bones found in Mongolia and Kazakhstan. Bones of a powerful arm once thought to have belonged to this dinosaur really came from another.

3 **Alioramus** ("other branch") may have been only half as long as *Tyrannosaurus*. It had a low head with bony knobs between the eyes and snout, and many sharp, curved fangs. Length: perhaps 20ft (6m). Place: Mongolia.

4 **Daspletosaurus** ("frightful lizard") had a great head, powerful body, small arms, and more teeth than *Tyrannosaurus*. Length: some 28ft (8.5m). Weight: perhaps up to 4 US tons (3.6 tonnes). Place: Alberta, Canada.

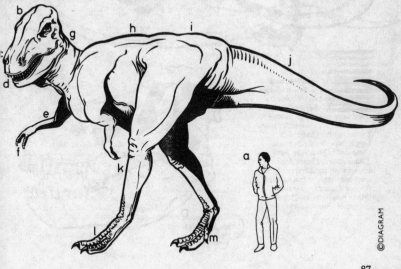

87

©DIAGRAM

Tyrannosaurids 2

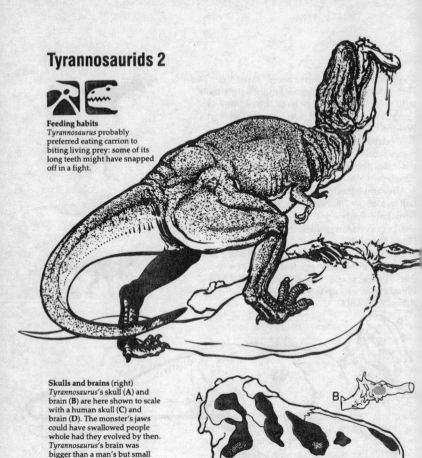

Feeding habits
Tyrannosaurus probably
preferred eating carrion to
biting living prey: some of its
long teeth might have snapped
off in a fight.

Skulls and brains (right)
Tyrannosaurus's skull (A) and
brain (B) are here shown to scale
with a human skull (C) and
brain (D). The monster's jaws
could have swallowed people
whole had they evolved by then.
Tyrannosaurus's brain was
bigger than a man's but small
compared to body size. Also
Tyrannosaurus's brain dealt
largely with sight and smell; the
cerebrum – the "thinking part"
(shown shaded) – was tiny.
(Many museums have remains
or casts of tyrannosaurids.)

5 **Indosuchus** ("Indian crocodile") has been called a medium-sized tyrannosaurid. It had more and shorter teeth than *Tyrannosaurus* and a more "old-fashioned" skull. It lived in central India.

6 **Prodeinodon** ("before the terror tooth") lived in Early Cretaceous Mongolia and China, before *"Deinodon"* (an old name for *Albertosaurus*). It may have been a megalosaurid ancestor of the tyrannosaurids.

7 **Tarbosaurus** ("alarming lizard") was a giant Asian carnosaur like *Tyrannosaurus* but less heavily built. Scientists have unearthed many *Tarbosaurus* skeletons in Mongolia. Length: 33–46ft (10–14m). Height: 14ft 6in–20ft (4.5–6m).

8 **Tyrannosaurus** ("tyrant lizard") was among the biggest, most powerfully armed carnosaurs. It measured 39ft (12m), towered 18ft 6in (5.6m) high and weighed as much as an African elephant: 7 US tons (6.4 tonnes). The skull alone measured 4ft (1.2m) and the saw-edged teeth were up to 7¼in (18.4cm) long. Arms were small but strong. Place: western North America and China.

Itemirids

First described in 1976, the itemirids were possibly fast-running, flesh-eating dinosaurs. In some ways they may have looked like the dromaeosaurids, but they more strongly resembled the huge tyrannosaurids, although much smaller and more agile. They probably also had better eyesight. Itemirids lived in Late Cretaceous Central Asia.

1 **Itemirus** is named for Itemir in central Kyzylkum where scientists found the small braincase of an adult. The lower part of the braincase resembled *Dromaeosaurus*'s. The upper part was more like that of *Tyrannosaurus*. The shape of the short high space inside the braincase shows that *Itemirus* had keen eyes and a well-developed sense of balance. The scientist describing *Itemirus* gave no estimate of size.

Itemirid homeland
This map shows where *Itemirus* was found.

©DIAGRAM

89

Segnosaurids

1
2
3

Strange saurischians (right)
Fossil finds prove segnosaurids were unusual saurischians (lizard-hipped dinosaurs).
A A *Segnosaurus* pubis – one of the bones making up the hip girdle – slanted back like an ornithischian's pubis (**a**) instead of jutting forward (**b**) like that of most saurischians.
B The skull had jaws like many an ornithischian's – ending in a toothless beak.
C Some scientists suppose this beak helped segnosaurids catch fish. The idea that they swam is hinted at by finds of tracks left by webbed, four-toed feet – prints quite possibly produced by segnosaurids.

This family is so unlike other flesh-eating dinosaurs that scientists place it in its own infraorder. Segnosaurids ("slow lizards") were lightly built, with hip bones aligned like those of the plant-eating, bird-hipped dinosaurs, and jaws with toothless beaks. Each foot had four toes (perhaps webbed), pointing forward and armed with long claws. Segnosaurids may have swum and hunted fish. They lived in Late Cretaceous East Asia.

1 **Erlikosaurus** ("Erlik's lizard") was named in 1980 for a legendary king of the dead. Its beaked jaws had short, sharp teeth. It was smaller than *Segnosaurus*, also from Mongolia.

2 **Segnosaurus** ("slow lizard") was described in 1979. It may have measured 30ft (9m) and stood taller than a man – perhaps 8ft (2.4m) high. *Segnosaurus* was found in southeast Mongolia.

3 **Nanshiungosaurus** ("Nanshiung lizard") may be a third East Asian segnosaurid, from China. Length: perhaps up to 13ft (4m).

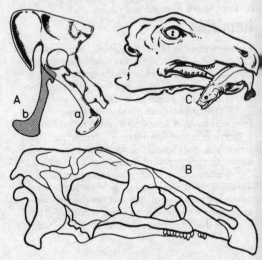

Therizinosaurids

Claws as savage as a sickle earned these "scythe lizards" their name. Jutting from an arm more massive than *Deinocheirus*'s and longer than a man, these weapons may have made their owners the most terrifying carnosaurs of all. The rest of the body remains mysteriously unknown.

Scythe lizards possibly evolved from ancestors of *Tyrannosaurus*, and may have used their mighty claws to kill duckbilled or armored dinosaurs. But perhaps they lived like giant anteaters, tearing open ants' nests with their claws to gobble up the teeming insect colonies inside. Only one Late Cretaceous genus from eastern Central Asia has been described.

1 **Therizinosaurus** ("scythe lizard") had arms over 8ft (2.4m) long, ending in fingers tipped with huge curved claws. One incomplete claw measured 27.6in (70cm) around its outer curve. Body length: unknown, perhaps 35ft (10.7m). Place: Nemegt Basin, southern Mongolia.

The missing monster (below)
A This illustration gives an idea of a therizinosaurid arm when its bones were clad in flesh. The ridge jutting forward half way along the upper arm bone provided a firm anchorage for powerful muscles that moved the arm.
B Huge claws like this projected from the fingers.
C A sickle held in a human hand is here drawn to the same scale.

Therizinosaurid finds
This map shows where *Therizinosaurus* was found.

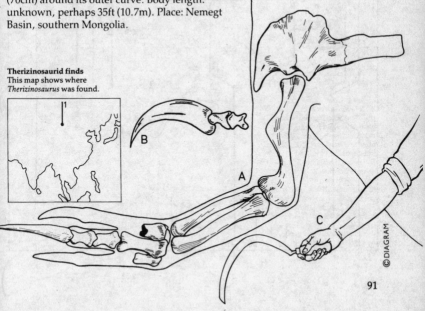

91

Strange killers

More than a dozen kinds of flesh-eating dinosaur are known only from teeth or pieces of bone that are so few or so broken that we cannot say what family they came from. Some may not belong to dinosaurs.

1 **Arctosaurus** ("Arctic lizard") is known from one vertebra, once thought to be a turtle's. Time: perhaps Late Triassic. Place: Cameron Island, Canada, north of the Arctic Circle.

2 **Chilantaisaurus** ("Ch'i-lan-t'ai lizard") was a big flesh-eating dinosaur with longish arms and hooked claws. It may have been a megalosaurid. Time: Late Cretaceous. Place: near Lake Jilantai, northwest China, and Kwangtung in the south.

3 **Colonosaurus** ("hill lizard") from Cretaceous western North America is a jaw that might be from a bird or a sea lizard.

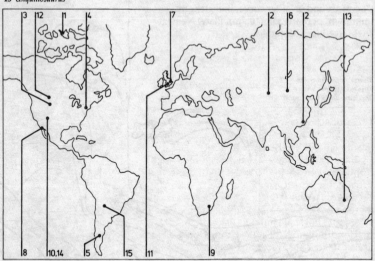

4 **Diplotomodon** ("double cutting tooth") is known from a tooth, once called a sea lizard's. Time: Cretaceous. Place: United States.

5 **Genyodectes** ("received under jaw") had small teeth but large jaws. Some think it was related to *Tyrannosaurus*. Time: Late Cretaceous. Place: Chubut province, southern Argentina.

6 **Hulsanpes** ("Chulsan foot") from Mongolia was a small theropod, described in 1982.

7 **Iliosuchus** ("crocodile hipped") may have been a small megalosaurid dinosaur. Time: Mid Jurassic. Place: Oxfordshire, England.

8 **Labocania** comes from Baja California's La Bocana Roja rock formation. It had a massive skull and may have resembled *Tyrannosaurus* but was stockier and smaller. Time: Late Cretaceous.

9 **Likhoelesaurus** ("Likhoele lizard") was an early theropod named in 1972 but not described. Time: Late Triassic. Place: Likhoele, Lesotho.

10 **Marshosaurus** ("Marsh's lizard") was an active hunter with sharp, curved, saw-edged teeth. Length: 16ft (5m) or less. Time: Late Jurassic. Place: Utah, USA.

11 **Palaeosauriscus** ("old lizard ancestor") was named from a tooth found near Bristol, England. Length: perhaps 20ft (6m). Time: Late Triassic.

12 **Paronychodon** ("alongside the nail tooth") is a poorly known dinosaur, named from a tooth found near the Judith River, Montana, USA.

13 **Rapator** ("plunderer") was an *Allosaurus*-size carnosaur. Length: perhaps 32ft (10m). Time: Early Cretaceous. Place: eastern Australia.

14 **Stokesosaurus** ("Stokes's lizard") was a small theropod, but maybe kin to *Tyrannosaurus*. Length: 13ft (4m). Time: Late Jurassic. Place: Utah, USA.

15 **Unquillosaurus** ("Unquillo lizard") was a big flesh-eater of Late Cretaceous northwest Argentina. Length: maybe 36ft (11m).

1
2
3
4
5
6
7
8
9
10
11
12
13
14
15

©DIAGRAM

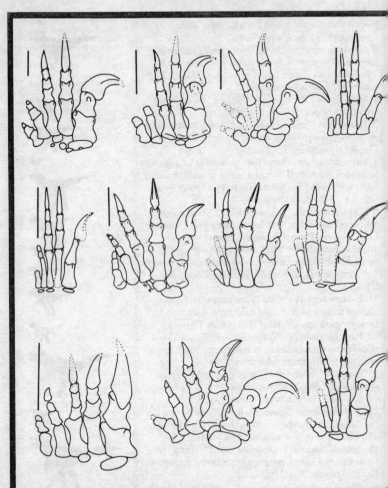

Section 3 PROSAUROPODS

This section describes seven families in the great group of mostly four-legged saurischians called sauropodomorphs ("lizard feet forms"). Here we call the seven families prosauropods ("before the lizard feet"). Some scientists prefer the name paleopods ("old feet"). The prosauropods (or paleopods) may have given rise to the mighty sauropods. (For general information about this section, see the chapter introduction on page 38.)

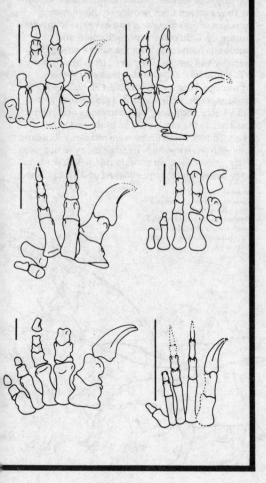

Seventeen drawings of the bones from prosauropods' hands betray the big, curved thumbs with spiky claws typical of these dinosaurs. Some hands were far larger than others, as the scale lines show; each line represents 5cm. Illustration after P.M. Galton and M.A. Cluver in *Annals of the South African Museum*, vol. 69, April 1976.

About prosauropods

Prosauropods ("before the lizard feet") included the first big, four-legged, plant-eating dinosaurs. Some say they evolved from two-legged, flesh-eating ancestors of *Staurikosaurus* and gave rise to the great sauropods. Others think prosauropods and sauropods both came from the same four-legged thecodont ancestors. They lived from Mid Triassic to Early Jurassic times and spread everywhere. Prosauropods ranged from about 7ft (2.1m) long to ones longer than the width of a tennis court. Most had a bulky body, long tail, fairly long neck, and small head. The massive hind limbs ended in five-toed feet. Front limbs were relatively short and slim with five-fingered "hands," many with a long, sharp, curved claw on each thumb, which stuck out sideways when its owner walked on all fours. The

Spiky thumbs (above)
A prosauropod's spiky thumb jutted in toward its body. Thumbs pointing away from fingers helped produce spreading hands on which these dinosaurs could rest the forepart of the body when walking on all fours. The long, hooked claws sprouting from their thumbs served as weapons, gouging tools, or both.

Desert trek (below)
When drought made food and water hard to find, herds of *Plateosaurus* seemingly crossed a desert in their search for more. Many died of thirst or hunger on the way.

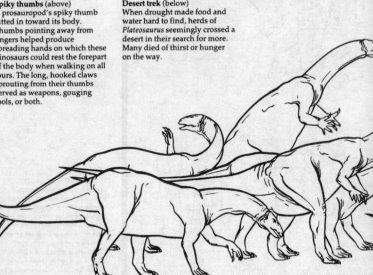

claw may have been used for rooting, hooking branches to the mouth, or jabbing at an enemy. At least some prosauropods could rear to browse or run, but most had to walk on all fours to support their bulky body with the big digestive system needed by plant-eating creatures. Prosauropods' triangular teeth seem poorly shaped for chewing, but small swallowed stones may have ground food in a gizzard. Bacteria in special "stomachs" probably helped digest the pulp. Some prosauropods might have eaten meat as well as or instead of plants.

These dinosaurs appear to have died out because they could not compete for food with bird-hipped dinosaurs – beasts with more efficient jaws.

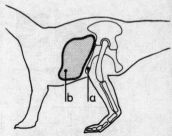

Forced onto all fours? (above) A plateosaurid's pubic bone (a) kept the digestive system's food mass (b) ahead of the hind legs. Walking on all fours helped body balance.

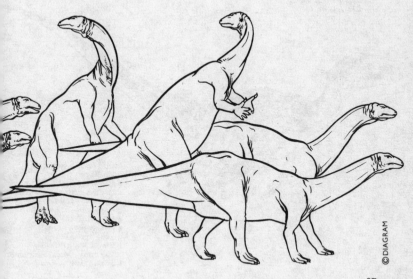

©DIAGRAM

Staurikosaurids

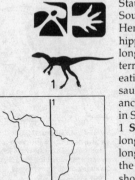

Staurikosaurids ("Cross lizards") are named for the Southern Cross star group, best seen in the Southern Hemisphere. These are the earliest-known lizard-hipped (saurischian) dinosaurs: two-legged hunters, longer than a man yet no heavier than a big bull terrier. They share some features with the flesh-eating theropods, and some with the plant-eating sauropods. They may have been related to the ancestors of both. The only genus yet described lived in South America.

1 **Staurikosaurus** ("Cross lizard") had a slim body, long, slender tail, and sprinter's legs, with shins longer than thighs. Sharp, flesh-eater's teeth armed the jaws of its rather large head. There were probably short arms, five-fingered hands, and five-toed feet. Middle toes and fingers may have been the longest. Length: 6ft 6in (2m). Weight: up to 66lb (30kg). Time: late Middle Triassic. Place: Santa Maria, in southern Brazil.

Staurikosaurid discovery
This map shows where *Staurikosaurus* was found.

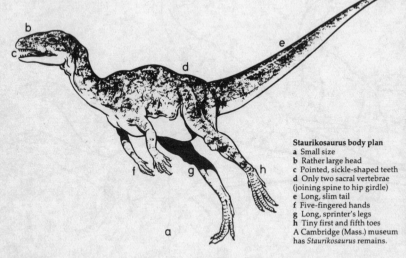

Staurikosaurus body plan
a Small size
b Rather large head
c Pointed, sickle-shaped teeth
d Only two sacral vertebrae (joining spine to hip girdle)
e Long, slim tail
f Five-fingered hands
g Long, sprinter's legs
h Tiny first and fifth toes
A Cambridge (Mass.) museum has *Staurikosaurus* remains.

Herrerasaurids

Herrerasaurids were early, sharp-toothed lizard-hipped dinosaurs much like staurikosaurids. They lived later and had rather different types of hip and leg bone, with longer thighs than shins, and maybe longer arms. The largest grew nearly twice as long as a man and weighed more than most men. Some scientists believe it was the ancestor of the sauropods. Known herrerasaurids lived in Late Triassic South America and China.

1 **Herrerasaurus** ("Herrera lizard") from northwest Argentina had pointed, sickle-shaped teeth and a large lower jaw. Length: 10ft (3m). Weight: 220lb (100kg). Time: early Late Triassic.

2 **Ischisaurus** ("Ischigualasto lizard") comes from the early Late Triassic Ischigualasto rock formation of northwest Argentina. It measured perhaps 7ft (2m).

3 **Sinosaurus** ("Chinese lizard") measured perhaps 8ft (2.4m) and lived in Late Triassic or maybe Early Jurassic southern China.

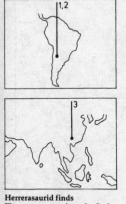

Herrerasaurid finds
These two maps show the finds.
1 *Herrerasaurus*
2 *Ischisaurus*
3 *Sinosaurus*

Herrerasaurus body plan
a Rather large lower jaw
b Pointed, sickle-shaped teeth
c Some bones (of neck, hip girdle, thigh, shin, and foot) differing from prosauropods'
d Parts of hips, thigh, and shin differing from theropods'
e Sauropod-type shin bone

©DIAGRAM

Anchisaurids

Anchisaurids were small, lightly built prosauropods, longer than a man yet less than half **his** weight. They had a lightly built skull, longer hind limbs than front limbs, and narrow feet and hands, with huge claws on the thumbs. One scientist thinks that they were just the young of the bigger, broader-footed plateosaurids. They were active hunter-foragers of dry uplands, and sometimes ran on their hind legs. Their fossils have been found in eastern North America, western Europe, southern Africa, and northeastern Australia. The family may have thrived from Middle Triassic to Middle Jurassic times.

Fossil finds
Dots show anchisaurid finds.
1 *Anchisaurus*
2 *Efraasia*
3 *Nyasasaurus*
4 *Thecodontosaurus*

1 **Anchisaurus** ("near lizard") had short feet, sturdy limbs, and more teeth than *Thecodontosaurus*, also distinctive vertebrae and hip bones. Its rather blunt teeth may have chewed both plants and flesh.
Length: 7ft (2.1m). Weight: 60lb (27kg). Time: Late Triassic or Early Jurassic. Place: northeast USA and South Africa.

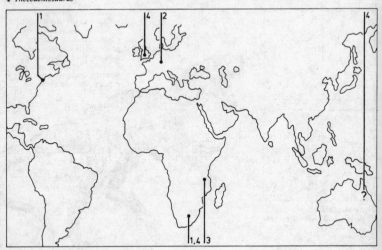

2 **Efraasia** was named in honor of E. Fraas, who discovered it in 1909. Only two vertebrae linked spine to hips (fewer than in any other lizard-hipped dinosaur except the very early, primitive *Staurikosaurus*). Its hip bones and tail bones differed from *Anchisaurus*'s and its hands were longer. Length: 8ft (2.4m). Time: Late Triassic. Place: southwest West Germany.

3 **Nyasasaurus** ("Nyasa lizard") from near Lake Nyasa, in Tanzania, is one of the earliest of all known dinosaurs, but few bones have been discovered. Unlike *Efraasia* it had three vertebrae linking spine to hips. Length: perhaps 7ft (2.1m). Time: Middle Triassic.

4 **Thecodontosaurus** ("socket-toothed lizard") had rather short neck bones, more teeth than *Anchisaurus* and a narrower, longer hand. Length: perhaps 7ft (2.1m). Time: Late Triassic and Early Jurassic. Place: west-central England, and maybe South Africa and northeast Australia.

Efraasia body plan
a Light skull, smaller than a human skull
b Only two sacral vertebrae (joining spine to hip girdle)
c Narrow, five-fingered hands with a big, curved thumb claw
d Long hind limbs
e Narrow feet
f Long, slim tail with bones unlike *Anchisaurus*'s
New Haven, Amherst, and Cape Town have museums housing anchisaurid fossils.

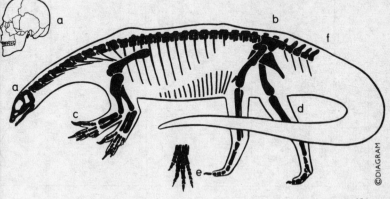

101

Plateosaurids

Plateosaurids ("flat lizards") were built like anchisaurids, but most were larger, with bigger, stronger skulls, jaws hinged in a more effective way, and broader hands and feet. Their legs may have stuck out slightly sideways and they usually walked on all fours. Their blunt teeth chewed plants and sometimes meat. They lived from Late Triassic to Early Jurassic times in the Americas, Europe, Africa, and Asia.

1 **Ammosaurus** ("sand lizard") from Connecticut and Arizona, USA, had small feet but big hands with stout thumbs tipped by formidable claws. Length: perhaps 8ft (2.4m). Time: Late Triassic or Early Jurassic.

2 **Aristosaurus** ("best lizard") had hip and spinal bones unlike other plateosaurids'. This small beast lived in Late Triassic or Early Jurassic South Africa. Length: 5ft (1.5m).

3 **Coloradisaurus** ("Colorados lizard") from northwest Argentina's Los Colorados rock formation had a shorter snout than *Plateosaurus*. Length: perhaps 13ft (4m). Time: Late Triassic.

1 ➧

2 ➧

3 ➧

Where they lived
Plateosaurid finds are indicated on this map.
1 *Ammosaurus*
2 *Aristosaurus*
3 *Coloradisaurus*
4 *Euskelosaurus*
5 *Lufengosaurus*
6 *Massospondylus*
7 *Plateosaurus*

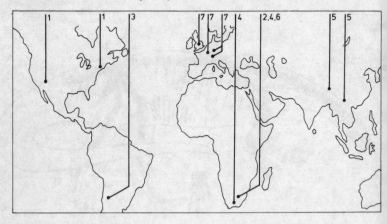

4 **Euskelosaurus** ("well-limbed lizard") may be the same kind of dinosaur as most others often called melanorosaurids. Such dinosaurs were big, four-footed creatures once thought to have given rise to the great sauropods. Length: 40ft (12.2m). Weight: 2 US tons (1.8 tonnes). Time: Late Triassic. Place: South Africa.

5 **Lufengosaurus** ("Lufeng lizard") from Lu-feng, southern China, had massive hands, broad feet, a rather short neck, and widely-spaced teeth. Length: up to 20ft (6m). Time: Late Triassic or Early Jurassic.

6 **Massospondylus** ("massive vertebra") had massive hands with spreading fingers and a great curved claw on each thumb. It was southern Africa's most widespread prosauropod. Time: Late Triassic to Early Jurassic. Length: 13ft (4m).

7 **Plateosaurus** ("flat lizard") was a big broad-footed prosauropod with a small, strong head, flattened, pointed teeth and rather short neck. Length: 26ft 3in (8m). Time: Late Triassic. Place: Germany, France, Switzerland, and England.

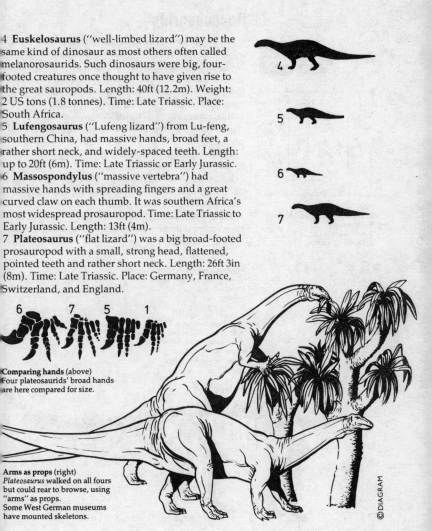

Comparing hands (above)
Four plateosaurids' broad hands are here compared for size.

Arms as props (right)
Plateosaurus walked on all fours but could rear to browse, using "arms" as props.
Some West German museums have mounted skeletons.

©DIAGRAM

103

"Roccosaurids"

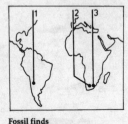

A South African paleontologist named this family to include those prosauropods with unusually sharp fangs and an especially strong joint linking hips with the backbone. But "roccosaurids" and plateosaurids like *Euskelosaurus* may belong to another family: the melanorosaurids ("black mountain lizards").

1 **Riojasaurus** ("Rioja lizard") from northwest Argentina's La Rioja province was a big, four-footed prosauropod with solid limb bones but vertebrae hollowed out for lightness. Length: perhaps 19–36ft (6–11m). Time: Late Triassic.

2 **Roccosaurus** ("Rocco lizard") from southern Africa had four vertebrae linking spine to hips, and fangs like carnosaurs'. Time: Late Triassic.

3 **Thotobolosaurus** ("Thotobolo lizard") was a big prosauropod that lived in early Late Triassic Lesotho, southern Africa.

Fossil finds
Dots show "roccosaurid" finds.
1 *Riojasaurus*
2 *Roccosaurus*
3 *Thotobolosaurus*

"Roccosaurid" features
Those given here are based on
Roccosaurus or *Riojasaurus*.
a Large size
b Four legged
c Solid limb bones
d Hollow vertebrae
e Four sacral vertebrae (joining spine to hip girdle) – twice as many as in *Efraasia*
f Carnosaur-like fangs

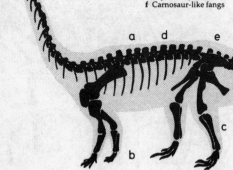

Prosauropod oddities

Mussaurids ("mouse lizards") may have been the smallest dinosaurs that ever lived. The largest in a nest of young discovered near the southern tip of South America was no bigger than a blackbird – although full-grown individuals must have been considerably larger.

"Blikanasaurids" seem to have been an unusual family of African prosauropods that would have left four-toed footprints, not three-toed prints like other prosauropods.

1 **Mussaurus** ("mouse lizard") is the smallest known dinosaur. Neck and head were relatively short for a prosauropod. Length: 8in (20cm), for young, but adults may have reached 10ft (3m). Time: Late Triassic. Place: southern Argentina.

2 **"Blikanasaurus"** ("Blikana lizard") from Blikana in South Africa's Cape Province had unusually short, strong ankle bones, and a "big toe" that pointed forward. Time: Late Triassic.

Fossil finds
This map shows *Mussaurus* (**1**) and *Blikanasaurus* (**2**) finds.

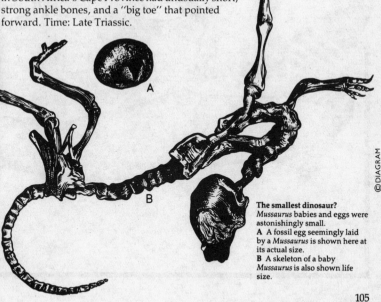

©DIAGRAM

The smallest dinosaur?
Mussaurus babies and eggs were astonishingly small.
A A fossil egg seemingly laid by a *Mussaurus* is shown here at its actual size.
B A skeleton of a baby *Mussaurus* is also shown life size.

105

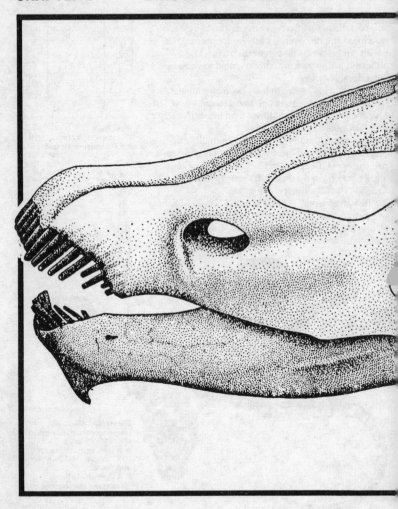

Section 4 SAUROPODS

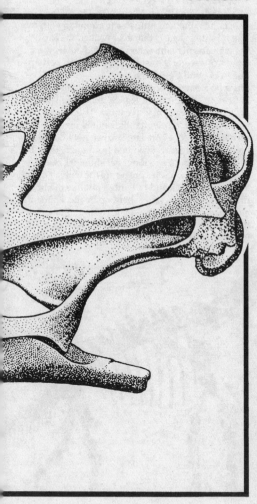

Sauropods ("lizard feet") were giants among dinosaurs and were the only large saurischian group whose members all were plant-eaters. Experts place them with prosauropods (or paleopods) in the saurischian suborder sauropodomorphs ("sauropod forms"). Various experts group sauropods differently. Here we give five main families, plus those sauropods that fit in none of these.
(For general information about this section, see the chapter introduction on page 38.)

The skull of *Diplodocus* was small compared with the huge size of this sauropod's body. Nostrils (or one nasal opening) lay above the eyes, and there were no teeth in the sides of its jaws. Sauropods have been known for many years, but their unusual skulls still puzzle scientists.
Illustration from *The Dinosaurs* by W.E. Swinton (George Allen and Unwin).

What sauropods were

Sauropods – the "lizard feet" – had five-toed feet, like lizards, but had little else in common with them. The mightiest beasts that ever walked the earth, these peaceful plant-eaters included giants the length of several buses, and heavier than perhaps a dozen big bull elephants.

Their bodies were engineered to bear and shift enormous weight. Four legs as thick as pillars underpinned each massive torso. The legs looked somewhat like an elephant's, but the first three toes on each hind foot bore large claws, not hoof-like nails, and a big claw sprouted from each "thumb." A mighty hip girdle and long, flat shoulder blades supported the muscles powering the limbs. From the torso, a long neck and tail jutted out like the boom projecting from a crane – held up by the ligaments attaching muscles to the spinal column. Spinal bones interlocked in ways that allowed the pull of muscles to lift or drop the neck or tail, or swing them left or

Sauropod body plan
a Small head
b Long neck that could be raised and lowered like the boom of a crane
c Light, hollowed vertebrae
d Massive body
e Pillar-like limbs with heavy, thick-walled bones
f Short, stout hind feet with long claws on toes 1–3
g One claw on each "thumb"
h Long tail, often raised
i Hind limbs, hips, and tall sacral vertebrae served as a suspension bridge tower to support the rear of the spine

right. Although the limb bones needed to be thick and solid to support the body, in many sauropods the backbone was deeply hollowed out for lightness. Some sauropod heads were smaller than a horse's – tiny for the great size of the body – and some skulls housed brains no larger than a kitten's. Some had jaws that seem poorly furnished with rather few, weak teeth. Strangely, nostril openings lay high up on the head, far behind the snout.

These giants probably evolved from small, two-legged ancestors, perhaps before the Triassic Period ended, 193 million years ago. By Late Jurassic times sauropods ranked among the most abundant of all plant-eating dinosaurs in lands as far apart as western North America, East Africa, and China. Sauropods of one kind or another persisted all through the following Cretaceous Period, but the Late Jurassic was their heyday.

Heads and brains
Compared with a sauropod (1), a horse (2) seems small and a kitten (3), minute. Yet many a sauropod had a head (4) roughly the size of a horse's (5), and a brain no bigger than a kitten's (6). Bulk for bulk, sauropods had smaller brains than all other backboned beasts. Yet probably they were not particularly unintelligent.

©DIAGRAM

109

How sauropods lived

Sauropods seem to have been most at home where lush vegetation clothed the banks of pools and of rivers snaking lazily across warm, low-lying plains. Experts used to think that these dinosaur giants had almost always wallowed in the water. Scientists argued that their legs could not have borne their massive weight unless water buoyed up their ponderous bodies. They thought only water plants would have been soft enough for sauropods' cropping teeth to tackle. They believed, too, that sauropods on land would have been at the mercy of the ferocious, large-fanged carnosaurs. All these notions now stand challenged. Studies show that sauropods were better built for walking on dry land than feeding in deep water, although no doubt they took a dip to rid their skins of parasites as elephants do today. It is likely that most used their long necks as giraffes use theirs: to browse high up among the trees. Some even might have reared up to reach the highest twigs. Vegetation snipped off by the teeth passed to a gizzard to be ground up by deliberately swallowed stones, or was chemically broken down inside the stomach by bacteria. Techniques like these made up for having teeth that could not chew.

As sauropods stripped one area of food they would have roamed in search of more. Their fossil footprints suggest that they tramped about in herds, perhaps holding their tails up to stop them being trampled on. Footprints hint, too, that young ones ambled in the middle of the herds, where they were safest from attack by carnosaurs. If their keen sense of smell warned of a nearby enemy, sauropods may not have plunged in water to escape, for a big flesh-eating dinosaur could swim after them. Instead, the great, thick-skinned bulls may have lashed out with their whip-like tails, as certain threatened lizards do, or reared and brought down their forelimbs in the same way that elephants are said to crush a tiger. Much of

Stomach stones
Such stones (shown actual size) may have helped sauropods' digestions. The dinosaurs supposedly swallowed rough stones that ground food to pulp inside a gizzard. In time the stones were ground smooth. Scientists have found thousands of such so-called gastroliths in rocks rich in dinosaur remains.

our information about these fascinating monsters must be guesswork, for most of the fossil clues so far discovered can be explained in several ways. Also, each family of sauropods was somewhat differently designed – maybe for a different style of life. While some lived mostly on hard ground, others could well have browsed in muddy shallows.

Sauropod tracks (above)
Preserved in mud that hardened into stone, these elephantine footprints (**1**) and bird-like tracks (**2**) show where a huge sauropod was chased by a big flesh-eating carnosaur.

Built for buoyancy? (left)
If sauropods had lived in water, the light backbone would have buoyed them up, while their heavy legs may have served like divers' weighted boots to keep them upright (**A**). But massive legs and lightweight spine would just as well have helped them stand and walk on land.

Dinosaur giraffes
If sauropods browsed as giraffes do they nipped off all the twigs and leaves that they could reach (**B**). The resulting "browse line" would have given a distinctive shape to conifers across the countryside.

Counterattack
Shown here (**C**) are two ways in which a sauropod might use its bulk to beat off a carnosaur.
1 Lashing the long, powerful tail from side to side – some types of sauropod had long whip-like tails
2 Rearing and bringing the forelimbs down upon the carnosaur to crush it by sheer body weight

©DIAGRAM

111

Sauropod family tree

Family tree
This is largely guesswork, for many sauropods are known only from a handful of bones that give a poor idea of their owner's body shape. Experts disagree about how many families there were and how closely one family related to another. Some people group all sauropods into two families, each divided into subfamilies. Dr John McIntosh – a leading American expert on sauropods – believes there were at least five families: cetiosaurids, brachiosaurids, titanosaurids, camarasaurids, and diplodocids, plus maybe barapasaurids. Our family tree shows when all six flourished.

a *Barapasaurids*
b *Cetiosaurids*
c *Camarasaurids*
d *Brachiosaurids*
e *Diplodocids*
f *Titanosaurids*

Triassic	Jurassic	Cretaceous
225 million years ago	193	136

Cetiosaurids 1

Cetiosaurids ("whale lizards") get their name from the discovery in central England in 1809 of great bones thought to have belonged to a huge aquatic beast. The first sauropods discovered, cetiosaurids also rank among the first to have evolved. Most lived in Jurassic times, though some persisted later. They lived worldwide. Cetiosaurids were 40–70ft (12–21m) long. Even a small one weighed as much as two or three Asian elephants.

The cetiosaurids had a long back, moderately long neck, shortish tail, and probably a short, blunt head, with teeth somewhat like thick flattened spoons. The backbone was almost solid – unlike those of more highly evolved sauropods like *Brachiosaurus* which were hollowed out for lightness. Not all scientists believe cetiosaurids form a separate family.

Fossil finds
Cetiosaurid finds are indicated on this map.

1 *Amygdalodon*
2 *Austrosaurus*
3 *Cetiosaurus*
4 *Chinshakiangosaurus*
5 *Dystrophaeus*
6 *Haplocanthosaurus*
7 *Patagosaurus*
8 *Rhoetosaurus*
9 *Shuosaurus*
10 *Volkheimeria*

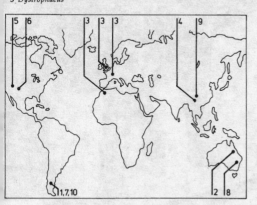

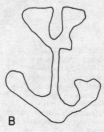

Two types of spinal bone
End-on views of a cetiosaurid and a brachiosaurid vertebra help to show these families were built in different ways.
A A thick, solid vertebra from a *Cetiosaurus* backbone
B A *Brachiosaurus* vertebra deeply scooped out at the sides

©DIAGRAM

113

Cetiosaurids 2

1 **Amygdalodon** ("almond tooth") was a primitive sauropod and is known only from almond-shaped teeth, vertebrae, and bone fragments. Time: Middle Jurassic. Place: southern Argentina.

2 **Austrosaurus** ("southern lizard") was possibly a late cetiosaurid. Scattered finds of worn bones turn up in Early-Middle Cretaceous rocks of northeast Australia. Length: 50ft (15m).

3 **Cetiosaurus** ("whale lizard") grew very large. It had a longish neck (shorter than in some later sauropods), long back, rather short, light tail, and probably a blunt head and spoon-shaped teeth. Length: 45–60ft (14–18m) or more. Weight of a 45ft (14m) specimen: about 10 US tons (9 tonnes). A huge skeleton found in Morocco in 1979 had a thigh bone about 79in (200cm) long – longer than all but the tallest men. Its 65in (165cm) shoulder blade was as high as an average woman. Time: Middle to Late Jurassic. Place: western Europe and North Africa.

Cetiosaurid body plan
a Head not well known
b Teeth like flat spoons
c Moderately long neck
d Front limbs ⅔–⅘ length of hind limbs
e Relatively short tail
f Spinal bones had almost solid centers and were not forked at the top.
Cleveland Museum has a good *Haplocanthosaurus* skeleton.

4 **Chinshakiangosaurus** ("Kinsha-kiang lizard") comes from Yunnan in southern China. (*Kinsha-kiang* is the Chinese name for the upper Yangtze River.) Described in 1975, it lived in Late Triassic or Early Jurassic times, making it one of the earliest of all known sauropods.

5 **Dystrophaeus** ("wasted one") is known only from pieces of bone from arm, hip, or shoulder. It was a big dinosaur, possibly the same kind as another already named. Time: Late Jurassic. Place: Utah, USA.

6 **Haplocanthosaurus** ("single spined lizard") was big and much like *Cetiosaurus*. It had a long back, fairly high shoulders, longish neck, and short tail. The spine jutting up from each vertebra was single, not forked as in some sauropods. Length: up to 72ft (21.5m). Time: Late Jurassic. Place: Colorado, USA.

7 **Patagosaurus** ("Patagonian lizard") resembled *Cetiosaurus* but had rather different tail and hip bones. It was built in a more "old-fashioned" way than *Haplocanthosaurus* but less so than *Amygdalodon*. Time: Late Jurassic. Place: southeast Argentina.

8 **Rhoetosaurus** ("Rhoetos lizard") gets its name from a giant of Greek myth. It probably had a long neck and measured over 39ft (12m). It came from Middle Jurassic eastern Australia.

9 **Shuosaurus** ("Shu lizard") was dug up in Szechuan, China in 1979. (*Shu* was the name of an old Chinese kingdom.) This Early-Middle Jurassic sauropod measured 30ft (9m) or more. It may have resembled India's *Barapasaurus*.

10 **Volkheimeria** ("Volkheimer's") is known from bones of a beast less than half the size of *Patagosaurus* and with a more "old-fashioned" spine. Both were described in 1979, lived in the Late Jurassic, and were found in the same part of Argentina.

©DIAGRAM

Brachiosaurids 1

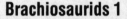

These "arm lizards" probably evolved from creatures like *Cetiosaurus*, but they had a relatively longer neck, higher shoulders, and longer "arms." Built like immense giraffes, they may have been able to browse high among leafy branches just by lifting their long necks. Some people once supposed they must have been too huge to live on land, arguing that leg bones would have cracked beneath their weight. Indeed, brachiosaurids included the heaviest-ever land animals. Some may have weighed more than 20 large elephants – as much as a blue whale, the mightiest animal alive today. The biggest brachiosaurids may have been longer than *Diplodocus*, often thought to be the longest dinosaur. They lived from Mid Jurassic to Cretaceous times, perhaps in every continent.

1 **Astrodon** ("star tooth") may have been smaller than most brachiosaurids, but some *"Astrodons"* have proved to be the young of other sauropods. Length: over 33ft (10m). Time: Early Cretaceous. Place: Maryland and Texas, USA, and maybe France and England.

2 **Bothriospondylus** ("excavated vertebrae") was probably larger than *Astrodon* but smaller than *Brachiosaurus*. Length: 49–66ft (15–20m). Time: Mid Jurassic-Early Cretaceous. Place: Western Europe and Madagascar.

3 **Brachiosaurus** ("arm lizard") was one of the most massive of all dinosaurs. Length: 75ft (23m), perhaps up to 90ft (27m), making it one of the longest dinosaurs. Head height: about 40ft (12m). Weight: 85 US tons (77 tonnes), maybe up to 112 US tons (102 tonnes). Time: Late Jurassic. Place: Colorado, USA, Algeria, and Tanzania.

A Puzzling skull

A Bony struts (1) helped lighten *Brachiosaurus*'s skull, which had raised nasal openings (2) above the eyes. Some creatures with such openings have trunks, so perhaps *Brachiosaurus* had one too. Or maybe blood flowing through skin that lined the inside of the nostrils shed heat in hot weather fast enough to cool the brain.

B An old idea was that nostrils high on the head let this dinosaur breathe with its body submerged in deep water. In fact water pressure would have crushed its lungs.

Brachiosaurid body plan

a Colossal size (in scale here with a giraffe and a man)
b Nostrils opening from a ridge above the eyes
c Low, broad snout
d Very long neck
e Shoulders higher than hips (as in the giraffe)
f Thickset tail, much shorter than in, say, diplodocids
g Front limbs as long as or longer than hind limbs

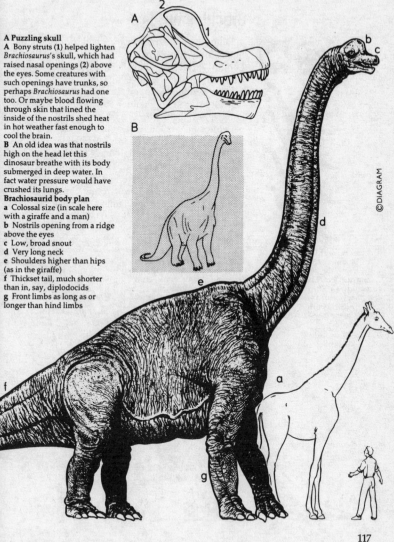

©DIAGRAM

117

Brachiosaurids 2

4 **Dinodocus** ("terrible beam") had slim forelimbs, but is known only from broken limb and hip bones. Length: 72ft (22m). Time: Early Cretaceous. Place: Kent, England.

5 **"Hughenden sauropod,"** awaiting a description, was found near Hughenden, in northeast Australia. Length: 80ft (24m). Time: Early Cretaceous.

6 **Pelorosaurus** ("monstrous lizard") seems to have had a skin studded with small, flat, six-sided tubercles. (Other brachiosaurids might have had them too.) Length: perhaps 80ft (24m). Time: Late Jurassic-Early Cretaceous. Place: western Europe.

7 **Rebbachisaurus** ("Rebbachi lizard") lived in Early Cretaceous Morocco and Tunisia. Some of its back vertebrae were about 5ft (1.5m) tall.

Giants among giants
A "Ultrasaurus" was a quarter larger than the largest mounted dinosaur; it may have weighed as much as a blue whale.
B "Supersaurus" reached maybe 79ft (24m) if a brachiosaurid, or 92ft (28m) if a diplodocid.

C *Brachiosaurus* perhaps included individuals as large as "Ultrasaurus." Dwarfing all three was *Breviparopus*, a Moroccan dinosaur named from tracks made by a beast 157ft (48m) long. Perhaps it was the longest-ever backboned animal.

8 "Supersaurus" ("super lizard") outstripped all known brachiosaurids when found in 1972. Estimated head height: 54ft (16.5m); shoulder height: 26ft (8m); neck length: 39ft (12m). Main shoulder bone: 8ft (2.4m) long. Largest vertebra: nearly 5ft (1.5m) long. Total body length: 80–100ft (24–30m). Possibly a diplodocid, it may have weighed much less than *Brachiosaurus*. Time: Late Jurassic. Place: western Colorado, USA.

9 "Ultrasaurus" ("ultra lizard") proved even larger than "Supersaurus" when found nearby in 1979. It may have been the largest-ever dinosaur, but both giants have yet to be scientifically named and studied. Length: maybe over 100ft (30.5m). Weight: possibly up to 150 US tons (136 tonnes). Time: Late Jurassic.

10 Zigongosaurus ("Zigong lizard") was a sauropod described in 1976. Time: Late Jurassic. Place: Zigong, Szechuan, China.

Where Brachiosaurids lived
Finds are located on the map.
1 *Astrodon*
2 *Bothriospondylus*
3 *Brachiosaurus*
4 *Dinodocus*
5 "Hughenden sauropod"
6 *Pelorosaurus*
7 *Rebbachisaurus*
8 "Supersaurus"
9 "Ultrasaurus"
10 *Zigongosaurus*
Brachiosaurid fossils can be seen in East Berlin and Paris.

©DIAGRAM

119

Camarasaurids 1

Hollow chambers in the backbone earn this family its name, which means "chambered lizards." Camarasaurids had a rather short, deep body, a long, flexible neck, and a long tail – but shorter than that of many sauropods. Front legs were somewhat shorter than back legs, but in some beasts the back sloped down to the tail. Big nostrils opened on top of the head, which in some camarasaurids was rather large and deep, with a short, blunt face. Dozens of big, strong teeth shaped like thick, flattened spoons rimmed the jaws. Many a camarasaurid measured about 40ft (12m) and weighed as much as three big bull elephants. These sauropods lived in western North America and East Asia. Those described here include ones sometimes listed in another family: the euhelopodids or "good marsh feet."

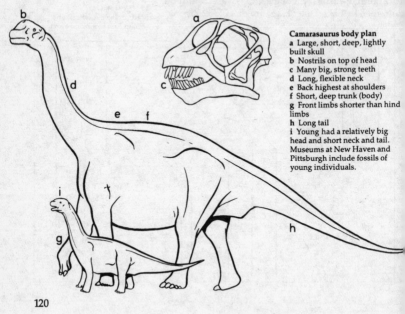

Camarasaurus body plan
a Large, short, deep, lightly built skull
b Nostrils on top of head
c Many big, strong teeth
d Long, flexible neck
e Back highest at shoulders
f Short, deep trunk (body)
g Front limbs shorter than hind limbs
h Long tail
i Young had a relatively big head and short neck and tail. Museums at New Haven and Pittsburgh include fossils of young individuals.

1 **Asiatosaurus** ("Asian lizard") is known from teeth discovered in Early Cretaceous rocks of Mongolia and China.

2 **Camarasaurus** ("chambered lizard") was heavily built, and higher at shoulders than hips. Its rather large, blunt head had a short face, big eyes, and four dozen great cropping teeth. Long nasal openings on top of its skull suggest to some it may have had some kind of trunk. Length: up to 60ft (18m). Usual weight: perhaps 20 US tons (18 tonnes). Time: Late Jurassic. Place: USA (Colorado, Oklahoma, Utah, and Wyoming).

3 **Chiayüsaurus** ("Chia-yü lizard") comes from Chia-yü-kuan in northwest China. The animal is known only from teeth, similar to teeth from Kansas, USA. It is possible that these teeth all came from *Euhelopus*. *Chiayüsaurus* lived during Late Cretaceous times.

Where camarasaurids lived
The map shows fossil finds.
1 *Asiatosaurus*
2 *Camarasaurus*
3 *Chiayüsaurus*
4 *Euhelopus*
5 *Omeisaurus*
6 *Opisthocoelicaudia*
7 *Tienshanosaurus*

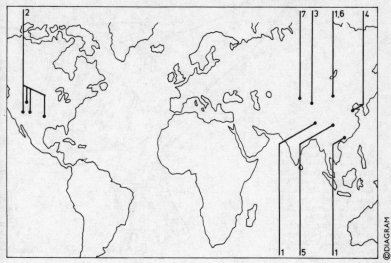

Camarasaurids 2

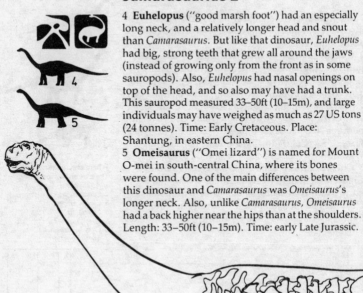

4 **Euhelopus** ("good marsh foot") had an especially long neck, and a relatively longer head and snout than *Camarasaurus*. But like that dinosaur, *Euhelopus* had big, strong teeth that grew all around the jaws (instead of growing only from the front as in some sauropods). Also, *Euhelopus* had nasal openings on top of the head, and so also may have had a trunk. This sauropod measured 33–50ft (10–15m), and large individuals may have weighed as much as 27 US tons (24 tonnes). Time: Early Cretaceous. Place: Shantung, in eastern China.

5 **Omeisaurus** ("Omei lizard") is named for Mount O-mei in south-central China, where its bones were found. One of the main differences between this dinosaur and *Camarasaurus* was *Omeisaurus*'s longer neck. Also, unlike *Camarasaurus*, *Omeisaurus* had a back higher near the hips than at the shoulders. Length: 33–50ft (10–15m). Time: early Late Jurassic.

A "headless" monster
By studying its bones and how they must have been arranged, a Polish scientist decided that *Opisthocoelicaudia* would have looked like this (**A**). Neck and head, for which no bones were found, are guesswork. The scientist felt that the streamlined body may have been designed for swimming. (Illustration after Borsuk-Bialynicka.)

6 **Opisthocoelicaudia** ("tail vertebrae cupped at the rear") was discovered when Polish scientists found a largely complete skeleton in the Gobi Desert of Mongolia. They think this dinosaur walked with an almost level back, and its tail held out stiffly behind. Unluckily, the neck and head are missing. The *Nemegtosaurus* skull found some miles away leads some experts to suggest that *Nemegtosaurus* and *Opisthocoelicaudia* are two names for one kind of animal. But the head may not match *Opisthocoelicaudia*'s type of body. Length: 40ft (12m). Time: Late Cretaceous.

7 **Tienshanosaurus** ("Tien Shan lizard") comes from near the Tien Shan mountain range in northwest China. Fossil hunters found most of the skeleton, but not its skull. Illustrations of this dinosaur suggest it had a long neck and tail and an almost level back. Length: 40ft (12m). Time: Early Cretaceous or Late Jurassic.

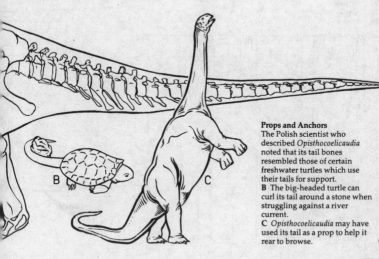

Props and Anchors
The Polish scientist who described *Opisthocoelicaudia* noted that its tail bones resembled those of certain freshwater turtles which use their tails for support.
B The big-headed turtle can curl its tail around a stone when struggling against a river current.
C *Opisthocoelicaudia* may have used its tail as a prop to help it rear to browse.

© DIAGRAM

123

Titanosaurids 1

Despite their name, which means "giant lizards," some titanosaurids were quite small. Unhappily, most are known from very incomplete remains. They seem to have had a wide, steeply sloping head with peg-shaped teeth, on a neck with rather short bones. Front legs were three-quarters as long as back legs and there was a long, slim "whiplash" tail. Titanosaurids' vertebrae were less hollowed out (for lightness) than those of other late sauropods. This makes them "old fashioned," yet they seem to have been novel in at least one way. Certain kinds had small armored shields set in their hides – something unknown for other sauropods. Titanosaurids form the largest sauropod family. All may have lived in the Cretaceous Period, many of them in southern continents.

Where titanosaurids lived
This map shows sites of fossil finds – some experts disagree about what some finds really represent.

1 *Aegyptosaurus*
2 *Aepisaurus*
3 *Alamosaurus*
4 *Algoasaurus*
5 *Antarctosaurus*
6 *Argyrosaurus*
7 *Campylodoniscus*
8 *Chondrosteosaurus*
9 *Hypselosaurus*
10 *Laplatasaurus*
11 *Macrurosaurus*
12 *Microcoelus*
13 *Saltasaurus*
14 *Succinodon*
15 *Titanosaurus*
16 *Tornieria*

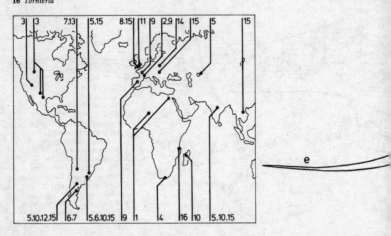

1 **Aegyptosaurus** ("Egyptian lizard") is known from limb bones found in Late Cretaceous rocks of northern Egypt, and others found in northwest Africa. Length: 52ft 6in (16m).

2 **Aepisaurus** ("elephant lizard") was a small sauropod. An arm bone was found in Early Cretaceous rocks of southern France. Length: 49ft (15m).

3 **Alamosaurus** ("Alamo lizard") comes from New Mexico, Utah, Texas, and Montana. Time: Late Cretaceous (70 million years ago). Length: 69ft (21m). Weight: 30 US tons (27 tonnes).

4 **Algoasaurus** ("Algoa lizard") seems to have been a small sauropod: its thigh bone was only 19½in (50cm) long. *Algoasaurus* comes from near Algoa Bay, South Africa. Length: 30ft (9m). Time: Early Cretaceous.

Titanosaurid features
a Steeply sloping face
b Peg-shaped teeth
c Short neck bones
d Armor (in some)
e Long "whiplash" tail
f Front limbs ¾ length of hind limbs
Most titanosaurids are known only from a few bones. Museums in Argentina, England, France, India, Sweden, and the United States have specimens. (Illustration after Bakker.)

Titanosaurids 2

5 **Antarctosaurus** ("not northern lizard") may have been among the largest dinosaurs: one had a thigh bone 7ft 6in (2.3m) long. These dinosaurs had slim hind legs, a short, sloping face, big eyes, and a broad snout. Length: 60ft (18m), maybe more. Time: Late Cretaceous. Place: Argentina, Uruguay, Brazil, India, and Kazakhstan.

6 **Argyrosaurus** ("silver lizard") was a massive dinosaur named for Argentina ("silver"). One fossil thigh bone is longer than an average man. Length: maybe 70ft (21m) or more. Time: Late Cretaceous. Place: Uruguay and Argentina.

7 **Campylodoniscus** ("bent toothed") may be the same as *Argyrosaurus* or another titanosaurid. Part of its jaw was found in southern Argentina. Size: very large. Time: Late Cretaceous.

8 **Chondrosteosaurus** ("bony cartilage lizard") is known only from pieces of hollow-backed vertebrae from England's Isle of Wight. Size: very large. Time: Early Cretaceous.

9 **Hypselosaurus** ("high ridge lizard") was an average-sized titanosaurid and has sometimes been shown with high hips, blunt head, and long tail. Its peg-like teeth were small and weak. Its bones have been found in southern and central France and Spain. Many sauropod eggs may be *Hypselosaurus* eggs – the only sauropod eggs probably traceable to the kind of animal that laid them. Length: 40ft (12m). Time: Late Cretaceous.

10 **Laplatasaurus** ("La Plata lizard") was larger and slimmer than *Titanosaurus*. Length: maybe 60ft (18m). Time: Late Cretaceous. Place: Argentina, India, and Madagascar.

11 **Macrurosaurus** ("long tail lizard") gets its name from 40 tail bones in two groups found miles apart, yet seemingly both from the same long-tailed individual. Length: maybe 40ft (12m). Time: Early Cretaceous. Place: near Cambridge, England.

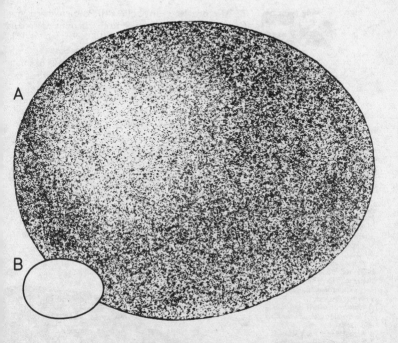

A

B

Big eggs
A *Hypselosaurus* probably laid big eggs like this – actual size 1ft (30cm) long by 10in (25cm) across, with a 5.8 pint (3.3 liter) capacity. Probably no dinosaur laid eggs any larger.
B A chicken egg is here shown to the same scale.
C A magnified cross section through a *Hypselosaurus* egg shell shows a bumpy surface. (Illustration after Colbert.)

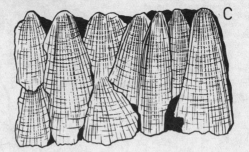

C

©DIAGRAM

127

Titanosaurids 3

12 Microcoelus ("tiny hollow") is known only from a few bones found in west-central Argentina. It lived in Late Cretaceous times.

13 Saltasaurus ("Salta lizard") is from Salta province, northwest Argentina. Thousands of small bony studs and a few larger bony plates guarded its broad back and sides. This was the first armored sauropod to be described as such (in 1980). Its body-build suggests that this sauropod may have reared to bring its mouth in reach of leaves high up on tall trees. *Saltasaurus* was a medium-sized titanosaurid, about 40ft (12m) long. Time: Late Cretaceous.

14 Succinodon ("narrow tooth") is known from a piece of jaw found in Late Cretaceous rocks southeast of Warsaw, Poland.

An armored sauropod
Piecing together bones from five incomplete skeletons helped scientists judge what *Saltasaurus* looked like, though they found no skull.
a Broad back
b Strong, broad upper tail bones may have helped the tail serve sometimes as a prop
c Rather flat feet
d Hundreds of tiny bony studs set in the skin guarded the back and flanks
e Actual size of bony studs
f A few bony plates, maybe capped by horny spikes, helped protect the back
g Actual size of a bony plate
(Illustrations **e** and **g** after Bonaparte and Powell.)

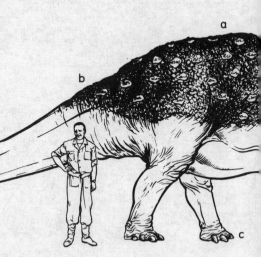

15 **Titanosaurus** ("titanic lizard") gets its name from the titans, giants of Greek myth. In fact it was much smaller than many sauropods. *Titanosaurus* was rather heavily built, probably with a broad, low, armored back, like *Saltasaurus*, and a whiplash tail. Length: 40ft (12m). Time: Late and maybe Early Cretaceous. Supposedly it lived in Europe, India, Indochina, and South America.

16 **Tornieria** is named for Gustav Tornier, a German scientist. It lived in Late Jurassic times, which makes it possibly the first titanosaurid, but some scientists consider that it was in fact a diplodocid. Place: Tanzania and possibly Malawi.

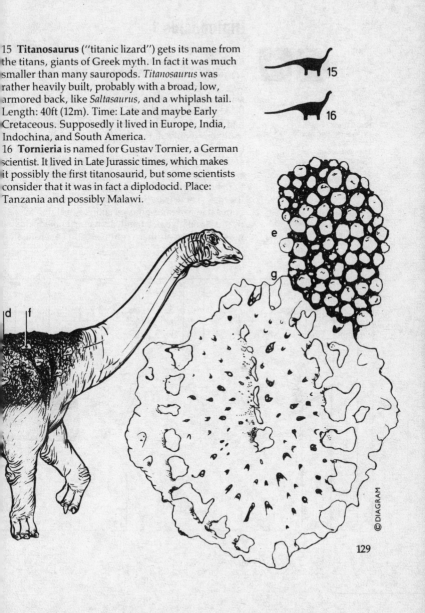

129

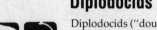

Diplodocids 1

Diplodocids ("double beams") included possibly the longest of all dinosaurs – even longer than a tennis court. Yet some were lightweight giants: the longest weighed only half as much as many another sauropod merely half its length. A deeply hollowed backbone helped to cut down weight. Diplodocids had long, low, sloping heads, with weak, pencil-like teeth found only at the front of the jaws. They breathed through nostrils opening from a single hole at the top of the skull, between the eyes. The neck was long and snaky. Front legs were much shorter than hind legs and the back may have been highest at the hips. There was a long, "whiplash" tail. Many tail bones had fore-and-aft projections – the "double beams" that give this family its name. Diplodocids mostly lived in northern continents, in Late Jurassic times.

Fossil finds
Diplodocid finds are located on this map.
1 *Amphicoelias*
2 *Apatosaurus*
3 *Barosaurus*
4 *Cetiosauriscus*
5 *Dicraeosaurus*
6 *Diplodocus*
7 *Mamenchisaurus*
8 *Nemegtosaurus*
9 Unnamed diplodocid
Many museums have diplodocid fossils or casts of the skeleton of *Diplodocus*.

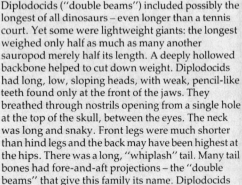

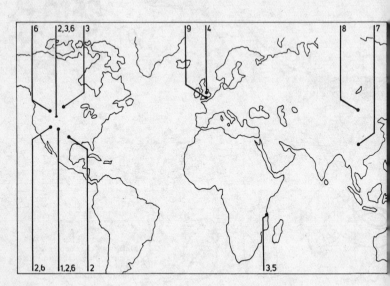

1 **Amphicoelias** ("with hollow-ended vertebrae") was long and slim-limbed. Its incomplete remains in fact may be a *Barosaurus*'s or *Diplodocus*'s. Time: Late Jurassic. Place: Colorado, USA.

2 **Apatosaurus** ("deceptive lizard") had a very long neck, short body, and very long tail. It was shorter than *Diplodocus* but three times heavier, and was once called *Brontosaurus* ("thunder lizard") from the way it supposedly made the ground shake as it walked. Length: 70ft (21m). Shoulder height: 14ft 6in (4.5m). Weight: 33 US tons (30 tonnes). Time: Late Jurassic. Place: USA (Colorado, Oklahoma, Utah, and Wyoming).

3 **Barosaurus** ("heavy lizard") was slim-limbed like *Diplodocus*, but with shorter tail bones and longer neck bones – the longest measured 3ft (nearly 1m). Its neck was very long indeed. Total length: maybe 75–90ft (23–27m). Time: Late Jurassic. Place: USA (South Dakota and Wyoming) and Tanzania.

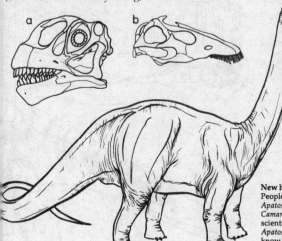

© DIAGRAM

New head for old
People once thought that *Apatosaurus* had a skull like *Camarasaurus*'s (**a**). In the 1970s scientists identified a true *Apatosaurus* skull (**b**), so we now know that *Apatosaurus* had a low, diplodocid, head (**c**).

131

Diplodocids 2

4 **Cetiosauriscus** ("whale lizard") was a primitive diplodocid with a whiplash tail and longish neck. Length: 49ft (15m). Time: Late Jurassic. Place: southern England.

5 **Dicraeosaurus** ("forked lizard") gets its name from high, forked spines jutting up from some vertebrae, anchoring muscles. *Dicraeosaurus* was shorter than *Diplodocus*, with a relatively shorter neck and tail. Length: 43–66ft (13–20m). Time: Late Jurassic. Place: Tendaguru, Tanzania.

6 **Diplodocus** ("double beam") is named from middle tail bones, with fore-and-aft skids protecting blood vessels if the tail dragged on the ground. This was one of the longest dinosaurs, yet slim-limbed and rather light. Total length: up to 87ft 6in (27m), mostly snaky neck and whiplash tail. Weight: only 11.7 US tons (10.6 tonnes). Time: Late Jurassic. Place: USA (Colorado, Montana, Utah, and Wyoming).

Diplodocid skull
These two views show the position of the nostrils (1) and the peg-like teeth (2). Teeth were mostly at the front of the mouth, and may have been used to sieve tiny organisms from fresh water. Yet many teeth were worn, which suggests that diplodocids used them to comb leaves from twigs.

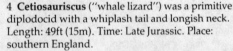

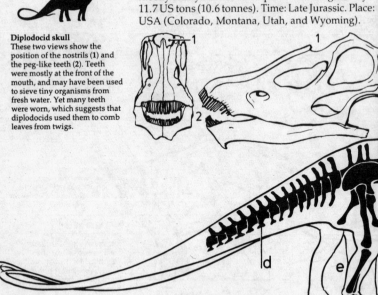

7 **Mamenchisaurus** ("Mamenchi lizard") from Mamenchi in south-central China had possibly the longest neck of any animal. No known dinosaur had as many neck vertebrae (19). From many of them, long, slender struts overlapped the vertebrae behind. This reinforced and stiffened the neck except where it joined the head and chest. Some experts put this dinosaur in its own family. Total length: 72ft (22m). Time: Late Jurassic.

8 **Nemegtosaurus** ("Nemegt lizard") from Mongolia's Nemegt Basin is known only from a sloping skull somewhat like *Diplodocus*'s. The body might have been similarly light and long. Time: Late Cretaceous (much later than other diplodocids).

9 **Unnamed diplodocid** A distinctive tail bone from a diplodocid has been found on the Isle of Wight in southern England. Body length: 54ft (16.6m). Time: Early Cretaceous.

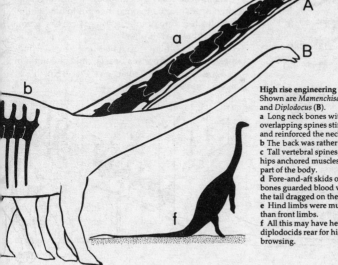

©DIAGRAM

High rise engineering
Shown are *Mamenchisaurus* (**A**) and *Diplodocus* (**B**).
a Long neck bones with overlapping spines stiffened and reinforced the neck.
b The back was rather short.
c Tall vertebral spines above the hips anchored muscles in that part of the body.
d Fore-and-aft skids on tail bones guarded blood vessels if the tail dragged on the ground.
e Hind limbs were much longer than front limbs.
f All this may have helped diplodocids rear for high-level browsing.

133

Assorted sauropods

A few sauropods fit no family so far described. Others are known only from puzzling fragments.

1 **Atlantosaurus** ("Atlas lizard") is named for a giant in Greek myth. Length: 75ft (23m). Time: Late Jurassic. Place: Colorado, USA.

2 **Barapasaurus** ("big leg lizard") is one of the earliest known sauropods. It had slim limbs, a short, deep head, spoon-shaped, saw-edged teeth, and unusual hollows in the backbone. Certain bones were "old-fashioned" like a prosauropod's. It may belong in its own family, the barapasaurids. Length: up to 60ft (18m). Time: Early Jurassic. Place: central India.

3 **Chubutisaurus** ("Chubut lizard") from Chubut province, southern Argentina was described in 1974 and put in a new family: chubutisaurids. It had shorter forelimbs than hind limbs, big hollows in its backbone, and probably a short tail. Length: 75ft 6in (23m). Time: Late Cretaceous.

4 **Clasmodosaurus** ("fragment tooth lizard") is known only from teeth once thought to have come from a flesh-eating dinosaur. Time: Late Cretaceous. Place: southern Argentina.

5 **Hypsibema** ("high step") was first named from bones that came from two beasts, only one of them a sauropod. Time: Late Cretaceous. Place: North Carolina and Missouri, USA.

Sites of fossil finds
This map locates finds of sauropods described on these two pages.
1 *Atlantosaurus*
2 *Barapasaurus*
3 *Chubutisaurus*
4 *Clasmodosaurus*
5 *Hypsibema*
6 *Loricosaurus*
7 *Mongolosaurus*
8 *Ohmdenosaurus*
9 *Sanpasaurus*
10 *Vulcanodon*
A *Barapasaurus* skeleton is on show in Calcutta but most of the other fossils are too few for museums to display.

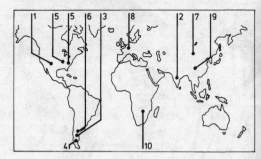

134

6 **Loricosaurus** ("armored lizard") was probably an armored titanosaurid, maybe *Titanosaurus*. Only its bony skin-plates have been found. Time: Late Cretaceous. Place: southern Argentina.

7 **Mongolosaurus** ("Mongolian lizard") from Early Cretaceous Mongolia is known only from teeth and pieces of skull and backbone.

8 **Ohmdenosaurus** ("Ohmden lizard") was a very small, early sauropod. A broken leg bone was found near Ohmden, southwest West Germany. Length: 13ft (4m). Time: late Early Jurassic.

9 **Sanpasaurus** ("Sanpa lizard") of Late Jurassic south-central China is named from bones from a young sauropod and maybe an iguanodontid.

10 **Vulcanodon** ("volcano tooth") was found in Zimbabwe in Early Jurassic rocks sandwiched by lava flows from a volcano. Its small, saw-edged teeth were like a prosauropod's, yet it had a sauropod's limbs. The back may have sloped down from the shoulder. Length: 20ft (6.5m).

"Big-leg lizard"
Barapasaurus may have looked like this. Among its strangest features were unusual chambers in its dorsal vertebrae, as well as normal hollows known to scientists as pleurocoels.

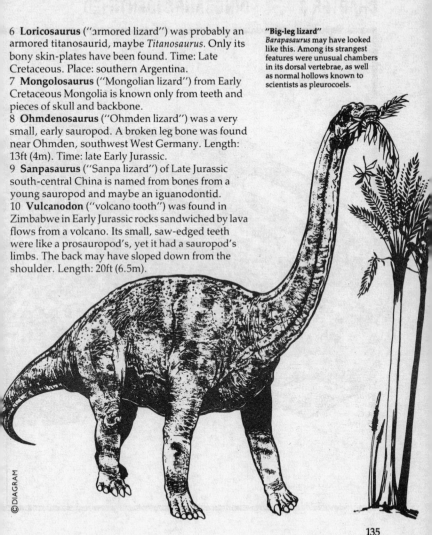

©DIAGRAM

135

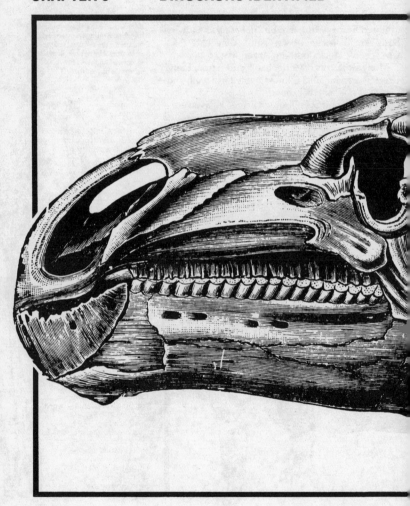

Section 5 ORNITHOPODS

Ornithopods ("bird feet") were the only ornithischian dinosaurs capable of walking or running on their hind legs. Most paleontologists rank them as one of four ornithischian suborders, though some put the boneheaded ornithischians in a suborder of their own. This book describes nine families of ornithopods. One of these, the hadrosaurids, is divided into two subfamilies.
(For general information about this section, see the chapter introduction on page 38.)

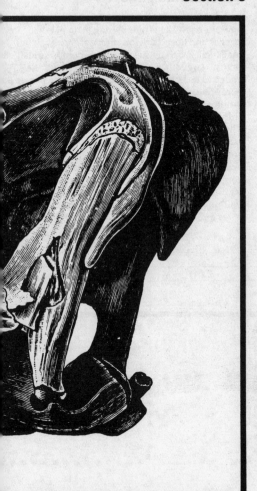

An old illustration of *Iguanodon*'s skull reveals a toothless beak suitable for cropping leaves, and flattened cheek teeth designed for grinding plants to pulp. Ornithopods and other ornithischians were the equivalents of today's horses, cows, sheep, and deer. Illustration after L. Dollo, appearing in *Dinosaurs* by W.E. Swinton (British Museum, Natural History).

About ornithopods

These "bird-footed" bird-hipped bipeds were mostly dinosaur equivalents of browsing mammals like gazelles and deer. Early ornithopods included the small, agile fabrosaurids and heterodontosaurids; some no larger than a dog. Hypsilophodontids also tended to be lighter than a man. But as time passed there appeared ever bigger browsers: first camptosaurids, then iguanodontids, and lastly hadrosaurids, some as heavy as an elephant. While ornithopods increased in size they also changed in other ways. The head grew relatively large, but teeth vanished from the front of the jaws, which ended in a toothless, horny beak designed for cropping vegetation. Cheek teeth, though, evolved as efficient grinders for crushing leaves, and early on ornithopods evolved with cheek pouches – useful stores for leaves that they had cropped but not yet

Ornithopod family tree
Scientists have a clearer idea of how ornithopod families related to each other than they have for most dinosaur groups. But camptosaurids may have been iguanodontids, and thescelosaurids may have been hypsilophodontids. Also when some families evolved remains a puzzle. Fabrosaurids and heterodontosaurids may have appeared in the Triassic Period, or maybe not until Jurassic times.

Triassic Period	Jurassic Period		
Late	Early	Middle	Late

Fabrosaurids

Camptosaurids

Heterodontosaurids

chewed. In many of the later ornithopods, the first
and fifth toes and fingers had shrunk or vanished.
Most of these dinosaurs had three-toed feet ending in
blunt claws or hoof-like nails.
Ornithopods could walk or run on their long hind
legs, balancing the body with the tail held off the
ground; many had a tail stiffened with the help of
bony tendons. The small ornithopods probably ran
faster than their bulkier relatives, and some or even
most of these may have spent a good deal of their
lives plodding slowly on all fours, using hands as
feet, not as grasping tools.
Ornithopods evolved late in the Triassic Period, or
just maybe not until Jurassic times. Efficiently
equipped for munching plants and hurrying away
from danger, they included some of the longest-lived
and most successful families of dinosaurs.

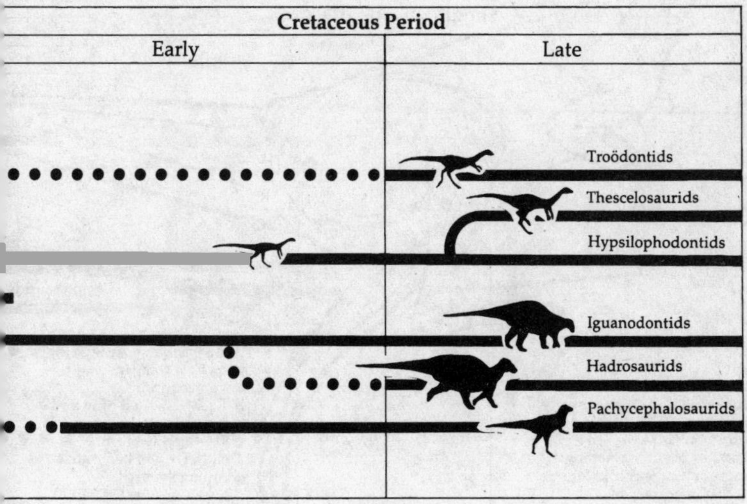

Cretaceous Period	
Early	Late

Troödontids

Thescelosaurids

Hypsilophodontids

Iguanodontids

Hadrosaurids

Pachycephalosaurids

©DIAGRAM

Fabrosaurids

Small beasts like these may have given rise to all other bird-hipped dinosaurs. They were lightly built, with hollow limb bones, long tails, and long legs with four-toed feet. Most had small arms with tiny, five-fingered hands. Ridged teeth rimmed their jaws, so there were no cheek pouches. The lower jaw ended in a toothless bone.

Fabrosaurids lived in Europe, North America, and southern Africa. Appearing in Late Triassic times, they survived for 55 million years.

1 **Azendohsaurus** from Azendoh village in Morocco's Atlas Mountains was larger than the better known fabrosaurid *Lesothosaurus*. Length: perhaps 6ft (1.8m). Time: Late Triassic.

2 **Echinodon** ("prickly tooth") was smaller than *Lesothosaurus*. It had a shorter head, relatively larger teeth – two of them long and sharp – and fewer front teeth. Among the last-known of its family, it lived in southern England at the end of the Jurassic Period. Length: maybe 2ft (60cm).

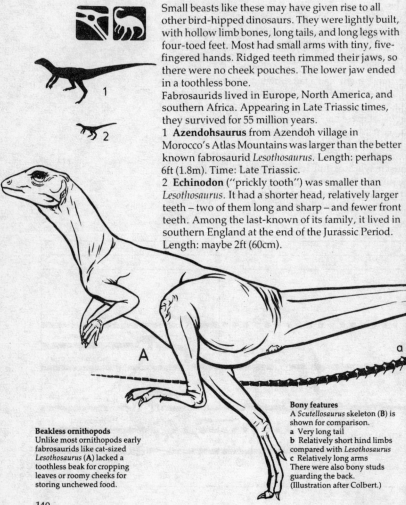

Beakless ornithopods
Unlike most ornithopods early fabrosaurids like cat-sized *Lesothosaurus* (**A**) lacked a toothless beak for cropping leaves or roomy cheeks for storing unchewed food.

Bony features
A *Scutellosaurus* skeleton (**B**) is shown for comparison.
a Very long tail
b Relatively short hind limbs compared with *Lesothosaurus*
c Relatively long arms
There were also bony studs guarding the back.
(Illustration after Colbert.)

140

3 **Fabrosaurus** ("Fabre's lizard") seemingly had lower, broader teeth than those of *Lesothosaurus*, and a broader jaw bone with holes for new teeth that grew to replace old. Length: 3ft 4in (1m). Time: Late Triassic or Early Jurassic. Place: Lesotho, Africa.

4 **Lesothosaurus** ("Lesotho lizard") may be another name for *Fabrosaurus*. *Lesothosaurus* was built for running: with short arms but long legs with longer shins than thighs. Toes and fingers were tipped with claws. Front teeth grew smooth and pointed. The cheek teeth looked like small, jagged arrowheads. Length: 3ft 4in (1m). Time: Late Triassic or Early Jurassic.

5 **Scutellosaurus** ("small shield lizard"), described in 1981, is the only known armored fabrosaurid. Hundreds of small bony studs guarded its back, adding to its weight. It had a very long tail for balancing, and long arms, maybe sometimes used as extra legs. Length: 4ft (1.2m). Time: Early Jurassic. Place: Arizona, southwestern USA.

6 **Trimucrodon** ("three-pointed tooth") is a fabrosaurid from Late Jurassic Portugal.

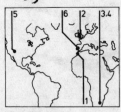

Where they lived
Fabrosaurid finds are shown.
1 *Azendohsaurus*
2 *Echinodon*
3 *Fabrosaurus*
4 *Lesothosaurus*
5 *Scutellosaurus*
6 *Trimucrodon*

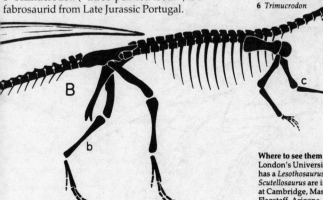

Where to see them
London's University College has a *Lesothosaurus*; fossils of *Scutellosaurus* are in museums at Cambridge, Mass., and Flagstaff, Arizona.

©DIAGRAM

141

Heterodontosaurids

These "different-teeth lizards" were small, early bird-hipped bipeds resembling fabrosaurids, their likely ancestors. But many had three kinds of teeth: sharp teeth like a carnivore's in the front upper jaw; rows of ridged cheek teeth for grinding plants; and – between both these – males at least had pairs of long, sharp tusks that fitted into special sockets. At least some kinds also had muscular cheeks. Most of these little dinosaurs measured about 4ft (1.2m), and lived in Late Triassic or perhaps Early Jurassic southern Africa.

1 **Abrictosaurus** ("awake lizard") from Lesotho may have been a primitive heterodontosaurid but many think it was a female *Heterodontosaurus* because the first fossil named *Abrictosaurus* had no tusks.

2 **Geranosaurus** ("crane lizard") had tusks but no sockets for them in its upper jaw. It came from South Africa's Cape Province.

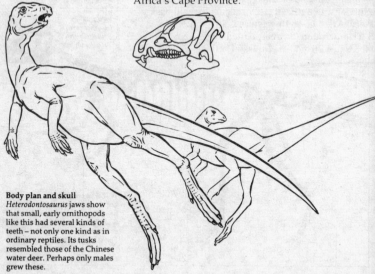

Body plan and skull
Heterodontosaurus jaws show that small, early ornithopods like this had several kinds of teeth – not only one kind as in ordinary reptiles. Its tusks resembled those of the Chinese water deer. Perhaps only males grew these.

142

3 **Heterodontosaurus** ("different-teeth lizard") was an advanced member of its family, with close-packed, long-crowned, ridged cheek teeth, and sharp, curved tusks. Tooth wear shows its jaws could chew from side to side, not just up and down like fabrosaurids' jaws. It comes from South Africa's Cape Province.

4 **Lanasaurus** ("wool lizard") had teeth sharpened by grinding on each other until they looked like chisels. New teeth grew to replace old in groups of three. *Lanasaurus* comes from Orange Free State, South Africa.

5 **Lycorhinus** ("wolf snout") had sharp tusks, and teeth like *Heterodontosaurus*'s and may have been that kind of animal. It comes from Cape Province, South Africa.

6 **Pisanosaurus** ("Pisano's lizard") had pointed teeth and maybe no tusks. Many experts consider this to be the oldest-known bird-hipped dinosaur. It lived in Late Triassic northwest Argentina. Length: maybe 3ft (90cm).

7 **Tatisaurus** ("Ta-Ti lizard") from southern China had a big lower jaw with well-worn overlapping teeth.

Heterodontosaurid finds
The map shows fossil finds.
1 *Abrictosaurus*
2 *Geranosaurus*
3 *Heterodontosaurus*
4 *Lanasaurus*
5 *Lycorhinus*
6 *Pisanosaurus*
7 *Tatisaurus*
A Cape Town museum displays a *Heterodontosaurus* skull.

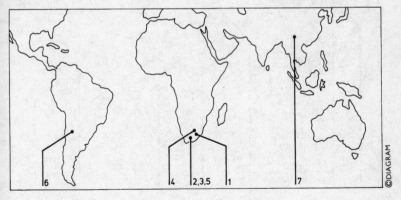

©DIAGRAM

143

Hypsilophodontids 1

Small, slim, and speedy, these were dinosaur "gazelles." All may have had five-fingered hands and four-toed feet. Their arms were short, but they had long, agile legs, with shins far longer than the thighs, as in many animals that sprint.

Hypsilophodontids were among the fastest runners of the Age of Dinosaurs. A long, tendon-stiffened tail helped them keep their balance as they raced away on their toes from the carnivores that chased them. Hypsilophodontids cropped vegetation with their horny beaks (some also had small teeth in the front of the upper jaw). They chewed this food with the ridged, high-crowned cheek teeth that give the family its scientific name, meaning "high ridge teeth." Among the most successful of all dinosaurs, the hypsilophodontids flourished for about 100 million years – perhaps longer than any other family of dinosaurs.

The hypsilophodontids' homes
The map shows fossil finds.
1 *Alocodon*
2 *Dryosaurus*
3 *Fulgurotherium*
4 "*Gongubusaurus*"
5 *Hypsilophodon*
6 *Loncosaurus*
7 *Nanosaurus*
8 *Othnielia*
9 *Parksosaurus*
10 *Phyllodon*
11 *Valdosaurus*
12 *Zephyrosaurus*
Museums in East Berlin, London, New Haven, Pittsburgh, and Tübingen show fossil hypsilophodontids.

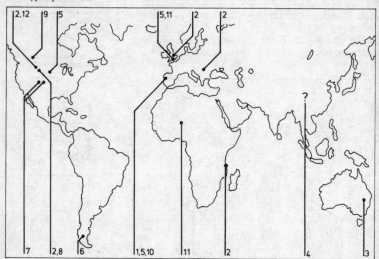

1 **Alocodon** ("wing tooth") gets its name from the distinctive shape of its teeth. At first they were mistaken for a fabrosaurid's. *Alocodon* lived in Late Jurassic Portugal. Length: maybe about 3ft 3in (1m).

2 **Dryosaurus** ("oak lizard") was one of the biggest hypsilophodontids. Its jaws lacked teeth at the front and its skull differed in other ways from beasts like *Hypsilophodon*. Length: 9–14ft (2.7–4.3m). Time: Middle-Late Jurassic. Place: western USA, eastern England, Tanzania, and Romania.

3 **Fulgurotherium** ("lightning beast") comes from Lightning Ridge in New South Wales, Australia. Known only from a broken thigh bone, it may really be a *Kangnasaurus* species. Length: perhaps 7ft (2m). Time: Early Cretaceous.

4 **"Gongubusaurus"** comes from the Japanese name for a Jurassic hypsilophodontid yet to be described.

Body, skull, and teeth
Dryosaurus was one of the largest hypsilophodontids.
a Its jaws had cheek teeth but no teeth at the front.
b A *Dryosaurus* tooth – such long, ridged teeth earned hypsilophodontids their name.

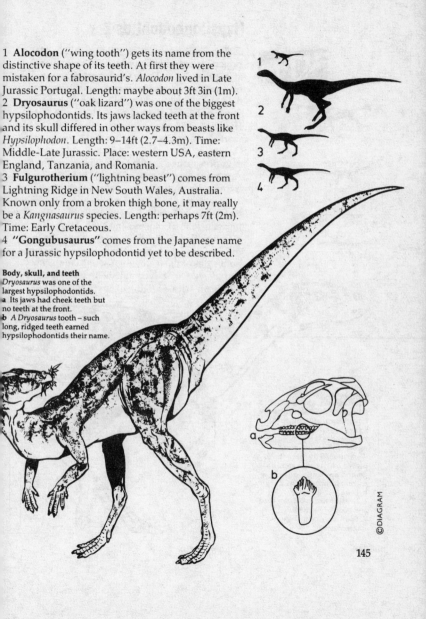

©DIAGRAM

145

Hypsilophodontids 2

5 **Hypsilophodon** ("high ridge tooth") had long, ridged, self-sharpening cheek teeth and more teeth at its horny beak. There were short arms with five-fingered hands, and long, sprinter's legs with four-toed feet. Two rows of bony studs may have run down its back. Length: 4ft 6in–7ft 6in (1.4–2.3m). *Hypsilophodon* ranged across the Early Cretaceous world from southern England and Portugal to South Dakota, USA.

6 **Loncosaurus** ("Lonco lizard") from southern Argentina may have been a Late Cretaceous hypsilophodontid. Length: perhaps 7ft (2m).

7 **Nanosaurus** ("dwarf lizard") may have been the smallest in its family. Length: 3ft (90cm). Time: Late Jurassic. Place: Colorado and Utah, USA.

8 **Othnielia** was small. Its name honors the fossil hunter Othniel Charles Marsh. Enamel hardened both sides of the teeth, not just one side as in *Hypsilophodon*. It lived in Late Jurassic western North America. Length: 4ft 6in (1.4m).

A dinosaur "gazelle"
Hypsilophodon was a small "old-fashioned" dinosaur with more fingers, toes, and teeth than some Cretaceous dinosaurs. People thought it perched or roosted in trees (see small illustration, right) until study proved that it had been a ground-dwelling sprinter.
a Long sprinter's shins
b Long four-toed feet
c Tail stiffened to balance head and body while running
d Short arms, with five-fingered hands

9 **Parksosaurus** ("Parks's lizard") had a skull and teeth differently designed from those of other hypsilophodontids. It also lived later than almost all the rest. Length: 8ft (2.4m). Weight: perhaps 150lb (68kg). Time: Late Cretaceous. Place: Alberta, Canada.

10 **Phyllodon** ("leaf tooth") is named from a tooth like those of *Nanosaurus*. It came from a lignite mine in central Portugal. Length: perhaps only 3ft (90cm). Time: Late Jurassic.

11 **Valdosaurus** ("Weald lizard") was a large hypsilophodontid with thigh bones like those of its ancestor *Dryosaurus*. It lived in Early Cretaceous southern England and Niger in West Africa. Length: about 10ft (3m).

12 **Zephyrosaurus** ("west wind lizard") from the western USA (Montana) had teeth at the front of its jaws like *Hypsilophodon*, but an unusual braincase. Length: perhaps 6ft (1.8m). Time: Early Cretaceous.

©DIAGRAM

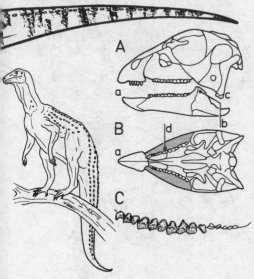

Jaws and teeth
Hypsilophodontids had jaws and teeth that were better built to crop and chew plants than those of the early ornithopods. Shown here from the side (**A**) and from below (**B**) is a *Hypsilophodon* skull. Various features are apparent.
a Horny cropping beak
b Bony coronoid process to anchor strong jaw muscles
c Jaw "pivot" below the level of the tooth row, helping all top teeth to meet all bottom teeth at once
d Teeth set in from the rim, leaving space for cheeks (shown shaded) where extra food was stored
Shown here actual size (**C**) are cheek teeth of *Zephyrosaurus*. Grinding against each other sharpened top and bottom teeth but wore them down; new teeth kept growing to replace them. (Illustrations after Galton and Sues.)

147

Where Troödon lived
The map shows fossil finds.

Troödon tooth
Views of a *Troödon* tooth from the sides (**a, b**) and front (**c**) show flattened sides, a pointed tip, and curving, saw-edged front and back that remind us of the teeth of theropods – the flesh-eating saurischian dinosaurs. Like their teeth, this tooth seems designed for slicing flesh not chewing plants. Understandably people once thought *Troödon* must have been some kind of theropod.

An ornithopod oddity
In fact, as shown here, *Troödon* may have been a small, flesh-eating ornithopod related to the hypsilophodontids. Proof is a supposed hypsilophodontid thigh bone now known to have been *Troödon*'s. The owner of the bone seems to have had unusually small, four-toed feet.

Troödontids

For nearly a century all that people knew about this family was a strange, small, pointed, saw-edged tooth. In the 1940s part of a lower jaw turned up. Then, in 1979 and 1980, fossil hunters John Horner and Robert Makela found more such teeth, a jaw, other bits of skeleton, and fossil troödontid eggs and babies. They realized that troödontids in some ways had resembled those harmless plant-eaters, hypsilophodontids. Yet the teeth were shaped for cutting flesh not crushing leaves. These bird-hipped dinosaurs had been meat-eaters – animals as unbelievable as a carnivorous cow. Troödontids may deserve placing in a dinosaur suborder all their own.

1 **Troödon** ("wounding tooth") was a small hunter with "steak-knife" teeth, two long, slim legs, and short, narrow four-toed feet unlike those of any other two-legged, bird-hipped dinosaur. It lived in Late Cretaceous Alberta and Montana. Length: maybe 8ft (2.4m).

Thescelosaurids

Among the last of the dinosaurs, thescelosaurids ("wonderful lizards") come from the topmost Mesozoic rock layer. These creatures grew as long as a small car. Some experts see them as among the bulkiest hypsilophodontids. Legs resembled those of the much larger iguanodontids, which sometimes went around on all fours. Some say either family may have given rise to thescelosaurids, but they seem different enough to belong to neither. They lived in North America. Scientists have described only one kind.

1 **Thescelosaurus** ("wonderful lizard") was long, low, and two-legged. The back had rows of bony studs. There were teeth in the front of its top jaw as in *Hypsilophodon*, but both sides of each tooth were enamel-coated. Thigh bones were longer than shin bones, as in *Iguanodon*. Length: 11ft (3.4m). Time: very late Late Cretaceous. Place: western North America (Alberta, Saskatchewan, Montana, and Wyoming).

Fossil finds
The map shows sites of fossil finds of *Thescelosaurus*.
A skeleton is on show at the National Museum of Natural History, Washington, DC.

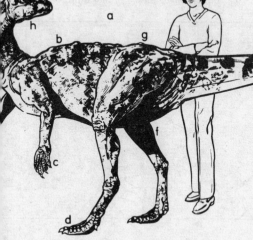

©DIAGRAM

Thescelosaurid body plan
a Moderate size
b Long, low body
c Five-fingered hand
d Five-toed foot
e Long, stiffened tail
f Long thigh bones
g Bony studs set in the skin
h Cheek teeth plus teeth in the front of the upper jaw (unusual in later ornithopods)

149

Camptosaurids

Camptosaurids ("bent lizards") were bigger and less agile than their ancestors – tiny, bird-hipped bipeds like *Hypsilophodon*. Some think they were just small iguanodontids. Each had a bulky body with large, strong hind legs and short, sturdy forelimbs. Each foot had four toes with hoof-like claws. The first three fingers of each hand also ended in a hoof-like claw. The head was long and flat, the teeth ridged and tightly packed. The front of the mouth was a sharp, toothless beak.

1 **Callovosaurus** ("Callovian lizard") was named in 1980 from the Callovian rock bed that its thigh bone came from. This early camptosaurid measured about 11ft 6in (3.5m) and lived in Middle Jurassic southern England.

2 **Camptosaurus** ("bent lizard") ranged in length from 4 to 23ft (1.2–7m) and weighed up to 1100lb (500kg) or more. Time: Late Jurassic to Early Cretaceous. Place: western Europe and western North America.

3 **"Honghesaurus,"** named and pictured in Japan, was probably a Chinese camptosaurid.

Sites of fossil finds
This map shows sites of camptosaurid fossil finds.
1 *Callovosaurus*
2 *Camptosaurus*
3 "Honghesaurus"
Some North American museums show *Camptosaurus* fossils.

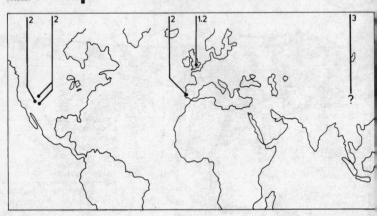

Camptosaurid footprints found preserved in rocks show that these dinosaurs often walked on their hind legs. They could also have gone down on all fours. The hooves on their fingers make this seem likely. So do their thigh bones, which grew bent not straight. Camptosaurids probably went down on all fours to browse on low-growing plants, but reared up to travel in a hurry. Running was their best chance of escaping powerful enemies.

Camptosaurids were harmless plant-eaters, and may have had a long tongue to pull leaves inside the mouth. The horny beak cut off the leaves, then the cheek teeth ground them up. While it chewed, a camptosaurid could keep breathing because a bony palate separated its mouth from the passages that let air from its nose travel to its lungs. This was true for many other dinosaurs.

Because *Camptosaurus* lived in North America and Europe, scientists believe these continents were joined in Late Jurassic times.

Living lassos
Camptosaurids and their kin, the iguanodontids, had a broad groove in the lower jaw. Maybe it held a long, mobile tongue. They may have used the tongue, giraffe-like, to lasso twigs and pull them to the mouth as shown below.

Camptosaurus body plan
a Long, low, broad skull with ridged cheek teeth
b Toothless beak
c Sturdy forelimbs capable of bearing weight
d Five fingers: 1–3 with hoof-like nails, 4–5 tiny
e Long, strong hind limbs
f Four toes, with tiny hooves
g Stiffened tail

©DIAGRAM

151

Iguanodontids 1

Iguanodontids ("iguana teeth") tended to be bigger than camptosaurids, with straighter thigh bones, relatively larger arms, and more cheek teeth. Some were as heavy as an elephant, and would have reared as high as an upstairs window, but walked mainly on all fours. *Iguanodon*, the best-known kind, roamed a warm, swampy countryside where herds of big males and smaller females browsed on horsetails. They may have used their spiky thumbs in mating or to jab into the eyes of an attacking carnosaur. Iguanodontids all lived in Cretaceous times. They spread to every continent. Scientists have found their footprints in South America and even Spitsbergen, now a snowy island group north of the Arctic Circle.

Iguanodontid fossil finds
Sites are shown on the map.
1 *Anoplosaurus*
2 *Craspedodon*
3 "*Gadolosaurus*"
4 *Iguanodon*
5 *Kangnasaurus* (possibly a hypsilophodontid)
6 *Mochlodon*
7 *Muttaburrasaurus* (possibly a camptosaurid)
8 *Ouranosaurus*
9 *Probactrosaurus*
10 *Vectisaurus*
11 *Tenontosaurus* (possibly a hypsilophodontid)
12 Iguanodontid footprints Brussels, London, and some other European cities have *Iguanodon* skeletons or casts.

1 **Anoplosaurus** ("not armored lizard"). Worn, broken bones of this Early Cretaceous dinosaur were found in eastern England in the 1800s.

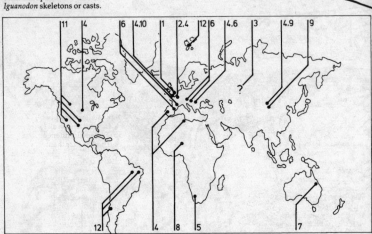

152

2 **Craspedodon** ("edge tooth") is known only from its five-ridged teeth, flattened from side to side. They may have chewed even more effectively than *Iguanodon*'s. This Late Cretaceous creature lived in Belgium.

3 **"Gadolosaurus"** is a small Russian iguanodontid, not yet officially described.

4 **Iguanodon** ("iguana tooth") had teeth like those of modern iguana lizards, but far larger. Its spiky thumb was its only weapon of defense. This Early Cretaceous dinosaur was the biggest, most plentiful, and most widespread of all the iguanodontids. Length: up to 29ft 6in (9m). Erect height: 16ft 6in (5m). Weight: up to 5 US tons (4.5 tonnes). Place: western Europe, Romania, western North America, North Africa, and Mongolia.

©DIAGRAM

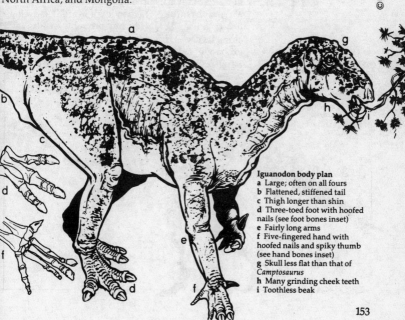

Iguanodon body plan
a Large; often on all fours
b Flattened, stiffened tail
c Thigh longer than shin
d Three-toed foot with hoofed nails (see foot bones inset)
e Fairly long arms
f Five-fingered hand with hoofed nails and spiky thumb (see hand bones inset)
g Skull less flat than that of *Camptosaurus*
h Many grinding cheek teeth
i Toothless beak

153

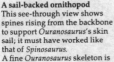

Iguanodontids 2

5 **Kangnasaurus** ("Kangnas lizard") is the name given to a tooth and leg bone found in Cretaceous rocks of Namaqualand, South Africa.

6 **Mochlodon** ("bar tooth") from Late Cretaceous southern and eastern Europe in some ways resembled *Camptosaurus* more than *Iguanodon*. Some experts think it belonged to neither of their families. Length: about 13ft (4m).

7 **Muttaburrasaurus** ("Muttaburra lizard"), possibly a camptosaurid, was first described in 1981. It had a low, broad head with an upward-bulging hollow muzzle, and teeth that sliced like shears; it might have eaten flesh as well as plants. It lived in Mid-Late Cretaceous times, and its fossil skeleton was found near Muttaburra in central Queensland, Australia. Length: 23ft (7m). Hip height: 10ft (3m).

8 **Ouranosaurus** ("brave monitor lizard") had a flat head, "duckbill" muzzle, and probably a skin "sail" along its back. This may have worked as a heat exchanger to keep its body at an even temperature. Length: 23ft (7m). Time: Early Cretaceous. Place: Niger, West Africa.

A sail-backed ornithopod
This see-through view shows spines rising from the backbone to support *Ouranosaurus's* skin sail; it must have worked like that of *Spinosaurus*.
A fine *Ouranosaurus* skeleton is on show in Niamey, Niger.

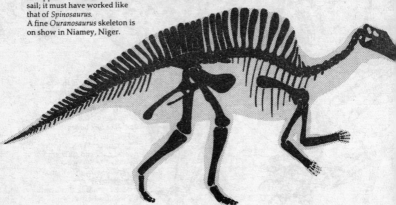

9 **Probactrosaurus** ("before the Bactrian lizard") was a Mongolian iguanodontid that looked rather like a flat-headed hadrosaurid. Scientists think it gave rise to the family of "duckbilled dinosaurs." Length: 19ft 6in (6m). Time: Late Cretaceous. Place: China and Mongolia.

10 **Vectisaurus** ("bar lizard") had longer spines rising from its backbone than *Iguanodon*. Like that dinosaur, it lived in Early Cretaceous southern England. Length: at least 13ft 6in (4m).

11 **Tenontosaurus** ("sinew lizard") has been called an iguanodontid but may have been a hypsilophodontid. It had a deep and enormously long tail – far longer than the rest of its body. It also had long front limbs, and often must have walked on all fours. Fossil finds suggest it was liable to be attacked by packs of *Deinonychus* – a fierce flesh-eater much smaller than itself. Length: 21ft 3in (6.5m). Weight: 1 US ton (907kg). Time: Early Cretaceous. Place: USA (Montana, Oklahoma, Texas, and Arizona).

The victim
Bones of *Tenontosaurus* and *Deinonychus* have been found mixed up – did *Deinonychus* packs sometimes attack a *Tenontosaurus*, or were the bones simply dumped together by flooding?
Tenontosaurus remains are on show in the Peabody Museum, New Haven, Connecticut.

©DIAGRAM

155

Hadrosaurids (duckbills)

These "big lizards" get the nickname "duckbills" from their broad, toothless beaks; yet, farther back, their jaws were crammed with batteries of grinding teeth – more teeth than any other dinosaurs possessed. Duckbills resembled their iguanodontid ancestors, but had deeper tails and longer limbs. Most had a bony head crest. Many weighed as much as a cow elephant. Standing on hind legs, a few

Hadrosaurid family tree
Hadrosaurids, or "duckbills," were an ornithopod family with two subfamilies. Skulls of most of their members appear on this family tree.
Hadrosaurines:
  1 *Mandschurosaurus* (also called *Gilmoreosaurus*)
  2 *Aralosaurus*
  3 *Brachylophosaurus*
  4 *Hadrosaurus*
  5 *Lophorhothon*
  6 *Prosaurolophus*
  7 *Saurolophus*
  8 *Claosaurus*
  9 *Tanius*
  10 *Shantungosaurus*
  11 *Edmontosaurus*
  12 *"Edmontosaurus copei"*
  13 *Secernosaurus*
  14 *Telmatosaurus*
Lambeosaurines:
  15 *Jaxartosaurus*
  16 *Lambeosaurus*
  17 *Corythosaurus*
  18 *Hypacrosaurus*
  19 *Bactrosaurus*
  20 *Tsintaosaurus*
  21 *Parasaurolophus*
Compared for size (below)
The largest and smallest of the duckbills are here shown to scale with a man.

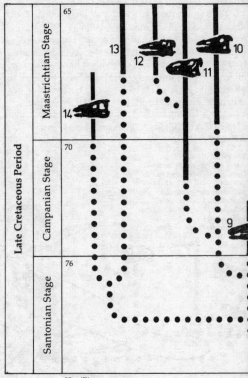

82 million years ago

towered as high as a house, although one was tiny. Duckbills' footprints have been found in western Canada's Early Cretaceous rocks, but their known fossils all date from Late Cretaceous times. Evolving possibly in Asia, these harmless browsing bipeds reached Europe and South America, and became among the most abundant dinosaurs of North America.

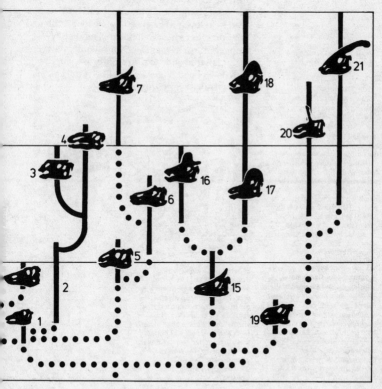

157

How hadrosaurids lived

Duckbills probably stood on their hind legs to browse from trees, but went down on all fours to crop low vegetation. While their powerful jaws were chewing one mouthful they could store extra unchewed food in their bulging cheeks.

Duckbills had no real defense against powerful enemies, yet their keen eyes, ears, and nostrils gave them early warnings of an attack. If a fierce carnosaur drew near, a duckbill resting or browsing on all fours rose on its long, strong hind legs and hurried away, head held low and balanced by the long, stiffened tail. Sometimes, a scared duckbill might have plunged into a lake or river, and swum by sweeping its flat tail from side to side as it thrust water back with its webbed fingers. More likely, duckbills escaped out of sight through forests of

Jaws and teeth
People used to think that duckbills ate soft waterweed, yet fossil duckbills have been found with stomach contents preserved well enough to show that this was not so. The animals had been chewing tough foods such as twigs and pine needles as well as fruits and seeds. A diet of this kind was made possible by these dinosaurs' jaws and teeth.

Shown here are a duckbill's skull (1) and lower jaw (2). Behind its duck-like beak (a) a duckbill's jaws bore pavements of packed rows of teeth (b). Each visible tooth crowned a vertical row of new teeth growing up to replace those that wore out. One duckbill could have as many as 2000 teeth, all told. Arrows show the pull of muscles that (c) opened and (d) closed *Corythosaurus*'s jaws, and (e) moved the lower jaw back and forth.

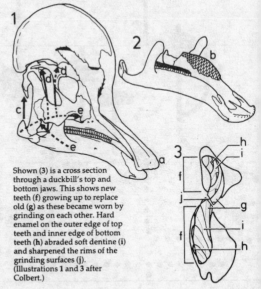

Shown (3) is a cross section through a duckbill's top and bottom jaws. This shows new teeth (f) growing up to replace old (g) as these became worn by grinding on each other. Hard enamel on the outer edge of top teeth and inner edge of bottom teeth (h) abraded soft dentine (i) and sharpened the rims of the grinding surfaces (j).
(Illustrations 1 and 3 after Colbert.)

broadleaved or needle-leaved trees where many made their homes.

Some ranged north of the Arctic Circle in their search for tender young leaves. Winters were less cold then than now, but plant food **became** scarce in the long, dark northern winters. Quite likely these Arctic hadrosaurids migrated south when summer faded, as caribou herds do now.

At mating time, head crests, facial skin flaps blown up like balloons, or bellowing calls probably helped males and females of the same species to find and recognize each other. After mating, females seem to have laid their eggs in broad, saucer-shaped mud mounds. Most may have protected and maybe even fed their hatchlings.

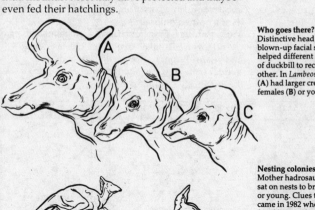

Who goes there?
Distinctive head crests, or blown-up facial skin flaps, helped different kinds and sexes of duckbill to recognize each other. In *Lambeosaurus*, males (**A**) had larger crests than females (**B**) or young (**C**).

© DIAGRAM

Nesting colonies
Mother hadrosaurids may have sat on nests to brood their eggs or young. Clues to this behavior came in 1982 when an American fossil hunter described a group of hadrosaur mud nests each a hadrosaur length apart. Mothers sitting on these nests would have been almost within "pecking distance" of their neighbors, like the nesting seabirds in a gannet colony. While some adults foraged for food, those that remained in the colony would have guarded eggs and young.

159

Hadrosaurine duckbills 1

The hadrosaurines' homes
The map shows fossil finds.
 1 *Aralosaurus*
 2 *Brachylophosaurus*
 3 *Claorhynchus*
 4 *Claosaurus*
 5 *Edmontosaurus*
 6 *Hadrosaurus*
 7 *Lophorhothon*
 8 *Maiasaura*
 9 *Mandschurosaurus*
10 *Microhadrosaurus*
11 *Notoceratops*
12 *Orthomerus*
13 *Prosaurolophus*
14 *Saurolophus*
15 *Secernosaurus*
16 *Shantungosaurus*
17 *Tanius*
18 *Telmatosaurus*
Many North American museums have duckbill skeletons.

Hadrosaurine duckbills had flat heads or skulls with *solid* bony humps or crests, a long, straight lower jaw, and long, slender limbs. Most may have had "nose flaps" they could blow up like balloons.

1 **Aralosaurus** ("Aral lizard") was an early hadrosaurid found near the Aral Sea in Central Asia. Its skull is incomplete but had a low bulge ahead of the eyes, like *Hadrosaurus*.

2 **Brachylophosaurus** ("short ridge lizard") of Alberta, Canada, had a steep face and flat skull roof formed by a bony, spade-shaped plate jutting back as a short spike. It had long forelimbs. Body length: about 23ft (7m).

3 **Claorhynchus** ("branched beak") of Montana is known only from part of a skull. People once mistook it for a horned dinosaur's.

4 **Claosaurus** ("branched lizard"). At about 12ft (3.7m) this was a small, early and "old-fashioned" hadrosaurid from Kansas, with slim body and slender feet. Toes and teeth somewhat resembled those of its iguanodontid ancestors.

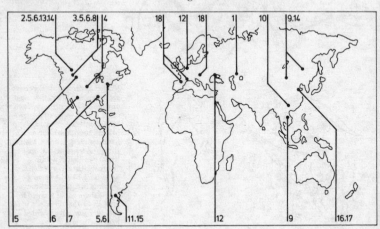

5 **Edmontosaurus** ("Edmonton lizard") from Alberta, Montana, and New Jersey was one of the largest duckbills, up to 42ft 6in (13m). It weighed 3.4 US tons (3.1 tonnes). Its flat face may have had loose skin that could be blown up to help it make a loud bellowing call. Long-headed *"Edmontosaurus* (or *Anatosaurus) copei"* is a "new" genus to be described in print and renamed.

6 **Hadrosaurus** ("big lizard") measured 26–32ft (8–10m). It had a deep, narrow face with a rounded hump before the eyes, probably covered with a thick, tough skin. (Females may have had no hump.) A soft frill ran down the back. Place: USA (New Jersey and New Mexico) and Canada (Alberta).

7 **Lophorhothon** ("crested snout") had a short snout and tiny pyramidal bump in front of its eyes. It may have reached 49ft (15m) but the only known specimens could be young *Parasaurolophus*. Place: Alabama, USA.

Hadrosaurids in action
Some experts believe that hadrosaurid dinosaurs may have adopted the attitudes shown.
a Low browsing
b Bipedal walking
c Quadrupedal walking
d High browsing
e Running

© DIAGRAM

161

Hadrosaurine duckbills 2

8 **Maiasaura** ("good mother lizard") of Montana, USA, reached 30ft (9m). A short bony spike jutted forward above its eyes. In 1978 scientists found a *Maiasaura* nest with babies, and clues suggesting that this dinosaur brought food to its young.

9 **Mandschurosaurus** ("Manchurian lizard") from northern China, Laos, and Mongolia measured 26ft (8m). It had a flat head, perhaps with a long, low narrow ridge along the middle of the face.

10 **Microhadrosaurus** ("tiny *Hadrosaurus*") was a tiny southern Chinese duckbill described in 1979.

11 **Notoceratops** ("southern horned face") is known only from part of a jaw found in southern Argentina. Some scientists think this came from a horned dinosaur.

12 **Orthomerus** ("having straight parts") is known from straight leg bones found in the Netherlands and southern Russia. *Orthomerus* may be the same as *Telmatosaurus*.

13 **Prosaurolophus** ("before *Saurolophus*") had a sloping face with bumps over the eyes and a broad, flat muzzle. This Canadian duckbill may have given rise to *Saurolophus*. Length: 26ft (8m).

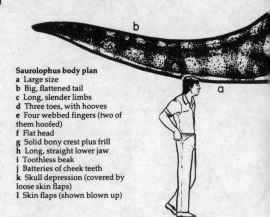

Saurolophus body plan
a Large size
b Big, flattened tail
c Long, slender limbs
d Three toes, with hooves
e Four webbed fingers (two of them hoofed)
f Flat head
g Solid bony crest plus frill
h Long, straight lower jaw
i Toothless beak
j Batteries of cheek teeth
k Skull depression (covered by loose skin flaps)
l Skin flaps (shown blown up)

14 **Saurolophus** ("ridged lizard") had a solid, spiky crest jutting from the back of the head. It may have been able to blow up skin balloons along the length of its face. It lived in East Asia and North America. Length: 30ft (9m).

15 **Secernosaurus** ("separate lizard") was probably a flat-headed duckbill only 10ft (3m) long. It lived in Argentina, far from the northern homes of most duckbilled dinosaurs.

16 **Shantungosaurus** ("Shantung lizard") reached 39–49ft (12–15m) long and 23ft (7m) high. This Chinese duckbill resembled *Edmontosaurus* but was even larger.

17 **Tanius** ("of the Tan"). This Chinese hadrosaurid was probably like *Edmontosaurus* but most of the front of its head remains unknown.

18 **Telmatosaurus** ("marsh lizard") had a deep skull much like *Hadrosaurus*'s. It is one of the few duckbills found in Europe: in Hungary, the Pyrenees, and southern France.

14

15

16

17

18

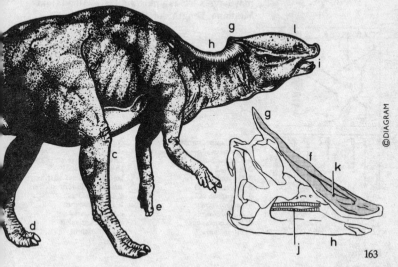

©DIAGRAM

163

Lambeosaurine duckbills

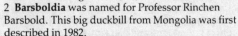

"Lambe's lizards" mostly had tall, showy head crests of hollow bone. Females and young had smaller crests than males of the same kind. Lower jaws and limb bones were relatively short.

1 **Bactrosaurus** ("Bactrian lizard") was an early lambeosaurine of Central and East Asia, possibly evolved from *Probactrosaurus*. Its low skull had a narrow bill. Length: 13ft (4m).

2 **Barsboldia** was named for Professor Rinchen Barsbold. This big duckbill from Mongolia was first described in 1982.

3 **Corythosaurus** ("helmet lizard") had a tall, hollow, narrow crest like a cocked hat. Young and females had small crests. Place: Alberta, Canada. Length: over 33ft (10m). Weight: 4.2 US tons (3.8 tonnes).

4 **Hypacrosaurus** ("below the top lizard") had a short, high skull and smaller, fatter crest than *Corythosaurus*. From the rear of the crest, a solid bony spike jutted back and down. A high ridge on its back may have acted as a radiator. Place: Alberta and Montana. Length: 30ft (9m).

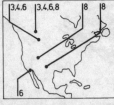

Bugle-like calls? (left)
This cutaway view shows the air passage in the skull of a female *Parasaurolophus*. When lambeosaurines called to one another their long air passages made the sound more resonant – acting rather like the long tube in a bugle or hunting horn. (Hadrosaurines produced a similar effect with facial skin flaps blown up like the vocal sacs of frogs.)

Where lambeosaurines lived
These maps show fossil finds.
1 *Bactrosaurus*
2 *Barsboldia*
3 *Corythosaurus*
4 *Hypacrosaurus*
5 *Jaxartosaurus*
6 *Lambeosaurus*
7 *Nipponosaurus*
8 *Parasaurolophus*
9 *Tsintaosaurus*

Characteristic crests (right)
Different kinds of lambeosaurines had differently shaped, hollow, head crests.
a *Corythosaurus*
b *Hypacrosaurus*
c *Lambeosaurus*
d *Parasaurolophus*
e *Tsintaosaurus*

5 **Jaxartosaurus** ("Jaxartes lizard") from Central Asia is poorly known. Length: 30ft (9m).

6 **Lambeosaurus** ("Lambe's lizard") had a hollow, hatchet-shaped crest jutting forward from the skull roof, and a spine jutting back, maybe supporting a neck frill. One species had a deep "swimmer's" tail. Length: perhaps up to 49ft (15m). Place: Alberta, Montana, and Baja California.

7 **Nipponosaurus** ("Japanese lizard") was a small hadrosaurid with a deep, short, broad head and a low crest. It may have been the young of another lambeosaurine. Its bones came from a mine on Sakhalin Island, once part of Japan.

8 **Parasaurolophus** ("beside *Saurolophus*") had a short muzzle and a curved, hollow horn up to 6ft (1.8m) long jutting back from its head. A frill might have run from horn to back. Length: 33ft (10m). Place: Alberta, Utah, and New Mexico.

9 **Tsintaosaurus** ("Tsintao lizard") had a long, spiky horn above its eyes. A showy skin flap might have stretched from horn to beak. This Chinese duckbill measured about 33ft (10m).

©DIAGRAM

Pachycephalosaurids (boneheads) 1

"Boneheads" were strange bipeds with thick skulls. These might have served as crash-helmets to protect the brain when rival males banged heads. Males probably grew bigger, thicker skulls than females. Boneheads had keen eyes and a sharp sense of smell. They walked with a level back and used the long, strong tail as a prop when standing. None ran fast. Many munched leaves, seeds, fruits, and maybe insects. Some grew sharper teeth than others and may have eaten different foods. Boneheads roamed hills, perhaps in herds ruled by strong males. The smallest kind was chicken-sized, the largest far larger than a man. Boneheads may have evolved from the same ancestors as horned dinosaurs. Most lived in Late Cretaceous North America and Asia. They might belong in their own suborder.

Bonehead fossil finds
This map shows finds of pachycephalosaurids.
 1 *Goyocephale*
 2 *Gravitholus*
 3 *Heishansaurus*
 4 *Homalocephale*
 5 *Majungatholus*
 6 *Micropachycephalosaurus*
 7 *Pachycephalosaurus*
 8 *Prenocephale*
 9 *Stegoceras*
 10 *Tylocephale*
 11 *Wannanosaurus*
 12 *Yaverlandia*

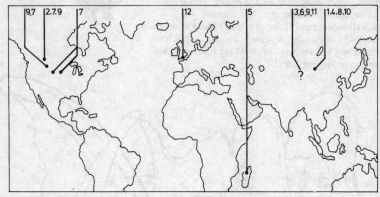

Comparative sizes
The largest, smallest, and a medium-sized bonehead are here drawn to the same scale as a man.

1 **Goyocephale** ("Goyot head") was a flat-headed bonehead from Mongolia, described in 1982. Some scientists put *Goyocephale* and *Homalocephale* in a new "flat-headed" family of boneheads.

2 **Gravitholus** ("heavy dome") had a big, thick, broad skull, with very little space inside for brain. Length: perhaps 10ft (3m) or more. Place: Alberta, Canada.

3 **Heishansaurus** ("Hei-shan lizard") comes from China. In 1953 one scientist described its remains as an armored dinosaur's. In 1979 another identified them as a bonehead's.

4 **Homalocephale** ("even head") from Mongolia had a flat head. The rough skull was patterned with pits and bony knobs. The hip bones' shapes suggest boneheads may have given birth to babies instead of laying eggs. Length: 10ft (3m).

Flat skull
This illustration shows the flat skull for which *Homalocephale* is named. This skull was found with other bones, which is unusual since most boneheads are known only from worn bits of braincase washed down by rivers from the uplands where many may have lived.
(Illustration after Maryanska and Osmólska.)

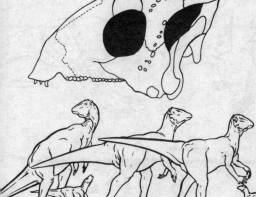

Family life
Herds or family groups of boneheads may have roamed the hills and mountains.

© DIAGRAM

Pachycephalosaurids (boneheads) 2

5 **Majungatholus** ("Majunga dome") had a skull with a thick, rough, dome-shaped top. This small, "old-fashioned" bonehead lived in Late Cretaceous Madagascar, which proves that northern boneheads could and did reach the Southern Hemisphere early in Cretaceous times. Its braincase was found in the early 1900s but not identified until 1979. Length: about 4ft 6in (1.4m).

6 **Micropachycephalosaurus** ("tiny thick-headed lizard") from China has one of the longest names and shortest bodies of any dinosaur. It was described in 1978. Length: about 20in (51cm).

7 **Pachycephalosaurus** ("thick-headed lizard") was the largest bonehead with the thickest, spikiest skull. Bone 10in (25cm) thick roofed its domed braincase. Bony spikes jutted from its low, narrow snout, and sharp knobs rimmed the back of the head. This bonehead lived in western North America. Length: 15ft (4.6m).

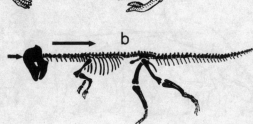

Head-banging

a Two rival *Stegoceras* males here crash head-on. The winner of the duel will rule a herd of females. Scenes like this took place where the Rocky Mountains stand today. Now bighorn rams bang heads with similar objectives.

b Arrows with this *Stegoceras* skeleton show that when its owner's head collided with another's, the force of impact traveled harmlessly through the thickest part of the skull, then straight on through the backbone. Neither brain nor spinal cord was jarred so harshly that it suffered damage.

8 **Prenocephale** ("sloping head") had a high, domed braincase, steeply sloping face and slim snout. Rows of tiny knobs ran around the sides and back of the head. Length: 8ft (2.4m). Place: Mongolia.

9 **Stegoceras** ("horny roof") was a small bonehead with a short, deep face. Its skull had a thick, smooth, domed roof and a frill of bony bumps around the back, but none on the sides. Most teeth were rather sharp. Length: 6ft 6in (2.5m). Weight: up to 120lb (54.4kg). Place: western North America, and maybe northwest China.

10 **Tylocephale** ("swollen head") looked like *Stegoceras* but its head's highest part lay farther back, and its teeth were relatively big. Length: about 6ft 6in (2.5m). Place: Mongolia.

11 **Wannanosaurus** ("Wannan lizard") was a small primitive Chinese bonehead described in 1977.

12 **Yaverlandia** came from Yaverland on England's Isle of Wight. This earliest known bonehead had a skull capped by two thickened areas of bone. It may have given rise to later boneheads. Length: perhaps 3ft (90cm). Time: Early Cretaceous.

Two bonehead skulls
Pachycephalosaurus had a much larger, more knobbly skull (**A**) than that of *Stegoceras* (**B**) which may have been its ancestor. Thick skulls left little space for brains.

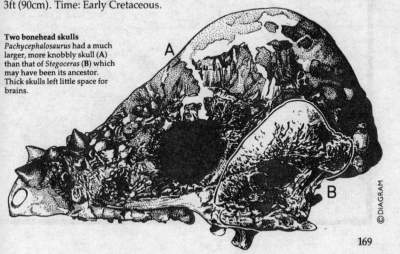

©DIAGRAM

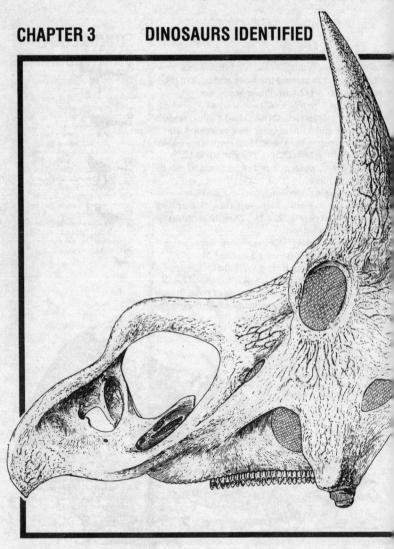

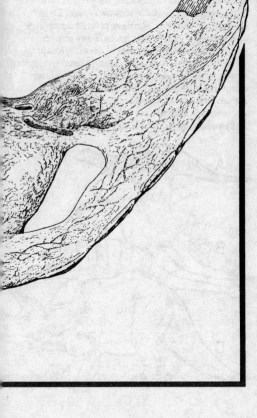

Section 6 FOUR-LEGGED ORNITHISCHIANS

Paleontologists usually group these plant-eaters in three suborders: the plated, armored, and horned dinosaurs – also known respectively as stegosaurs, ankylosaurs, and ceratopsians. Here are one family of stegosaurs, two families of ankylosaurs, and three families of ceratopsians. Also included in this section are the scelidosaurids. These may have given rise to the ankylosaurs, although some experts group scelidosaurids with those two-legged ornithischians the ornithopods. (For general information about this section, see the chapter introduction on page 38.)

Sharp brow horns and a bony neck frill protected this horned dinosaur's head and neck from enemy attack. Named *Diceratops* in 1905, the skull is really that of a *Triceratops*, a type of ornithischian dinosaur that had been named in 1889. Illustration after O.C. Marsh, appearing in *The Dinosaur Dictionary* by Donald F. Glut (Citadel).

About four-legged ornithischians

Like their ornithopod relatives, four-legged ornithischians ate plants and had horny beaks. The hip bones were arranged like those of birds, although the horned dinosaurs had a piece of bone that looked at first sight like the forward-jutting pubis of saurischian or "lizard-hipped" dinosaurs. These ornithischians may have moved more slowly than their biped kin. Instead of running to escape the sharp-fanged carnosaurs, they relied on armor to protect them. Scelidosaurs had rows of bony studs set in the skin. Stegosaurs had bony plates and spikes to guard their backs. Bony armor guarded most exposed parts of the ankylosaurs. Horns sprouted from most ceratopsians' snouts and brows, and the neck was protected by a massive bony frill. Although all had some sort of body armor, these quadrupeds came from two-legged ancestors. Scelidosaurs evolved first, stegosaurs and ankylosaurs next, and ceratopsians last.

Four types of protection
These four beasts represent the four main groups of four-legged ornithischians described in detail in this chapter. Each relied upon a somewhat different type of armor to protect the body.
A Scelidosaurs merely had bony studs in the skin.
B Stegosaurs had plates or spikes jutting upward from the back and a spiky tail, but poorly guarded flanks.
C Ankylosaurs had armored head, back, tail, flanks, and maybe outer sides of limbs. Some had belly armor, too.
D Ceratopsians developed huge heads with bony neck frills and formidable horns, but they lacked bony armor on the back and flanks.

Scelidosaurids

These "limb lizards" were low-slung, car-length dinosaurs. Their strong jaws worked ridged teeth that chewed low-growing plants. Slow moving, they relied for protection on rows of bony studs like those on the dinosaurs' early, crocodile-like ancestors. Another old-fashioned feature was lack of a prepubic process (a forward-jutting piece of hip bone found in most later bird-hipped dinosaurs). Both features occur among the ankylosaurs. Scelidosaurids might have given rise to those armored dinosaurs.

1 **Lusitanosaurus** ("Lusitania lizard") lived in Early Jurassic Portugal (once called Lusitania). It probably resembled *Scelidosaurus*.

2 **Scelidosaurus** ("limb lizard") had four strong legs with large feet. Its heavy body was highest at the hips. Seven rows of jaw-breaking bony studs and spikes set in the skin guarded its back. Length: 11ft 6in (3.5m). Time: Early Jurassic. Place: Lyme Regis, southern England and Tibet.

Where they lived
Shown are *Lusitanosaurus* (1) and *Scelidosaurus* (2) finds.

Scelidosaurid features
a Small head
b Heavy body
c Bony studs
d Strong legs
e Broad feet
Scelidosaurid hip bones
The pubis (f) lacked the prepubic process (g) found in most later ornithischians.

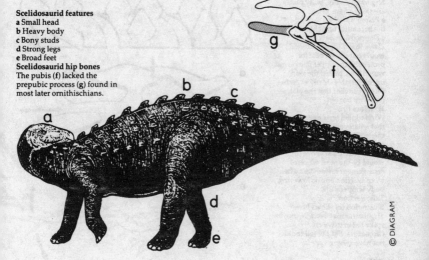

© DIAGRAM

173

Stegosaurids (plated dinosaurs) 1

Stegosaurids ("roof lizards"), the plated dinosaurs, formed a suborder all their own. Bony plates or spikes, or both, embedded in thick skin guarded neck, back, and tail. Big plates also may have shed unwanted body heat.

Stegosaurids usually walked on all fours but may have reared to browse on trees. Their short, weak teeth could only tackle soft, lush plants. Under attack they may have swung their spiky tails, but their flanks must have been vulnerable. These dinosaurs evolved from small, two-legged ornithischians with rows of bony studs along the back. Two types of stegosaurid evolved: one mainly plated; the other mostly spiny. The largest of them were twice as long as, yet lighter than, a large rhinoceros. Stegosaurids roamed North America, Europe, Africa, and Asia, and lived from Mid Jurassic to Late Cretaceous times.

Problems of the plates
Three possible arrangements of *Stegosaurus's* big, bony plates are shown here.
a Paired upright
b Alternating upright
c Flopped outward
Plates that flopped outward would have been best for protecting the upper flanks, but would have pulled the skin uncomfortably. Many experts think it likelier that the plates jutted up not out.

Heat loss fins
Wind tunnel tests have shown that whatever the direction of the wind an alternating arrangement of body plates, as shown here from above (**d**), would have been the most efficient arrangement for shedding heat by convection and so lowering body temperature.

Tail in action
Illustration (**e**) shows how *Stegosaurus* may have swung its spiky tail to drive off carnosaurs. But the tail could not have swung very far.

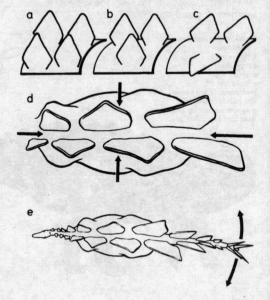

1 **Chialingosaurus** ("Chia-ling lizard") was a slim stegosaurid with rather long front legs and small spiky plates on back and tail. Time: Mid Jurassic. Place: near the Chia-ling River, southern China. Length: perhaps 13ft (4m).

2 **Craterosaurus** ("bowl lizard") is known from a bit of backbone with a bowl-shaped dip, first mistaken for a braincase. This dinosaur reached about 13ft (4m) and lived in southern England in Early Cretaceous times.

3 **Dacentrurus** ("pointed tail") had many paired spines, but perhaps no plates, along its back and tail. It had longer forelimbs and a lower back than most stegosaurids. Time: Middle to Late Jurassic. Place: western Europe.

4 **Dravidosaurus** ("Dravidanadu lizard") means "lizard from south India." Described in 1979, this small stegosaurid had plates, and unusual spines that bulged halfway up. Length: perhaps only 10ft (3m). Time: Late Cretaceous (it was the last known stegosaurid). Place: southern India.

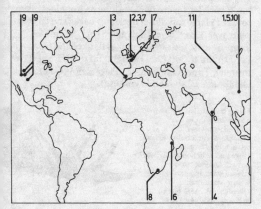

Fossil finds
Sites of stegosaurid fossil finds are shown on the map.
1 *Chialingosaurus*
2 *Craterosaurus*
3 *Dacentrurus*
4 *Dravidosaurus*
5 *Huayangosaurus*
6 *Kentrosaurus*
7 *Lexovisaurus*
8 *Paranthodon*
9 *Stegosaurus*
10 *Tuojiangosaurus*
11 *Wuerhosaurus*

© DIAGRAM

Stegosaurids (plated dinosaurs) 2

5 **Huayangosaurus** ("Huayang lizard") was described in 1982. It had plates, spines, and front teeth (not a toothless beak) and may have given rise to later stegosaurids. Length: 13ft (4m). Time: Middle Jurassic. Place: China.

6 **Kentrosaurus** ("pointed lizard") had pairs of short triangular plates on neck and shoulders and long spikes on the back and tail, with an extra pair guarding the tops of its thighs. Length: 17ft (5m). Time: Late Jurassic. Place: Tendaguru, Tanzania, East Africa.

7 **Lexovisaurus** ("Lexovi lizard") probably had fairly narrow, short plates on neck and back, and spines on its tail. Its name comes from the Lexovi tribe of northwest France. A pair of very long spines jutted back from the hips. Length: 17ft (5m). Place: England and France. Time: Mid Jurassic.

8 **Paranthodon** ("beside *Anthodon*") is known from a piece of skull with teeth ridged like *Kentrosaurus*'s. Length: about 17ft (5m). Time: Early Cretaceous. Place: Cape Province, South Africa.

9 **Stegosaurus** ("roof lizard") is the biggest known stegosaurid, with the largest plates. Hips were room-high; back legs were twice as long as front legs. Two rows of plates ran down neck and back. The largest plate was 30in (76cm) high and 31in (78.5cm) long. At least four heavy spikes flanked the tail. Length: up to 30ft (9m). Weight: up to 2 US tons (1.8 tonnes). Time: Late Jurassic. Place: USA (Colorado, Oklahoma, Utah, and Wyoming).

Stegosaurus body plan
a At least two pairs of bony spikes on the tail
b Heavy tail
c Two rows of tall bony plates, maybe sheathed in horn
d Narrow body, highest at the hips
e Spinal cavity above the hips probably holding a gland to help energize the hind limbs
f Long hind limbs
g Short front limbs
h Broad, short feet
i Four toes with hoof-like claws on each hind foot
j Five toes with hoof-like claws on each forefoot
k Head small and narrow with a walnut-sized brain
l Small, weak cheek teeth
m Horny, toothless beak

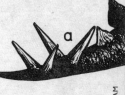

©DIAGRAM

10 **Tuojiangosaurus** ("Tuojiang lizard") had 15 pairs of triangular plates (some spiky) from neck to halfway down the tail. Two pairs of spikes guarded the end of the tail. A skeleton described in 1977 is the best preserved of any Asian stegosaurid. Length: 23ft (7m). Time: Late Jurassic. Place: Zhucheng County, south-central China.

11 **Wuerhosaurus** ("Wuerho lizard") had long, slim bony spines rising from the backbone above its hips, and long, low plates running down its back. Length: perhaps 20ft (6m). Time: Early Cretaceous. Place: Wuerho District, Sinkiang, northwest China.

Ankylosaurs (armored dinosaurs)

Ankylosaurs ("fused lizards") were low, squat, heavy-bodied beasts, many with short, massive limbs and barrel-shaped bodies. The smallest was the length of a man, the largest, the length of a bus and the weight of a small elephant. All were built like living battle tanks. A flexible armor of bony slabs, plates, and spikes, set in tough skin and sheathed with horn, guarded exposed parts of the body.

Ankylosaur family tree
This shows possible links between some members in each of the two families making up the ornithischian suborder of ankylosaurs or armored dinosaurs. Their ancestors may have been *Scelidosaurus*.
Nodosaurids included:
1 *Hylaeosaurus*
2 *Acantholis*
3 *Struthiosaurus*
4 *Sauropelta*
5 *Silvisaurus*
6 *Nodosaurus*
7 *Panoplosaurus*
Ankylosaurids included:
8 *Sauroplites*
9 *Talarurus*
10 *Pinacosaurus*
11 *Saichania*
12 *Tarchia*
13 *Euoplocephalus*
14 *Ankylosaurus*
Letters show stages of the Cretaceous Period:
A Berriasian
B Valanginian
C Hauterivian
D Barremian
E Aptian
F Albian
G Cenomanian
H Turonian
I Coniacian
J Santonian
K Campanian
L Maastrichtian

period	division	stage	EUROPE
Cretaceous	Upper	L 65	
		70	3
		K	
		J 76	•
		I 82	•
			•
		H 88	•
		G 94	2 •
	Lower	F 100	
		106	•
		E 112	•
		D	1 •
		C 118	•
		B 124	• • • • • •
		A 130	
		136	
		million years ago	• • • • • •

Ankylosaurs had small teeth and weak jaws. They probably ate soft, low-growing plants, but just might have lived mainly on insects. Protected from even the largest carnosaurs, two ankylosaur families flourished in northern lands during Cretaceous times. Including poorly known *Regnosaurus*, their 32 genera account for almost one in ten of all known kinds of dinosaur.

Comparative sizes
The largest and smallest ankylosaurs are shown here to scale with a man.

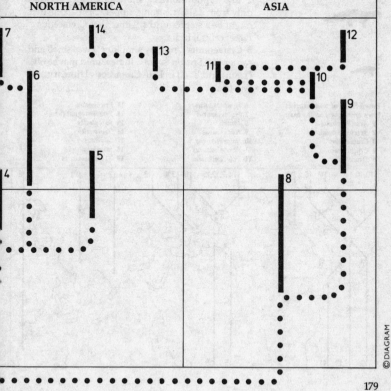

NORTH AMERICA	ASIA

7 14 13
6
4 5
8 9 10 11 12

©DIAGRAM

Nodosaurid ankylosaurs 1

Nodosaurids ("node lizards") had narrow snouts, solid armor plates, flank spines longer than broad, and relatively slim limbs. They may have held their bodies higher than ankylosaurids when walking. The tail tip was not armed with a club.

1 **Acanthopholis** ("thorn bearer") had rows of raised plates set in its skin, long neck spikes, and possibly plates on the tail. Length: 18ft (5.5m). Time: Early and Late Cretaceous. Place: southern England.

2 **Brachypodosaurus** ("short-foot lizard") is known only from a short, strong, upper "arm" bone that might be a stegosaurid's. Time: Late Cretaceous. Place: central India.

3 **Crataeomus** ("mighty shoulder") was small and rather like *Struthiosaurus*. It measured maybe 6ft (1.8m) and lived in Late Cretaceous Hungary and Austria.

Fossil finds of nodosaurids
Sites are shown on the map.

1 *Acanthopholis*	6 *Hoplitosaurus*	13 *Priconodon*
2 *Brachypodosaurus*	7 *Hylaeosaurus*	14 *Priodontognathus*
3 *Crataeomus*	8 *Minmi*	15 *Sarcolestes*
4 *Cryptodraco*	9 *Nodosaurus*	16 *Sauropelta*
5 *Dracopelta*	10 *Palaeoscincus*	17 *Silvisaurus*
	11 *Panoplosaurus*	18 *Struthiosaurus*
	12 *Polacanthoides*	19 "*Tenchisaurus*"

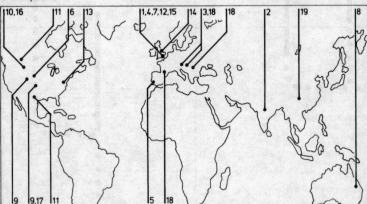

4 **Cryptodraco** ("hidden dragon") from Late Jurassic Cambridgeshire, England, had a massive thigh bone like *Hoplitosaurus*'s and might have resembled that beast.

5 **Dracopelta** ("armored dragon") had five types of armor. Named in 1980, this is the oldest well-preserved ankylosaur. It measured 7ft (2m) and lived in Late Jurassic western Portugal.

6 **Hoplitosaurus** ("hoplite lizard") was named for the hoplites – heavily armored infantry in ancient Greece. It had five types of armor: triangular, round, flat, keeled, and spined – most likely the spines jutted from its flanks. Time: Early Cretaceous. Place: Calico Canyon, South Dakota, USA.

7 **Hylaeosaurus** ("woodland lizard") from Early Cretaceous southeast England may have had spiky flanks, an armored back, and plates jutting up along the tail. Length: 20ft (6m).

8 **Minmi** is named for Minmi Crossing near Roma in southeast Queensland, Australia. Described in 1980, this is the first undoubted named ankylosaur found in the Southern Hemisphere, and the first found anywhere with bony plates developing in the body wall. Length: perhaps 7ft (2m). Time: Early Cretaceous.

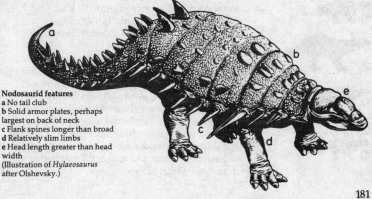

Nodosaurid features
a No tail club
b Solid armor plates, perhaps largest on back of neck
c Flank spines longer than broad
d Relatively slim limbs
e Head length greater than head width
(Illustration of *Hylaeosaurus* after Olshevsky.)

©DIAGRAM

181

Nodosaurid ankylosaurs 2

9 **Nodosaurus** ("node lizard") had alternating rows of large and small plates down the back and flanks. On the skin large plates between the ribs bore round bony nodes. Length: 18ft (5.5m). Time: early Late Cretaceous. Place: Kansas and Wyoming, USA.

10 **Palaeoscincus** ("old skink") from Late Cretaceous Montana is known from few remains, perhaps of *Panoplosaurus*. Length: 23ft (7m).

11 **Panoplosaurus** ("fully armored lizard") was one of the last North American nodosaurids. Hard plates encased its back and bony armor was fused to its skull. Length 23ft (7m). Weight: 3.8 US tons (3.5 tonnes). Time: Late Cretaceous. Place: Alberta to Texas.

12 **Polacanthoides** ("*Polacanthus* form") from Early Cretaceous southern England may have resembled *Hylaeosaurus*, but had a different type of shoulder blade. Length: maybe 16ft (5m).

13 **Priconodon** ("saw cone-shaped tooth") had teeth like *Sauropelta*'s and possibly resembled it. Length: perhaps over 20ft (6m). Time: Early Cretaceous. Place: Maryland, USA.

14 **Priodontognathus** ("saw-toothed jaw") is known only from a piece of jaw containing 18 fairly large teeth like *Sauropelta*'s. Once called an iguanodontid, then a stegosaurid, it was redescribed as a nodosaurid in 1980. Time: probably Early Cretaceous. Place: Yorkshire, England.

15 **Sarcolestes** ("flesh robber") is known only from scraps, including a piece of jaw with small teeth. This Mid Jurassic beast is the world's oldest known ankylosaur. Place: Cambridgeshire, England.

16 **Sauropelta** ("lizard shield") had a long, narrow skull. Bands of large and small shields ran across the back, and spines might have stuck out from its sides. One of the largest nodosaurids, at up to 25ft (7.6m), it weighed 3.5 US tons (3.2 tonnes). Time: Early Cretaceous. Place: Montana, USA.

17 **Silvisaurus** ("forest lizard") had large cheek bones and a rather long neck. Rows of thick, round or many-sided plates covered the back. Sharp spines stuck out from the shoulders, and probably jutted from its rather wide, flat tail. Length: 13ft (4m). Time: Early Cretaceous. Place: Kansas, USA.

18 **Struthiosaurus** ("ostrich lizard") had six types of armor plates including large spines guarding the shoulders and sharp plates guarding hips and tail. Only 6ft (1.8m) long, this is the smallest known ankylosaur. Like some modern dwarf cattle it may have lived only on islands, in what are now eastern Austria, Hungary, Romania, and southern France. Time: Late Cretaceous.

19 **"Tenchisaurus"** ("Tenchin lizard") has been shown and named in a Japanese book as an early nodosaurid, but has not been scientifically described. Time: Jurassic. Place: perhaps Tenchin Gomba, Szechuan, China.

Nodosaurid facts (below)
a *Panoplosaurus*'s narrow snout and those of other nodosaurids suggest they were choosy feeders like today's (narrow snouted) black rhinoceros.
b Bony armor fused to the skull made *Panoplosaurus*'s head resemble a sheep's head when seen from the side.
c Air flowed through simple passages to nodosaurids' lungs.
Comparative sizes (bottom)
A man is here shown to scale with the largest and smallest nodosaurids.
A *Struthiosaurus*, an island-dwelling genus, may have been the smallest nodosaurid.
B *Sauropelta*, one of the largest nodosaurids, is represented by this fossilized skin. Rows of bony studs protected the back and tail.

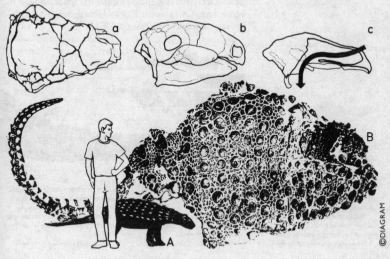

©DIAGRAM

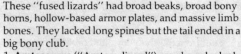

Ankylosaurid ankylosaurs 1

These "fused lizards" had broad beaks, broad bony horns, hollow-based armor plates, and massive limb bones. They lacked long spines but the tail ended in a big bony club.

1 **Amtosaurus** ("Amtgay lizard") may have looked like *Talarurus*, but was larger, at maybe 23ft (7m). It was found at Amtgay in Mongolia. Time: Late Cretaceous.

2 **Ankylosaurus** ("fused lizard") was the largest and last known ankylosaur. Its armored head had rounded nostrils and a horny, toothless beak. Rows of raised plates, some sharper and larger than others, protected back and flanks. It grew up to 35ft (10.7m) long and lived in Late Cretaceous Alberta, Canada, and Montana, USA.

3 **Euoplocephalus** ("well-armored head") had armored bands down its back, with rows of small shields, ridged plates, and blunt spines. This was the most common North American ankylosaur. Length: up to 23ft (7m). Weight: 2–3 US tons (1.8–2.7 tonnes). Time: Late Cretaceous. Place: Alberta, Canada, and maybe Sinkiang, northwest China.

Euoplocephalus body plan
a Large size (shown here to scale with a US M47 tank)
b Bony tail club, swung against attacking carnosaurs
c Tail carried raised
d Big, broad body
e Limbs directly below body
f No spines on side of body

g Bands of bony plates across back and tail, with small bony studs between the bands
h Plates jut up over the shoulder and back; armor may have floated in the skin as in crocodiles, or some may have had a horny sheath.
i Head broader than long

j Small eyes
k Broad muzzle
l This cross section through the armored skull shows how bony struts made it light yet strong. Looped nasal passages warmed breathed-in air before it reached the lungs.
(Illustration after Carpenter.)

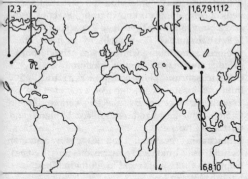

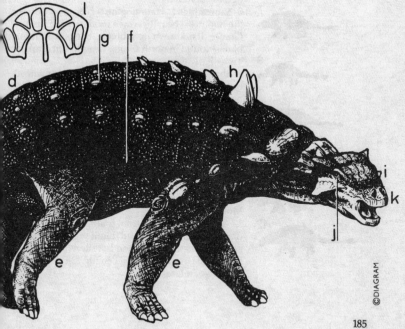

©DIAGRAM

185

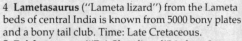

Ankylosaurid ankylosaurs 2

4 **Lametasaurus** ("Lameta lizard") from the Lameta beds of central India is known from 5000 bony plates and a bony tail club. Time: Late Cretaceous.

5 **Peishansaurus** ("Pei-Shan lizard") is from Late Cretaceous northwest China. It was named from a piece of jaw, maybe a young ankylosaur's.

6 **Pinacosaurus** ("plank lizard") was a rather lightly built ankylosaurid with slim feet, a rounded beak, three "nostrils," and very small feet. Length: 18ft (5.5m). Time: Late Cretaceous. Place: Mongolia and northern China.

7 **Saichania** ("beautiful") had heavy bony armor on its head, belly armor, and massive forelimbs. It comes from Late Cretaceous rocks in southern Mongolia. Length: 23ft (7m).

8 **Sauroplites** ("lizard hoplite") gets its name from the hoplites – heavily armed infantry of ancient Greece. It is known from broken bones and armored plates, found in north China. Length: 20ft (6m). Time: Early Cretaceous.

9 **Shamosaurus** is a Mongolian ankylosaur named but not described in 1981. Its head and beak were narrow compared with ankylosaurids like *Tarchia*. Length: maybe 23ft (7m).

10 **Stegosaurides** ("stegosaur form") was named from a few bones, now probably lost. Time: Late Cretaceous. Place: northern China.

11 **Talarurus** ("basket tail") had bands of thick plates and hollow spines protecting the back, hips, and tail. Its massive limbs bore small, hoof-like nails. Length: 20ft (6m). Time: Late Cretaceous. Place: Mongolia.

12 **Tarchia** ("brainy") from southern Mongolia had a massive skull with a broad, blunt snout. *Tarchia gigantea* was the largest and last surviving of all known Asian ankylosaurs. Length: 28ft (8.5m). Time: late Late Cretaceous.

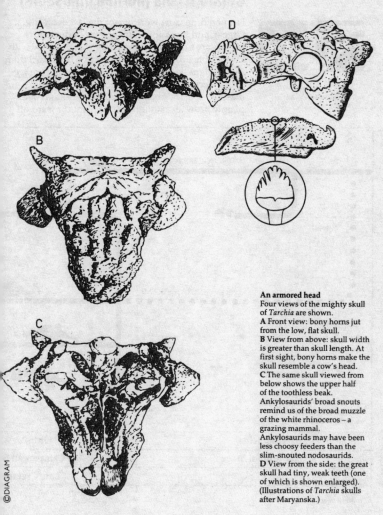

An armored head
Four views of the mighty skull
of *Tarchia* are shown.
A Front view: bony horns jut
from the low, flat skull.
B View from above: skull width
is greater than skull length. At
first sight, bony horns make the
skull resemble a cow's head.
C The same skull viewed
from below shows the upper half
of the toothless beak.
Ankylosaurids' broad snouts
remind us of the broad muzzle
of the white rhinoceros – a
grazing mammal.
Ankylosaurids may have been
less choosy feeders than the
slim-snouted nodosaurids.
D View from the side: the great
skull had tiny, weak teeth (one
of which is shown enlarged).
(Illustrations of *Tarchia* skulls
after Maryanska.)

187

Ceratopsians (horned dinosaurs)

Horned dinosaurs were one of the last evolved, largest, and most abundant groups of dinosaurs. Most were four-legged, with huge heads armed with formidable horns. A bony frill jutting backward from the skull masked the neck and provided anchorage for powerful muscles that worked jaws ending in a massive "parrot's beak." Horned dinosaurs could plainly browse on tough-leaved plants or ward off

PROTOCERATOPSIANS   2

1

CERATOPSIANS   12

8   9

10

*name in Asiamerica
**name in Europe

*Djadochta	*Oldman
**Santonian Stage	**Campanian S
	Late Cretace

82 million years ago   76

©DIAGRAM

188

ttacks by carnosaurs. They were dinosaurian "cattle" or "rhinoceroses."

From agile ancestors like *Psittacosaurus* these dinosaurs evolved fast – producing ever-larger species. Some bristled with horns and spikes, or sported enormously long frills. They ranged from creatures lighter than a man to monsters twice as long as a rhinoceros and as heavy as a big elephant.

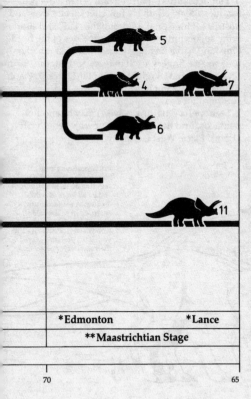

*Edmonton   *Lance

**Maastrichtian Stage

70   65

Ceratopsian family tree
Horned dinosaurs formed an ornithischian suborder evolved from ornithopods. This family tree includes members of two families: the protoceratopsids and the ceratopsids. The latter contained both long-frilled and short-frilled forms.
Examples of protoceratopsids:
  1 *Protoceratops*
  2 *Leptoceratops*
Long-frilled ceratopsids were:
  3 *Chasmosaurus*
  4 *Pentaceratops*
  5 *Anchiceratops*
  6 *Arrhinoceratops*
  7 *Torosaurus*
Short-frilled dinosaurs included:
  8 *Brachyceratops* (possibly just a form of *Monoclonius*)
  9 *Monoclonius*
  10 *Styracosaurus*
  11 *Triceratops*
  12 *Pachyrhinosaurus*
How horned dinosaurs began
(below) Some Asian scientists think families b–f evolved from ornithopod family a.
  a Heterodontosaurids
  b "Chaoyoungosaurids"
  c Pachycephalosaurids
  d Psittacosaurids
  e Protoceratopsids
  f Ceratopsids

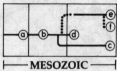

├── **MESOZOIC** ──┤

189

Psittacosaurids

Man sized or smaller, these "parrot lizards" had a broad, deep, hornless head, narrowing into a sharp beak like a parrot's. They could walk on all fours or hurry on their long, strong hind legs. Like the boneheads and protoceratopsids these Early Cretaceous beasts may have evolved in China from Jurassic dinosaurs like "Chaoyoungosaurus" and "Tianchungosaurus," still to be described.

1 **Psittacosaurus** ("parrot lizard") had a deep, toothless beak, relatively few cheek teeth, eyes and nostrils set high on the sides of the skull, and short bony spikes jutting back from the sides of the head. One kind had a tiny nasal horn. Each hand had only four sizable fingers, used in feeding. Length: 2ft 7in–5ft (80cm–1.5m). Weight: up to 50lb (22.7kg). Place: Mongolia, east and northwest China, and southern Siberia.

2 **Stenopelix** ("narrow pelvis") may be another psittacosaurid (its skull is unknown). Length: 5ft (1.5m). Place: West Germany.

Fossil finds
Finds of *Psittacosaurus* (**1**) and *Stenopelix* (**2**) are shown.

Psittacosaurus group
Here we see *Psittacosaurus* standing on its hind limbs (**A**) and on all fours (**B**) while feeding. A psittacosaurid's sharp, deep beak could slice through tough leaves and woody stems. Psittacosaurid young (**C**) probably stayed with their mother for protection.

Protoceratopsids

Protoceratopsids were small, primitive ceratopsians. They had clawed toes, and poorly developed horns or bumps in place of horns.

1 Bagaceratops ("small horned face") from Mongolia was small and squat. Length: 3ft 3in (1m).

2 Leptoceratops ("slim horned face") was lightly built with a flat frill, no horn, and short front limbs. It may have run on its long hind limbs. Length: 6ft (1.8m). Weight: 120lb (55kg). Height: 4ft (1.2m). Place: Alberta, Wyoming, and Mongolia.

3 Microceratops ("tiny horned face") from Mongolia and east China was small and slim.

4 Montanoceratops ("horned face of Montana") from Montana resembled *Protoceratops*, but with a well-formed nose horn. Length: 10ft (3m).

5 Protoceratops ("first horned face") is the earliest known horned dinosaur, with a big, beaked skull, a broad frill, and bumps above the eyes and snout (precursors of the ceratopsids' horns). Length: 6ft (1.8m). Weight 1.5 US tons (1.4 tonnes). Height: 30in (75cm). Place: Mongolia.

Fossil finds
Proceratopsid finds are shown.
1 *Bagaceratops*
2 *Leptoceratops*
3 *Microceratops*
4 *Montanoceratops*
5 *Protoceratops*

Nest and eggs
Protoceratops laid eggs in hollows dug in sand. Each female laid a clutch of 12 or more in a kind of horizontal spiral, with the eggs' narrow ends facing inward. Large clutches suggest two females used one nest.

©DIAGRAM

191

Long-frilled ceratopsids

Long-frilled ceratopsids were much larger than their protoceratopsid ancestors. From the skull a long, backswept bony crest or frill jutted out above the neck and shoulders. In some species it stretched over halfway down the back. Big, skin-covered holes in such frills tended to reduce their weight.

1 **Anchiceratops** ("near horned face") was larger than *Chasmosaurus* and had bigger brow horns. It roamed ancient marshes in Alberta, Canada.

2 **Arrhinoceratops** ("nose horned face") from Alberta had a shorter frill than *Anchiceratops* and avoided marshes.

3 **Chasmosaurus** ("cleft lizard") from Alberta and New Mexico had a small nose horn, but two larger horns above the brows. Huge "windows" in the frill reduced its weight. Length: 17ft (5.2m).

4 **Pentaceratops** ("five-horned face") was larger than *Chasmosaurus*, with longer horns, a shorter face, and smaller holes in its enormous frill. It had two large brow horns, a small horn on the snout and two bony outgrowths from the cheeks. Place: New Mexico.

5 **Torosaurus** ("bull lizard") was the largest in this group: 25ft (7.6m) long and weighing 8–9 US tons (7.3–8.2 tonnes). Range: Montana to Texas.

Massive skull
Torosaurus's huge three-horned skull is here shown to scale with a human skull.

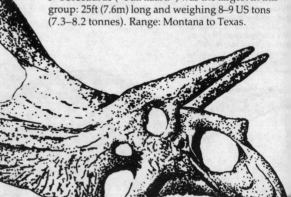

Short-frilled ceratopsids 1

Like long-frilled ceratopsids, most of these had horns, frills, scaly skins, and hoofed toes. But their frills were relatively short and some lacked holes. Some short-frilled ceratopsids had bony spikes. All species came from North America.

Agathaumas ("marvelous") of Wyoming may have resembled (or been) *Triceratops*.

Brachyceratops ("short-horned face") from Alberta and Montana had a small nose horn. Maybe a young *Monoclonius*, it measured only 6ft (1.8m).

Centrosaurus ("sharp point lizard") of Alberta had a nose horn bent forward. Length: 20ft (6m).

Ceratops ("horned face") from Colorado and Montana had a short, three-horned head.

Eoceratops ("earliest horned face") of Alberta had a short, deep, three-horned head.

Monoclonius ("one horned") had a large nose spike, small brow horns, and a short frill pierced by two big holes and rimmed by bony knobs. Length: 18ft (5.5m). Range: Alberta to Mexico.

Pachyrhinosaurus ("thick-nosed lizard") had no horns, just a rough, thick, bony bulge between the eyes. Length: 18ft (5.5m). Place: Alberta.

Styracosaurus ("spiked lizard") had a long, straight nose horn, tiny brow horns, and six long spikes jutting backward from its frill. Length: 18ft (5.5m). Place: Alberta and Montana.

Ceratopsid fossil finds
These two maps provide a comparison of where long-frilled and short-frilled ceratopsids were found.
A Long-frilled:
1 *Anchiceratops*
2 *Arrhinoceratops*
3 *Chasmosaurus*
4 *Pentaceratops*
5 *Torosaurus*
B Short-frilled:
1 *Agathaumas*
2 *Brachyceratops*
3 *Centrosaurus*
4 *Ceratops*
5 *Eoceratops*
6 *Monoclonius*
7 *Pachyrhinosaurus*
8 *Styracosaurus*
9 *Triceratops*

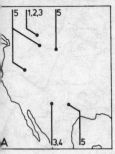

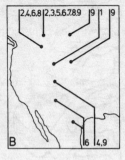

Short-frilled ceratopsids 2

9 **Triceratops** ("three-horned face") was one of the last and largest ceratopsids. It weighed 6 US tons (5.4 tonnes) and measured up to 30ft (9m). Nearly one-third of its length was a massive head with a short, solid frill and formidable brow horns longer than the nose horn. The bony horn cores alone measured up to 3ft (90cm) so the actual horns may have been much longer. Range: Alberta to Colorado, and Saskatchewan to South Dakota.

Many dinosaurs are known only from a few pieces of bone, but hundreds of *Triceratops* skulls have survived. These have helped scientists to identify *Triceratops* species as different from one another as horses are from zebras. So far, experts have identified 15 supposed *Triceratops* species and five *Triceratops*-like genera, but four of the genera are forms of *Triceratops* – some diseased.

Triceratops species
Shown here are the skulls of 10 *Triceratops* species. Those with small brow horns tended to have a big nasal horn and vice versa.
a *Triceratops horridus* was the largest species.
b *Triceratops flabellatus* had a deep face.
c *Triceratops prorsus* was the smallest species.
d *Triceratops serratus* had a less deep face than species b.
e *Triceratops elatus* was long-snouted.
f *Triceratops obtusus* had no nasal horn.
g *Triceratops calicornis* was long-snouted.
h *Triceratops hatcheri* had no nasal horn.
i *Triceratops eurycephalus* had long brow horns.
j *Triceratops albertensis* had upright horns.
(Illustrations after Steel.)

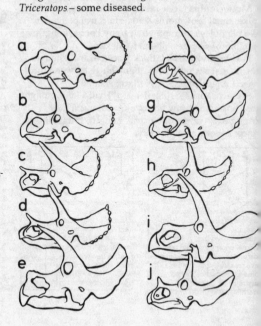

194

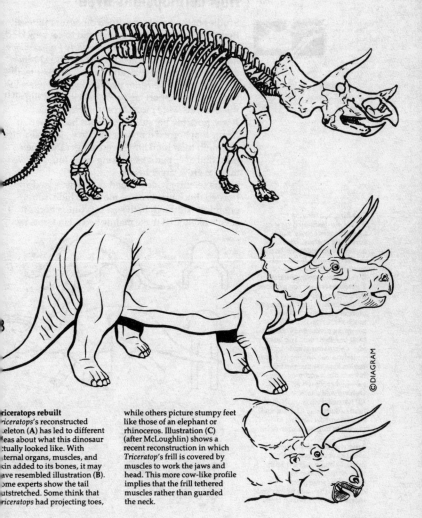

©DIAGRAM

riceratops rebuilt
riceratops's reconstructed keleton (**A**) has led to different eas about what this dinosaur ctually looked like. With ternal organs, muscles, and kin added to its bones, it may ave resembled illustration (**B**). ome experts show the tail utstretched. Some think that *riceratops* had projecting toes,

while others picture stumpy feet like those of an elephant or rhinoceros. Illustration (**C**) (after McLoughlin) shows a recent reconstruction in which *Triceratops*'s frill is covered by muscles to work the jaws and head. This more cow-like profile implies that the frill tethered muscles rather than guarded the neck.

How ceratopsians lived

Studies of the fossils of horned dinosaurs suggest that these evolved the way they did to eat new kinds of tough-leaved plants. Even the early *Protoceratops* had a relatively larger head, armed with a sharper, stronger, narrower beak and longer, sharper teeth than ancestors like *Psittacosaurus*. Even *Protoceratops* had a frill to support big jaw muscles. Later on, all these trends were much accentuated.

It was possibly because their heads had grown so heavy that horned dinosaurs had to walk on all fours, although their hind limbs were longer than their front limbs; or perhaps walking on all fours allowed them to grow larger heads.

Horns seemingly developed as size increased and horned dinosaurs became too big to hide from enemies. Although both sexes sprouted horns it seems likely that these mainly served in fights by

Standing and moving
A This old-fashioned view of *Chasmosaurus* shows it in a sprawling posture, with front legs stuck out sideways so that the feet are outside the body and support it inefficiently.
B This recent reconstruction of *Torosaurus* is based on a modern theory that most horned dinosaurs held their front legs more or less straight down – a much more effective way of propping up the body. Beasts built like this could run quite fast. Calculations made by the American paleontologist Robert Bakker suggest that the big horned dinosaurs may have galloped at 30mph (48km/h).

Defense and attack
1 If horned dinosaurs lived in herds adults may have formed an outward-facing ring to protect young from approaching predators.
2 Big well-armed ceratopsids could have charged any predator and gouged it with their horns. Giants like *Triceratops* were more dangerous than any other plant-eaters that ever lived on land.

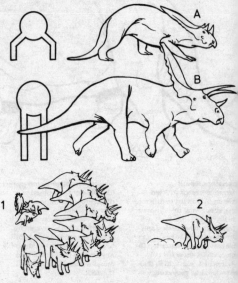

rival males. The variety of horns among ceratopsids reminds us of the variety of horns in African antelopes – beasts where males of different species have different horn types and joust in different ways. *Pachyrhinosaurus* could have used its bony head to topple small palm trees to get at their fronds. But rival males probably used their horns mainly in butting combats with one another; they could not cross horns like the males of long-horned species. Horned dinosaurs were evidently quiet, inoffensive animals unless attacked. People used to picture them as giant solitary rhinoceroses. But their fossils prove so plentiful in certain areas that scientists suspect beasts like *Triceratops* roamed upland groves in herds, as bison later roamed the prairies. Doubtless living in a group gave individuals the best protection.

The foods they ate (above)
Horned dinosaurs probably ate such foods as the fronds of the palm-like cycads (**a**) and the spiky fronds of true palm trees (**b**) whose milky sap is rich in nourishment. Palms were among the new, tough-leaved flowering plants that were spreading as older, soft-leaved plants like ferns grew scarcer.

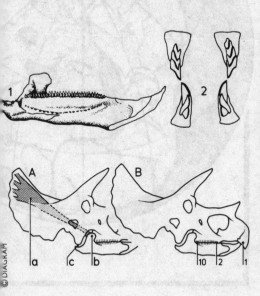

Their shearing teeth (left)
This lower jaw (**1**) and the cross section through top and bottom jaws (**2**) show how *Triceratops* and other horned dinosaurs coped with food cropped by their beaks. Sharp teeth meshed like scissor blades to slice fibrous or woody vegetation. New teeth were always growing up to replace old teeth as these fell out.

Muscle power for jaws
A Triceratops achieved powerful jaw leverage with help from a big muscle (**a**) stretched between the frill and the coronoid process – a bony projection (**b**) jutting up from the lower jaw above the part that acted as the fulcrum (**c**).
B Figures on this diagram show a 10:2:1 ratio between the pulling force available at *Triceratops*'s back teeth, front teeth, and beak.

© DIAGRAM

197

CHAPTER 4 — THEIR CHANGING WORLD

Lands and climates altered slowly through the Mesozoic Era or "age of middle life," which roughly tallies with the Age of Dinosaurs. Continents broke up, deserts shrank, seas invaded the land, mountains rose, and flowering plants began to spread. Change indirectly helped new kinds of dinosaur to replace old ones. Here we look at different groups of dinosaurs, and at other backboned animals flourishing in different periods of the Mesozoic Era. The chapter ends by probing the mystery of why all dinosaurs died out – perhaps in only a matter of months – after thriving for 140 million years.

These views picture the ancient world as imagined by the German meteorologist Alfred Wegener. Similar maps appeared in 1915 in his book *The Origin of Continents and Oceans*. Geologists at first ridiculed his idea that the continents had drifted apart, but recent study proves that Wegener's theory was correct. Illustration from Nigel Calder *Restless Earth* (BBC).

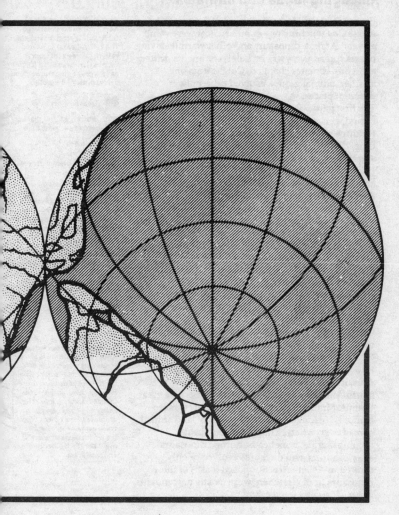

Changing lands and climates

For much of the Mesozoic Era, all of the great land masses lay touching one another; most were warm all year. At first, dinosaurs and other warmth-loving beasts spread everywhere. Later, continents drifted apart and climates changed. Cut off from one another, animal groups evolved differently in different places.

The first part of the Mesozoic Era, the Triassic Period, gets its name from the Latin *trias* ("three") for three rock layers formed in Germany at this time, 225–193 million years ago. The one vast supercontinent Pangaea ("All Earth") was breaking into two parts: Laurasia (North America, Europe, and Asia) and Gondwanaland (South America, Africa, India, Antarctica, and Australia). Dinosaurs could and did walk from one part to the other, but they found deserts in the huge inland areas far from the ocean's rain-bearing winds.

The Jurassic Period, 193–136 million years ago, gets its name from rocks formed at this time in the French and Swiss Jura Mountains. Gondwanaland was now breaking up but dinosaurs could still crisscross all the continents until at least late in the Jurassic Period, flourishing best in plant-rich lands with rainy seasons.

Chalky layers formed the floors of some seabeds in the Cretaceous Period, 136–65 million years ago. (*Creta* means "chalk.") Invading seas split Laurasia into Asiamerica (East Asia and western North America) and Euramerica (Europe and eastern North America). Southern continents became great islands. Mountains rose and seasons grew more marked. No longer could new kinds of land animal spread everywhere. Thus dromaeosaurids, tyrannosaurids, boneheads, horned dinosaurs, ankylosaurids, and duckbills evolved or only thrived in Asiamerica. Supposed fossils of these dinosaurs from elsewhere were mostly descendants of earlier common ancestors.

The Late Triassic world (A)
About 200 million years ago continents lay jammed together. The Tethys Sea (a) separated eastern Laurasia (b) from eastern Gondwanaland (c), but early types of dinosaur reached every corner of the world.

▨ Areas now dry land

▨ Submerged land that may ha been dry at some time

☐ Oceans

▨ Shallow prehistoric seas

The Mid Jurassic world (B)
About 160 million years ago sea-filled cracks were opening or widening between some land masses. The beginning of the Atlantic Ocean (d) had started to separate Africa from North America. India (e) was splitting away from Africa and Antarctica. Australia had begun to break away from Antarctica. Yet new types of saurischian and ornithischian dinosaur walked overland to all parts of the world during the Jurassic Period.

The Late Cretaceous world (C)
About 80 million years ago the continents were taking on their modern outlines and positions. Lands once joined had drifted far apart. Also, shallow seas invaded many regions. These changes cut off some groups of dinosaurs from others. New types evolving in what became the landmass Asiamerica (f) could not reach other continents, and vice versa.

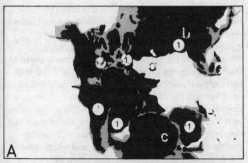

Triassic dinosaurs
Plateosaurid prosauropod (1) remains have come from North America, South America, Europe, Africa, Asia, and Australia. These early dinosaurs plainly traveled overland to every continent.

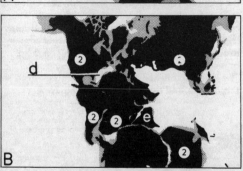

Jurassic dinosaurs
Cetiosaurid sauropods (2) are from North America, South America, Europe, Africa, Asia, and Australia. Like earlier dinosaurs, they colonized the world on foot before continents split up.

Cretaceous dinosaurs
Tyrannosaurid dinosaurs (3) are known only from Central and East Asia, western North America, and maybe India. Their homelands must have formed a huge island isolated from other continents.

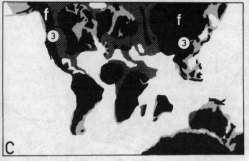

Life in the Triassic Period

The Late Triassic world that dinosaurs inherited looked very different from the world today. There were no grasses or flowering plants such as most trees. Moisture-loving ferns and horsetails flourished on damp watersides. Like many early land plants, ferns grow from spores that need wet soil for their survival. But gymnosperms ("naked-seed" plants) invaded drier lands – after falling on dry soil, their seeds could sprout months later when rain had soaked the ground. Among them were tall conifers related to the Norfolk pine and monkey-puzzle that thrust their massive trunks high above the ground. Yews appeared, and ginkgoes. Other trees or tree-like plants included cycads, with a crown of palm-like fronds sprouting from a stumpy trunk, and the bennettitaleans – somewhat similar to cycads but with leaf clusters growing on short branches.

The long-established mammal-like reptiles, thecodonts, and rhyncosaurs related to New

A Triassic landscape
All the animals and plants pictured here may have lived as the Triassic Period was ending.
a Prosauropod dinosaurs
b Shrew-like early mammals – just possibly mammals did not appear until after the Triassic Period
c Early crocodile
d Coelophysid – a small, flesh-eating dinosaur
e *Longisquama*, a strange pseudosuchian thecodont – its bones come from Early Triassic rocks but such beasts perhaps persisted until later
f Early pterosaur

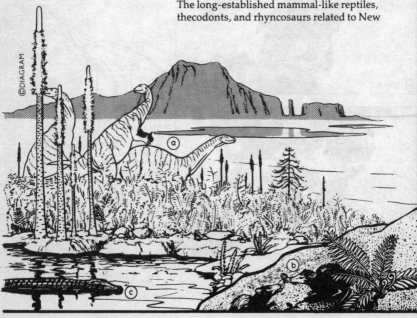

©DIAGRAM

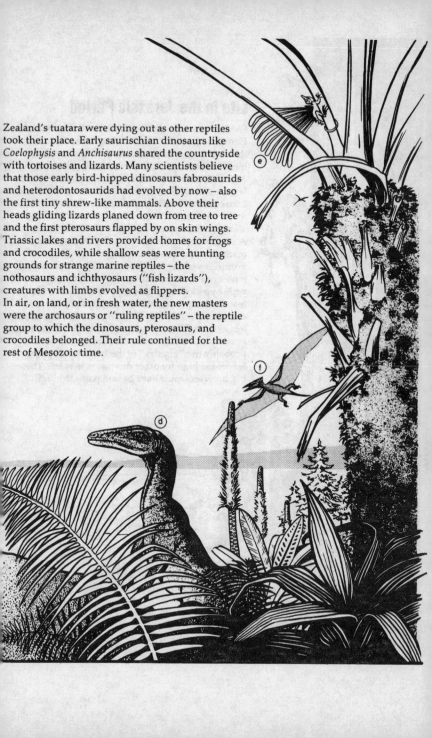

Zealand's tuatara were dying out as other reptiles took their place. Early saurischian dinosaurs like *Coelophysis* and *Anchisaurus* shared the countryside with tortoises and lizards. Many scientists believe that those early bird-hipped dinosaurs fabrosaurids and heterodontosaurids had evolved by now – also the first tiny shrew-like mammals. Above their heads gliding lizards planed down from tree to tree and the first pterosaurs flapped by on skin wings. Triassic lakes and rivers provided homes for frogs and crocodiles, while shallow seas were hunting grounds for strange marine reptiles – the nothosaurs and ichthyosaurs ("fish lizards"), creatures with limbs evolved as flippers.
In air, on land, or in fresh water, the new masters were the archosaurs or "ruling reptiles" – the reptile group to which the dinosaurs, pterosaurs, and crocodiles belonged. Their rule continued for the rest of Mesozoic time.

Life in the Jurassic Period

Shallow seas invaded much of North America and Europe in Jurassic times, and rains reached lands that had been deserts. Plants grew thickly along moist river banks. This period has been called the Age of Cycads, but those palm-like plants proved less successful than their relatives, bennettitaleans. Like conifers, ferns, and tree ferns, these flourished in the moister tropics, which then included southern Europe and southern North America. A variety of dinosaurs evolved to feed upon the many plants available. Among the bird-hipped group, low-slung, early armored dinosaurs may have munched ground-level ferns and fungi. Small, agile hypsilophodontids nipped off knee-high leaves. Camptosaurids and perhaps plated dinosaurs could have reared up on hind legs to strip leaves from the lower twigs of trees. But those huge lizard-hipped dinosaurs, the sauropods, were probably the "giraffes" of the Jurassic: cropping leaves too high for other dinosaurs to reach. These big browsers must have beaten paths through

orests, creating open spaces where smaller
dinosaurs could search for food. Also their
droppings fertilized the soil, nourishing seedlings
that eventually became trees.

Then there were the hunters. Small saurischian
carnivores like *Compsognathus* and *Coelurus* could
dart through thickets after lizards. Some of these
coelurosaurs probably scavenged from the great
kills made by their much larger relatives, the
megalosaurid and allosaurid carnosaurs.

It may be because dinosaur hunters proved so
successful that the only mammals to survive were
nocturnal or small enough to climb or burrow.
Dinosaurs themselves would have suffered from the
bites of insect pests and parasites.

Now, early birds were leaping in the air, where new
kinds of furry-bodied pterosaur flew on fragile
wings of skin and bone. Meanwhile, big short-
necked plesiosaurs with limbs like paddles shared
shallow seas with their streamlined reptile relatives,
the ichthyosaurs.

A Jurassic landscape
The animals and plants pictured
here lived in North America in
Late Jurassic times.
a "Bird dinosaur"
b *Brachiosaurus*
c Primitive mammal
d *Stegosaurus*
e *Dryosaurus*
f Winged insect
g Lizard
h *Allosaurus*
i *Coelurus*
j *Diplodocus*

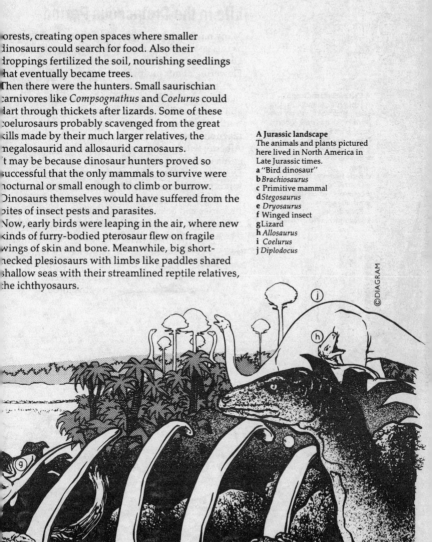

©DIAGRAM

Life in the Cretaceous Period

Many modern types of plant and animal appeared as this last and longest period in the Age of Dinosaurs was ending.

Flowering plants multiplied and spread. Their well-protected seeds survive cool winters better than some other seeds. Yet harsh winters remained still unknown 70 million years ago, even in the north. Then, forests of oaks, hickories, and magnolias sprawled near streams in what is now Alberta; with swamp cypresses, giant sequoias, and china firs in swampy areas.

Dinosaurs with teeth designed for chewing new kinds of tough-leaved plants grew numerous. Duckbills like *Hypacrosaurus* browsed among the hickories and oaks, while *Edmontosaurus* munched the leaves of broad-leaved and bald-cypress trees. The horned dinosaur *Anchiceratops* cropped

A Cretaceous landscape
All the animals and flowering plants pictured here may have lived in what is now Alberta, southwest Canada late in the Cretaceous Period.
a *Hypacrosaurus*
b Early gull
c Frog
d Early heron or egret
e *Quetzalcoatlus*
f Long-necked plesiosaur
g *Anchiceratops*
h Early ducks
i Saurornithoidid dinosaur

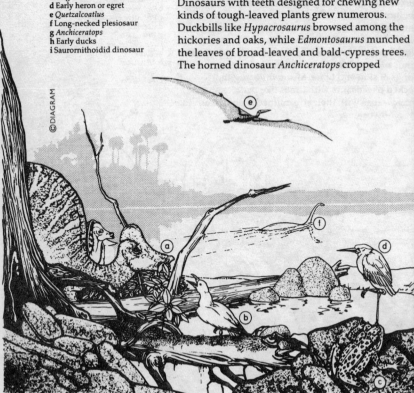

©DIAGRAM

streamside ferns and cycad cones. Each creature had its special feeding ground. (Higher, drier land was probably the main home of boneheads and perhaps armored dinosaurs.) By clearing undergrowth, duckbills left space for ostrich dinosaurs. Tyrannosaurids feeding on the duckbills kept down their numbers, and so saved forests from being over-browsed.

Above the dinosaurs soared pterosaurs like *Quetzalcoatlus*, with the wingspan of a World War II fighter aircraft. The big marine reptiles were now long-necked plesiosaurs, and mosasaurs – flippered lizards up to 33ft (10m) long. Other beasts included snakes, softshell turtles, frogs, salamanders, gulls, waders, and opossums. These last seven all have relatives alive today.

Death of the dinosaurs

Seventy million years ago dinosaurs seemed set to dominate the land for ever. Then, about 65 million years ago, they all died out – perhaps in only a matter of months. With them, went plesiosaurs, pterosaurs, and many other land and sea animals large and small (but mainly large).

To explain this natural calamity, many different reasons have been suggested. Theories that have now been disproved include the following: flesh-eaters ate all the plant-eaters and starved; dinosaurs evolved such clumsy bodies that they could not breed or perhaps even move; germs wiped out the dinosaurs; small mammals ate all their eggs; the new flowering plants poisoned them. None of these theories takes into account the fact that dinosaurs were as well designed to cope with life as any other animals. Nor do they show why so many other creatures disappeared.

This has led scientists to argue that the whole world must have altered in some deadly way. Cosmic rays from an exploding star might have deformed unborn animals, or deadly radiation poured in briefly when the Earth's magnetic field switched around. Or perhaps changes in their sizes, levels,

Mass extinctions
This diagram shows which of 18 groups of backboned animals did and which did not survive the end of the Cretaceous Period (the line marked **A**).
1 AMPHIBIANS
2–9 ORDINARY REPTILES:
    2 turtles
    3 ichthyosaurs
    4 plesiosaurs
    5 eosuchians
    6 rhynchocephalians
    7 lizards
    8 snakes
    9 crocodiles
10 PTEROSAURS
11–16 DINOSAURS:
    11 theropods
    12 sauropods
    13 ornithopods
    14 stegosaurs
    15 armored dinosaurs
    16 horned dinosaurs
17 BIRDS
18 MAMMALS

Million years ago

A
65

135

and positions chilled continents, killing dinosaurs with winter cold. If warm-blooded, they lacked fur or feathers to trap body heat. If cold-blooded, most were too big to hibernate in frost-free holes.

By 1980 more new theories were being proposed. Geologists suggested that about 65 million years ago a lump of rock about 6 miles (10km) across had streaked in from space and hit the Earth. The impact hurled dust and moisture up into the atmosphere, darkening the sky everywhere for months. Many plants and plant-eating creatures would have died. Perhaps the world froze briefly. Then it grew extremely hot, for although the dust settled, moisture still up in the sky served as a greenhouse roof that stopped the Sun's incoming heat escaping. Heat stress easily kills some creatures that cannot control their body temperature well; overheating may have wiped out any dinosaurs not already killed by cold or hunger.

For whatever reason, mass deaths replaced the Mesozoic with the Cenozoic Era ("Age of Recent Life"): the Age of Dinosaurs gave way to the Age of Mammals.

million years ago

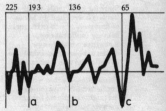

Life waxes and wanes (above)
This graph shows that numbers of known kinds of backboned animal rose and fell all through the Mesozoic Era; but the most dramatic fall came when that era ended.
a End of Triassic Period
b End of Jurassic Period
c End of Cretaceous Period

A "bomb" from space (below)
Here we compare Manhattan Island, New York with the likely size of an asteroid that indirectly may have killed the dinosaurs and many other forms of life.

©DIAGRAM

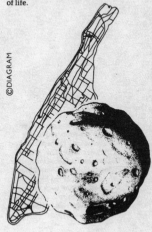

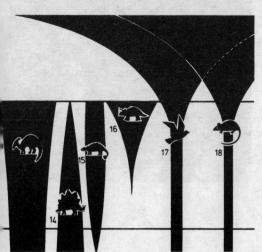

CHAPTER 5

DISCOVERING DINOSAURS

Since the early 1800s, fossil hunters have found the bones of dinosaurs buried in the rocks of every continent except Antarctica (and we know dinosaur bones must exist there as well). Our tour around the world takes in many of the richest sites. We start with northern lands once joined as the mighty continent Laurasia; then we turn to lands once making up the southern supercontinent Gondwanaland. First, though, we see how dinosaur bones became preserved in rocks; how fossil hunters find and free them; and how scientists work out a fossil's age. Only a handful of dinosaurs left fossils, and just a fraction of that fraction has been found – much of it since 1970. Who knows what astonishing discoveries still lie ahead?

Dinosaur hunters armed like gunfighters prepared to face hostile Indians in the Wild West of the later 1800s. This team's leader was the famous dinosaur collector Othniel Charles Marsh – the burly, bearded figure in the middle of the back row. Photograph reproduced by permission of Yale Peabody Museum.

How dinosaurs were fossilized

When creatures die their bodies usually rot.
Sometimes, though, the hard parts get preserved in
rocks as fossils. Fossils are the clues that tell us what
we know about the long-dead dinosaurs.

Fossils formed in several ways. The process often
started when a creature drowned, floated down a
river, and lodged on a sandbar. There, its flesh and
skin soon decomposed. But before its bones
decayed, particles of sand or mud covered them,
shutting out the oxygen needed by bacteria that
cause decay. Later, water saturated with dissolved
minerals seeped into the many tiny holes or pores
that are found in bone. Inside these tiny pipes the
water shed some of its load of minerals. In this way,
layers of substances such as calcite, quartz, iron
sulfide, or even opal gradually filled the holes in
bones and reinforced them, helping them survive
the weight of sediments piling up above.

Sometimes bones dissolved, leaving hollows that
preserved their shapes – fossils known as *molds*. If

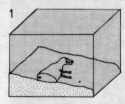 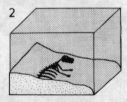 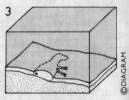

The story of a fossil (above)
These diagrams show stages in
the making, burying, and
uncovering of a fossil dinosaur.
1 A freshly dead dinosaur
lodges on a sandbank in the
shallows of a river.
2 Flesh rots, exposing bones.
3 Mud or sand dumped by the
river covers up the bones,
shutting out oxygen and so

preventing their decay.
4 Mud layers pile up above the
bones, now reinforced by
minerals brought by water
seeping from above.
5 Hardened into stone and
raised by uplift of the Earth's
crust, the layered rocks are worn
away by weather. Rain and frost
expose fossil bones that lay
beneath the surface.

Molds and casts (right)
A fossil mold (**A**) is produced
when a dinosaur bone dissolves
to leave a bone-shaped hollow
in rock that had formed around
it. If such a hollow is then filled
by minerals, the result is a fossil
cast (**B**).

©DIAGRAM

212

minerals filled a mold they formed a *cast*. Most dinosaur fossils were created by one or another of these methods. But not all fossils developed under water: some formed under sands heaped up by desert winds.

Unfortunately often only scattered fossil bones survive – remains of corpses torn apart by scavengers or floods. But besides bones, footprints, droppings, even skin were sometimes fossilized.

As a fossil hardens under water, layers of mud or sand may be piling up above it. Their crushing weight and the natural cements that they contain may change thick layers of mud or sand to thin beds of rock. Millions of years later, great movements of the Earth's crust may thrust up these layers to build high mountains. Rain and frost at once begin to wear them down. Slowly, weather bares the mountains' inner layers, and whatever fossils they contain.

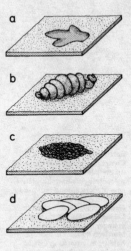

Four kinds of fossil (above) Besides bones, dinosaurs left other fossil traces.
a Footprints made in soft mud are preserved as fossils if the mud hardened into rock before rain or running water washed away the prints. (Creatures named from fossil footprints are known as ichnogenera.)
b Fossilized droppings bear the name of coprolites. The largest coprolites may have come from sauropods.
c Fossilized skins or skin impressions survive from some dinosaurs, usually ones that died in dry conditions. Some ankylosaurids and hadrosaurids are among those whose skins are partly known.
d The fossil eggs of some sauropods and horned and other dinosaurs have survived.

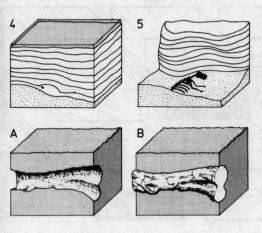

Dating fossil finds

As old kinds of dinosaur died out, new ones took their place. Finding out which dinosaurs lived when calls for careful detective work.

Among the most important clues are the rocks that hold the fossil dinosaurs – sedimentary rocks like sandstones, mudstones, chalk. Each rock layer or *stratum* holds fossils of the animals and plants living when that stratum was laid down. Looking at a quarry, cliff, or cutting you may see many strata bared like layers in a slice of layer cake. Usually the lowest strata are the oldest. Beasts preserved low down in a cliff may have lived many million years before those near its top. But similar fossils from strata found many miles apart probably lived at roughly the same time. By carefully comparing strata from around the world scientists know that, for example, *Tyrannosaurus* roamed North America while *Tarbosaurus* prowled Mongolia, and that both these dinosaurs lived long after *Scelidosaurus* ambled over southern England.

Rock strata are grouped in *systems* that give their names to the geological *periods* in which they

Relative dating
Comparing fossils from rocks of different levels and regions helps paleontologists find the relative ages of rocks around the world. In North America, *Hypsilophodon* fossils occur in Lakota Sandstone (1), a higher, younger rock layer than the Morrison Formation rocks (2) holding *Brachiosaurus* fossils. This indirectly helps to show that Europe's Wealden rocks (3) are younger than those at Tendaguru (4), East Africa.

formed. Each period is divided into Early, Middle, and Late to match the Lower, Middle, and Upper strata of the system that it represents.

Rock strata cannot tell us exactly when a creature lived, but scientists can date some rocks by studying certain radioactive elements inside them. In a given time – its "half-life" – half the substance in a radioactive element decays into another element. After another half-life (just as long) half of what remained will also have decayed, and so on. For dating rocks as old as dinosaurs scientists use the potassium-argon method. The half-life of the potassium isotope involved is 1310 million years: after that length of time half the potassium in a sample will have decayed to produce a measurable amount of argon. Such radiometric dating works best with rocks such as lava that have been molten and then quickly cooled and hardened. Lava flows often help us date fossil dinosaurs indirectly: the age of sedimentary rocks holding dinosaur fossils can be deduced by dating lava flows lying directly above or below them.

Radiometric dating
Half the mass of a quantity of potassium-40 decays by radiation into known proportions of stable argon-40 and calcium-40 in a period of 1310 million years (its half life). In the next 1310 million years half of what remains decays, and so on. This diagram shows the mass of potassium-40 in a newly formed rock (**A**), and the proportions of potassium-40 remaining after one half life (**B**) and a further half life (**C**).

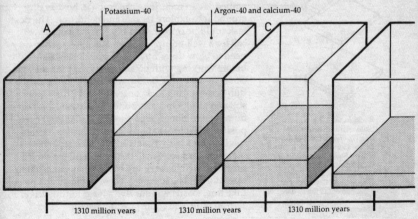

Potassium-40   Argon-40 and calcium-40

A   B   C

1310 million years   1310 million years   1310 million years

215

Quaternary

Tertiary

Cretaceous

Jurassic

Triassic

Permian

Carboniferous

Devonian

Silurian

Ordovician

Cambrian

Precambrian

TEXAS

Rocks in the USA
Slabs in this diagram show the
relative areas of rock of different
periods now exposed in the
United States; also shown for
comparison is the area of the
state of Texas. Only Triassic,
Jurassic, and Cretaceous rocks –
a fraction of the total – date from
the Mesozoic Era, the "Age of
Dinosaurs."

Excavating fossil dinosaurs

Fossil hunters search where weather has laid bare
rocks that date from the Age of Dinosaurs. In much
of the world these Mesozoic rocks have been worn
away, swamped by sea, or buried by later layers of
rock or soil. The best places for dinosaur hunts are
dry lands where erosion has stripped soil from
Mesozoic rocks. Some cliffs and quarries make fine
hunting grounds, too.

Although some dinosaurs grew immense, many
were small and most left only teeth or scraps of
bone. Finding these clues can prove laborious and
slow. Collectors trudge over weathered rock,
scanning cliffs and gullies for fossils washed down
from the rocks above. Often, their first reward is a
battered, discolored object resembling a stone and
small enough to fit in a matchbox. Only its shiny
surface or spongy inside may hint that this is bone –
and even experts make mistakes. The "dinosaur"
Aachenosaurus was named in 1888 from what later
proved to be a lump of fossil wood.

Searching a slope above his first fossil find, a lucky
collector may discover the rest of the skeleton still
embedded in rock. If he can reach it, he may dig
around it to explore its size and condition. The next
task could be immense. A big fossil dinosaur will
call for a well-equipped team of workers. They may
need to blow up or bulldoze a great mass of rock
before working with picks and shovels. As they get
closer to the brittle bones, workers carefully chisel
into surrounding rock, or scrape and brush away
soil and sand. Once the bones lie exposed, workers
number and photograph them and plot their exact
positions. To prevent breakage, collectors harden
fragile bones with dissolved resins or remove
blocks of hard rock with the bones still inside. To
protect these blocks or big bones, they cover them
carefully in plaster or pack them in plastic foam.
Like this, fossils will survive a long, jolting drive
across country to some far-off museum.

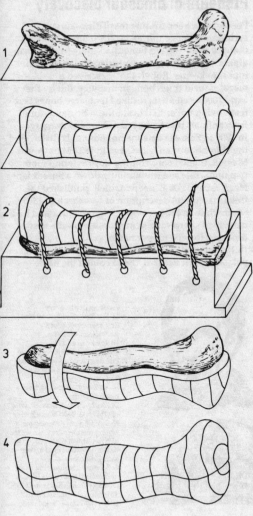

Digging up a dinosaur
These diagrams show the traditional way of removing a big fossil limb bone from soil and reinforcing it. (An effective new technique uses aluminum foil instead of wet paper, and polyurethane foam instead of plaster of Paris.)

1 Just over half the bone is exposed by digging away the surrounding soil.

2 After packing wet paper around the exposed bone, experts cover it in bandages soaked in plaster of Paris which hardens to provide a protective casing. Next they dig away the surrounding soil, leaving the bone embedded in a soil pedestal. Holes bored through the pedestal take ropes which secure the whole bone.

3 People remove the whole bone and turn it over.

4 They pack the unprotected bone with bandages and plaster of Paris.

5 This is a cross section of such a fully packaged bone.

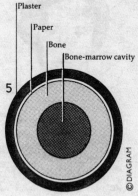

Plaster

Paper

Bone

Bone-marrow cavity

©DIAGRAM

217

Pioneers of dinosaur discovery

People have been finding fossil dinosaurs accidentally for centuries. At first some observers thought these big old bones had come from human giants. More than three centuries ago an English museum keeper, Robert Plot, described a megalosaurid thigh bone in that way. But by the early 1800s, scientists realized that large bones and teeth being unearthed in southern England came from animals that had lived millions of years ago. In 1809 in Sussex someone unknowingly discovered the shin bone of an *Iguanodon*. In 1822 Mary Ann Mantell, the wife of a country doctor, found more remains while she was strolling down a Sussex lane. Her husband, Dr Gideon Mantell, published the first (inaccurate) description of *Iguanodon* in 1825. Meanwhile in 1824 geologist William Buckland had described sharp-fanged *Megalosaurus* – the first dinosaur to get a proper name.

In 1841 at an important British scientific meeting, paleontologist Richard Owen coined the name

Pioneers in discovery
1a The Reverend Robert Plot, first keeper of Oxford's Ashmolean Museum.
1b The knee end of a megalosaurid thigh bone that Plot described and illustrated in 1677. This was the first dinosaur bone to be described (mistakenly, as coming from a human giant).
2a Mrs Mary Ann Mantell, wife of (**2b**) Dr Gideon Mantell. Her chance find of *Iguanodon* teeth among roadmenders' stones led him to publish what proved to be the first account of a plant-eating dinosaur.
2c Scientists banqueting in an unfinished, inaccurate lifesize model of an *Iguanodon* in 1853. This concrete monster is still in Crystal Palace Park, London.

Dinosauria or "terrible lizards" for these and similar gigantic prehistoric reptiles.

By then discoveries had taken place elsewhere. In 1787 at Philadelphia in the United States anatomist Casper Wistar reported on a mighty thigh bone – probably a duckbilled dinosaur's – unluckily now lost. In 1802 a Massachusetts farm boy, Pliny Moody, began finding tracks of huge "birds" imprinted in the sandstone near his home. Not until the 1860s did people realize that these footprints had been made by early dinosaurs.

The first American dinosaurs to be described were named in 1856 by a second Philadelphia anatomist, Joseph Leidy. They included *Palaeoscincus* and *Troödon*, but were known only from teeth, found the year before by Dr Ferdinand Vandiveer Hayden in what is now Montana. Then, in 1858, Leidy described *Hadrosaurus* from fossil bones discovered in New Jersey. By then the hunt for dinosaurs was on around the world.

5

©DIAGRAM

More pioneers
3 Dean William Buckland of Oxford University in 1824 described flesh-eating *Megalosaurus* – the first dinosaur to get a proper name.
4a Dr Richard Owen in 1841 invented the name Dinosauria for giant prehistoric beasts like *Iguanodon* and *Megalosaurus*.
4b Owen's mistaken notion of *Megalosaurus* as a quadruped was just one of many ways in which this scientist shaped early ideas about dinosaurs.
5 Some of the Connecticut River valley's many types of fossil dinosaur footprint named by geologist Edward Hitchcock (1793–1864). He wrongly thought they had been made by prehistoric birds.

219

Two famous fossil hunters

In the later 1800s, two wealthy rival American scientists sparked off the largest, longest-ever quest for dinosaurs in the United States up to that time. Othniel Charles Marsh and Edward Drinker Cope hired teams of fossil hunters whose finds amazed the world and showed just how huge, plentiful, and varied some groups of dinosaurs had been.

Their richest pickings came from Upper (Late) Jurassic rocks in the rugged, untamed West. But collecting here proved arduous and risky. Men worked armed against attack by Indians. Their leaders were so jealous of each other that each team tried to keep its finds a secret, and legend has it that Cope's and Marsh's men once came to blows.

The hunt became a race to find the most productive bone beds. In 1877 Marsh's men discovered bones near Morrison in Colorado. Meanwhile, near Canyon City, south of Morrison, Cope's men were mining huge bones from other outcrops of the same Morrison rock formation. But before that summer

Othniel Charles Marsh
1 Yale University's Professor Othniel Charles Marsh (1831–1899) spent huge sums hiring teams of men to find "new" dinosaurs. Seventeen genera still bear the names he gave them. Four of the best-known of Marsh's dinosaurs are shown here:
a *Diplodocus*
b *Allosaurus*
c *Stegosaurus*
d *Triceratops*

220

ended both sites were dwarfed by Como Bluff – a ridge in south Wyoming, where mighty fossil bones lay thickly clustered over seven miles (12 km). Here, Marsh's men spent years extracting dinosaurs from scores of quarries hacked into the solid rock, and discouraging attempts by Cope to do the same. Both teams achieved astonishing success. Between them they revealed colossal skeletons of sauropods like *Apatosaurus (Brontosaurus)*, *Barosaurus*, *Camarasaurus*, and *Diplodocus*. They found the small hunter *Coelurus* and the great carnosaur *Allosaurus*. They recovered remains of *Stegosaurus*, the first known plated dinosaur, and bird-hipped bipeds like *Camptosaurus* and *Nanosaurus* – no larger than a cat. Before Marsh and Cope began fossil hunting, only nine dinosaur species were known from North America. Between them they added 136 (Marsh 80, Cope 56). Some of Marsh's names duplicated Cope's and vice versa, but the two rivals had opened up a vast and unsuspected world of ancient life.

2

Edward Drinker Cope
2 Edward Drinker Cope (1840–1897) rivaled Marsh as the United States' greatest 19th-century discoverer of dinosaurs. Yet most of those he described have proved the same as kinds already named or of uncertain origin. Shown here are the best-known genera named and/or found by Cope:
e *Camarasaurus*
f *Monoclonius*
g *Coelophysis*

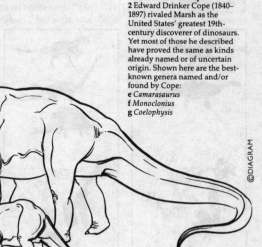

221

More discoveries in North America

Collectors working for museums have added greatly to Marsh's and Cope's discoveries of Late Jurassic dinosaurs. In Wyoming, the American Museum of Natural History's team by 1903 had wrested scores of tons of fossils from sites like Bone Cabin Quarry, named for a nearby shepherd's cabin actually built of fossil bones. In 1909 Earl Douglas, working for Pittsburgh's Carnegie Museum, began hacking a menagerie of Jurassic dinosaurs from Carnegie Quarry, carved in an upended rock layer east of Vernal, Utah.

The United States has also proved rich in dinosaurs from other times. Remains of the small flesh-eater *Coelophysis* came from Late Triassic rocks of New Mexico and Connecticut. Supposedly Triassic rocks of Connecticut Valley quarries have yielded fossil prosauropod bones and tracks. But Yale University's Paul Olsen and Peter Galton of Bridgeport University have argued that many of Connecticut's, and some of southern Africa's "Triassic" dinosaurs lived about 190 million years ago – just after the Triassic Period. If so, this fills a

Mesozoic North America
Three maps show areas with exposed Mesozoic rocks. Dinosaurs above each map lived when those rocks were being formed. Some rocks developed under seas and hold no dinosaur bones; some outcrops are too small to be shown.
A Triassic Period
(some rocks may be Jurassic)
a *Coelophysis*
b *Anchisaurus*
B Jurassic Period
a *Allosaurus*
b *Diplodocus*
c *Stegosaurus*
C Cretaceous Period
a *Tyrannosaurus*
b *Parasaurolophus*
c *Triceratops*

gap in our knowledge of dinosaurs living early in the next period, the Jurassic.

Since the mid 1960s John Ostrom, Peter Galton, and others have described Early and Late Cretaceous dinosaurs. We now know that the West was home to many duckbilled, horned, and carnivorous dinosaurs with close relatives in Central Asia.

By 1900 the most exciting dinosaur discoveries had come from the United States. Soon, though, a fossil "goldrush" began in Canada. Its goals were the skeletons of hundreds of beasts living 76–65 million years ago on what were then warm, well-wooded, swampy plains between the rising Rocky Mountains and an inland sea.

In 1889 geologist Thomas Chesmer Weston had gathered fossil bones exposed along the soft bare cliffs above the Red Deer River in what is now Alberta. Then, in 1910, the American Museum of Natural History paid fossil hunter Barnum Brown to sail along that river, piling bones onto a big flat-bottomed barge. Not to be outdone by the Americans, the Geological Survey of Canada soon sent the experienced Sternberg family to join the hunt. Luckily, Red Deer River cliffs held enough bones for both teams of collectors. The fossil harvest of Late Cretaceous duckbills, horned dinosaurs, and carnosaurs went on until 1917.

More recently, many finds have come from Dinosaur Provincial Park – a tract of barren hills and valleys straddling a section of Alberta's Red Deer River. In the late 1970s and early 1980s, paleontologists found fossil beds so rich that they could hardly move without stepping on the bones of herds of horned dinosaurs like *Centrosaurus*. Even greater discoveries may come from farther north. Early Cretaceous leaves lie here, pickled (not fossilized) by Alberta's oily tar sands. One day, scientists may also find the whole, pickled body of a dinosaur more than 100 million years old.

North American sites
These maps show where fossil dinosaurs were found. Symbols give their periods. Major sites include:
1 Connecticut Valley
2 Ghost Ranch, New Mexico
3 Como Bluff, Wyoming
4 Canyon City, Colorado
5 Dinosaur National Monument, Utah and Colorado
6 Hell Creek, Montana
7 Red Deer River, Alberta

O Triassic
● Jurassic
■ Cretaceous

©DIAGRAM

223

European finds

Since scientists first recognized fossil dinosaurs in England (see pages 218–219), collectors have scoured Europe's Mesozoic rocks for more. Several countries have produced exciting discoveries. Rocks beneath southwest Germany's rolling woods and fertile farmland have yielded some of the world's early dinosaurs. By 1837 paleontologist Hermann von Meyer had already described *Plateosaurus* – a big prosauropod that roamed Triassic Germany more than 200 million years ago. In 1921, Friedrich von Huene began finding thousands of *Plateosaurus* bones in a quarry near Trossingen. The dinosaurs had evidently died on a long desert trek in search of food. Also in southern Germany, fine-grained Jurassic limestone rocks preserve the actual impressions of feathers from the "bird dinosaur" *Archaeopteryx*, first found in 1860. Area for area, southern England probably held more kinds of dinosaur than anywhere on Earth early in Cretaceous times. Much of what we know about that period comes from fossils discovered in the Isle of Wight or nearby regions of the Weald. Rocks in

Mesozoic Europe
Three maps show rocks formed in the three periods of the Mesozoic Era and now exposed. Dinosaurs above each map lived when the rocks it shows were being formed. Some rock outcrops are too small to be shown and some developed under seas and hold no fossil bones of dinosaurs.
A Triassic Period
a *Procompsognathus*
b *Plateosaurus*
c *Teratosaurus*
B Jurassic Period
a *Compsognathus*
b *Scelidosaurus*
c *Cetiosaurus*
C Cretaceous Period
a *Megalosaurus*
b *Hypsilophodon*
c *Iguanodon*

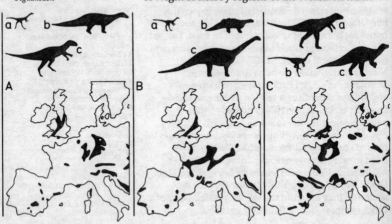

this area hold the remains of bird-hipped dinosaurs like bulky *Iguanodon*; small, agile *Hypsilophodon*; *Yaverlandia* (the earliest-known bonehead); and the armored dinosaur *Hylaeosaurus*. Here, too, lived big, ferocious *Megalosaurus*, and sauropods including mighty *Pelorosaurus*. All evidently roamed a marshy delta that sprawled to France and Belgium. Indeed in 1878 Belgian coalminers working 1,046ft (322m) below the surface made Europe's most outstanding dinosaur discovery: the skeletons of 31 *Iguanodon* that had fallen down a deep ravine and died.

Perhaps the most fascinating dinosaur discoveries from France have been the big fossil eggs dug up in Provence. Since the 1860s collectors have found whole batteries of eggs and many thousand fragments, evidently laid by the Late Cretaceous sauropod *Hypselosaurus*. Other interesting European finds include Late Cretaceous dinosaurs that lived in Austria, Hungary, Transylvania, and southern France on what was then a chain of islands.

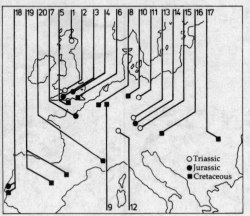

European sites
This map shows selected sites and areas where fossil dinosaurs were found. Symbols indicate their periods.
1 Elgin, Scotland
2 Bristol, England
3 Charmouth, England
4 Oxfordshire, England
5 Isle of Wight, England
6 Weald, England
7 Caen and Dives, France
8 Bernissart, Belgium
9 Maastricht, Netherlands
10 Bückeberg, West Germany
11 Halberstadt, East Germany
12 Trossingen, West Germany
13 Heroldsberg, West Germany
14 Solnhofen, West Germany
15 Pfaffenhofen, West Germany
16 Eastern Austria
17 Transylvanian Romania
18 West-central Portugal
19 North-eastern Spain
20 Provence, France

○ Triassic
● Jurassic
■ Cretaceous

225

Dinosaurs of Central Asia

Once, few people other than hardy nomadic shepherds roamed the wastes of Central Asia. Among its harshest regions is the Gobi Desert – burned by summer sun, seared by freezing winter winds. Yet since the 1920s its roadless tracts of rock and sand have drawn fossil hunters like a magnet – and with good reason. The great inland basins of southern Mongolia have proved among the richest boneyards anywhere.

Serious discovery began in 1922 when Roy Chapman Andrews led the first of five expeditions for the American Museum of Natural History. Scientists drove many hundred miles in rugged cars, backed by up to 125 camels carrying supplies. Their finds astonished paleontologists everywhere. Most famous were the eggs, nests, and fossil bones of the early horned dinosaur *Protoceratops*, discovered at Bayn-Dzak's red sandstone "Flaming Cliffs." There were small flesh-eating dinosaurs too: *Oviraptor*, *Velociraptor*, and *Saurornithoides*. Since World War II, Russians, Poles, and

Mesozoic Asia
Three maps show the exposed Mesozoic rocks of much of Asia and nearby parts of eastern Europe. (For China and India see pages 228–229 and 234–235 respectively.) Dinosaurs above a map lived when the rocks it shows were being formed. Some rocks that developed under the sea hold no fossil bones of dinosaurs. Some rock outcrops are too small to appear here. Almost all the dinosaurs discovered in this enormous area come from the Cretaceous rocks of Central Asia. (See maps on the opposite page.)
A Triassic Period
B Jurassic Period
C Cretaceous Period
a *Tarchia*
b *Saurolophus*
c *Oviraptor*

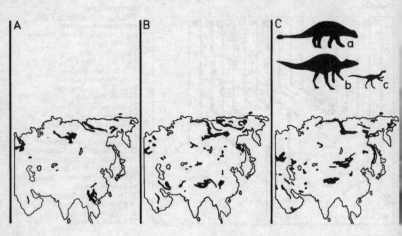

Mongolians have found much more. In the late 1940s, Professor Efremov led three Russian expeditions. In Mongolia's Nemegt Basin they found possibly the world's richest treasury of Late Cretaceous dinosaurs – great carnosaurs, sauropods, and duckbilled and armored dinosaurs, drowned in their thousands by floods 70 million years or so ago. Collectors filled 460 crates with fossils of beasts like *Saurolophus* and *Tarbosaurus*. In the 1960s Polish-Mongolian expeditions under Zofia Kielan-Jaworowska revealed new wonders, like *Opisthocoelicaudia*'s huge headless skeleton, *Deinocheirus*'s amazing arms, and bonehead skulls. By the 1980s collectors had found dozens of "new" dinosaurs in Mongolia and nearby Soviet and Chinese Central Asia. These finds shed light on how some groups of dinosaurs evolved. Discovery of similar dinosaurs in Central Asia and western North America showed, too, that both had formed one landmass in at least part of the Cretaceous Period.

Mongolian sites
The small map (above) shows the location of Mongolia, Central Asia's richest treasury of Late Cretaceous fossil dinosaurs.
The larger map (left) shows major sites and areas where teams have searched Mongolia for fossils.
1 Dzerguen Basin
2 Beguer- Nür
3 Nemegt Basin
4 Orog Nür
5 Chiréguin-Gachoun
6 Ochi-Noarov
7 Bayn-Dzak
8 Olgoi-Ulan-Tsab
9 Ergull Ubo
10 Bayn-Chiré
11 Khara-Khutul-Ula

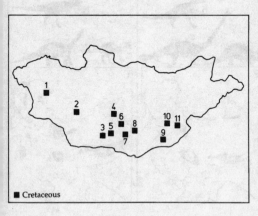

■ Cretaceous

© DIAGRAM

227

Fossil finds from China

Mesozoic China
Three maps show exposed
Mesozoic rocks of China.
Dinosaurs pictured above each
map lived when the rocks it
shows were being formed. Some
rocks that developed under seas
hold no fossil bones of
dinosaurs and some rock
outcrops are too small to be
shown here.
A Triassic Period
(some rocks may be Jurassic)
a *Lukousaurus*
b *Lufengosaurus*
c *Chinshakiangosaurus*
B Jurassic Period
a *Tuojiangosaurus*
b *Yangchuanosaurus*
c *Mamenchisaurus*
C Cretaceous Period
a *Tsintaosaurus*
b *Tyrannosaurus*
c *Asiatosaurus*

Before the 20th century no dinosaur discoveries had
been reported from that great East Asian nation,
China. Yet by 1981 paleontologist Dong Zhi-ming
could report finds from all provinces but one.
The first Chinese fossil dinosaur to be recovered
was *Mandschurosaurus*, a duckbill dug up in 1902 in
the northern region of Manchuria. Carted off to
Russia, it now adorns a Leningrad museum. Twenty
years after its discovery, collectors found a fossil
Euhelopus in the eastern province of Shantung.
(That sauropod migrated, too, to the exhibition hall
of Sweden's Uppsala University.) In 1939 Professor
Young Chung Chien chanced upon a wealth of early
dinosaurs near Lufeng, a town in south-central
China. The prosauropod *Lufengosaurus* and other
dinosaurs found here may date from Triassic times,
perhaps 200 million years ago, though certain
experts put them later.
Some Chinese dinosaurs have proved especially
remarkable. From Shantung province in 1950 came

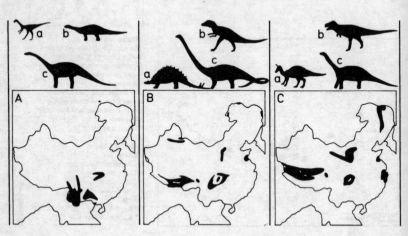

Tsintaosaurus, a duckbill with a horn resembling a unicorn's. In the 1970s Shantung also yielded *Shantungosaurus,* possibly the largest duckbill ever. Perhaps no province is so rich in dinosaurs as Szechuan; in 1956 this fertile farming region produced *Mamenchisaurus,* an unbelievably long-necked sauropod. From 1979 to 1981 workers took 200 crates of fossils from the Zigong area, where Chinese newspapers reported a Jurassic "burial pit" simply crammed with the remains of a rich variety of dinosaurs that had perished about 150 million years ago. From Zigong came skeletons of *Omeisaurus, Szechuanosaurus,* and *Tuojiangosaurus* – the best-preserved plated dinosaur from Asia. Meanwhile, in 1976, road-builders working in Tibet struck dinosaur fossils 13,770ft (4200m) above sea level, where rocks containing sauropods had been thrust up when India collided with the rest of Asia. By the mid 1970s, China and other Asian nations had yielded a quarter of all known dinosaurs.

Major Chinese sites
This map shows major finds of dinosaurs in China. Three kinds of symbol stand for the three periods of the Mesozoic Era. Some show isolated finds, others whole beds of fossil bones. Areas, regions, or provinces with important dinosaur discoveries include:
1 Manchuria
2 Shantung
3 Szechuan
4 Yunnan
5 Tibet
6 Inner Mongolia
7 Kansu
8 Sinkiang

○ Triassic
● Jurassic
■ Cretaceous

© DIAGRAM

229

South American discoveries

South American fossil hunters have been busiest in southern Brazil and western and southern Argentina, especially in that great southern tract of grassland and semidesert known as Patagonia. South America's first fossil dinosaur discovery came in Argentina in 1882. Soon, scientific study was led by the Ameghino brothers: Carlos, who collected, and Florentino, who described what Carlos found. By the 1920s, the Museum of La Plata's storerooms were filled with bones from several parts of Argentina. Many came from great sauropods and other dinosaurs that had roamed a low, hot land, with pools and rivers where lungfish, crocodiles, and turtles swam. All had flourished as the Age of Dinosaurs was ending.

By the late 1920s came hints that very early dinosaurs had also lived in South America. The German, Friedrich von Huene, found supposed prosauropod remains while searching Triassic rock gullies near Santa Maria in southern Brazil. From

Mesozoic South America
Three maps show exposed Mesozoic rocks in South America. Dinosaurs pictured above each map lived when the rocks it shows were being formed. Some rocks that developed under seas hold no fossil bones of dinosaurs and some rock outcrops are too small to be shown.
A Triassic Period
a *Staurikosaurus*
b *Pisanosaurus*
B Jurassic Period
a *Amygdalodon*
b *Piatnitzkysaurus*
C Cretaceous Period
a *Saltasaurus*
b *Noasaurus*
c *Secernosaurus*

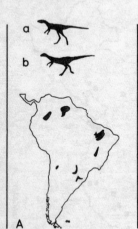

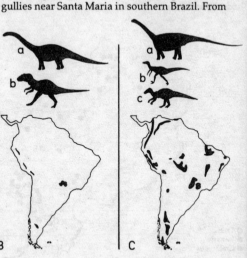

here, later, came *Staurikosaurus,* one of the very earliest dinosaurs; while Rioja in northwest Argentina yielded *Pisanosaurus,* perhaps the earliest of all known bird-hipped dinosaurs. In 1979, José Bonaparte of Argentina filled a gap by describing Jurassic dinosaurs from Patagonia. A big *Allosaurus-*like flesh-eater and two kinds of sauropod were relatives of kinds found elsewhere in the world. Their discovery proved that dinosaurs could come and go between South America and other continents in Jurassic times.

By the 1980s, South America's 30 or so known genera of dinosaurs included three surprises: *armored* sauropods; duckbills, members of a family once unknown from the Southern Hemisphere; and *Noasaurus,* a small hunting dinosaur with a big, wicked-looking, switchblade toe claw.

Perhaps the most exciting finds still lie ahead. South America may prove to be the place where all the dinosaurs began.

O Triassic
● Jurassic
■ Cretaceous

©DIAGRAM

South American sites
This map shows selected finds of South American dinosaurs. Symbols show which period each came from. Some symbols stand for isolated finds, but most represent whole beds of fossil bones. Numbered areas or rock formations are:
1 Laguna Umayo, Peru
2 Bauru Formation, Brazil
3 Santa Maria Formation, Brazil
4 Andean Basin, Argentina
5 Ischigualasto Formation, Argentina
6 Neuquén Basin, Argentina
7 Chubut Province, Argentina
8 Chubut Province, Argentina

231

Bone beds of Africa

Africa – the continent where man had his beginnings – was also home to many early dinosaurs. Their discoverers have mostly come from the European nations that once ruled much of Africa. By 1866, British scientists had described *Massospondylus* and *Euskelosaurus* – prosauropods from what is now South Africa. In the early 1900s, more discoveries were made by Robert Broom, a Scottish doctor who tramped South Africa's hot, rugged countryside dressed like a city businessman. Later came "Fuzz" Crompton, Alan Charig, and others.

Some hunted in Lesotho. This small nation's Jurassic and Triassic strata form the topmost, smallest, and youngest in a nest of great rock "saucers" making up the Karroo Basin that covers most of southern Africa. From Lesotho's rocks scientists have coaxed the fragile fossils of small, agile dinosaurs like *Lesothosaurus* – creatures close to the ancestors of all bird-hipped bipeds. Elsewhere, French scientists like Albert de

Mesozoic Africa
Three maps show exposed Mesozoic rocks of Africa and the island of Madagascar. Dinosaurs above each map lived when the rocks it shows were being formed. Some rocks that developed under seas hold no fossil bones of dinosaurs, and certain outcrops are too small to be shown.
A Triassic Period
(some rocks may be Jurassic)
a *Euskelosaurus*
b *Syntarsus*
c *Lesothosaurus*
B Jurassic Period
a *Dryosaurus*
b *Kentrosaurus*
c *Brachiosaurus*
C Cretaceous Period
a *Spinosaurus*
b *Aegyptosaurus*
c *Ouranosaurus*

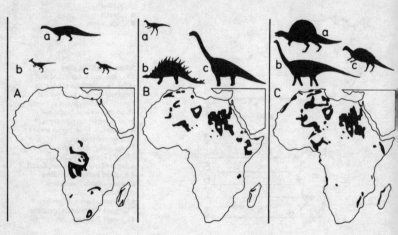

Lapparent and Philippe Taquet have studied dinosaurs that once ranged what are now the hot and arid Sahara Desert, the Atlas Mountains of Morocco, and the great offshore island of Madagascar.

Africa's richest treasury of fossil dinosaurs was found at Tendaguru Hill, now in Tanzania. From 1909 to 1912, German expeditions led by Werner Janensch paid up to 500 Africans at a time to dig pits from which they rescued many thousand bones. Their haul included mighty sauropods like *Brachiosaurus* and *Dicraeosaurus*, the plated dinosaur *Kentrosaurus*, and smaller dinosaurs. Most were Late Jurassic relatives of dinosaurs already known from North America. The dinosaurs appeared to have lived and died near a rivermouth. Floods might have drowned them, then washed their corpses onto mudbanks where their bones were buried and preserved. All told, collectors shipped to Germany 1000 boxes of fossils, totaling 250 tons.

©DIAGRAM

O Triassic
● Jurassic
■ Cretaceous

Selected African sites
Numbers indicate nations with Mesozoic rocks where people have found fossil dinosaurs. Three kinds of symbol show finds from the three periods of the Mesozoic Era. (Some "Triassic" sites may date from Jurassic times.)
1 Morocco (mainly in the Atlas Mountains)
2 Algeria (in the Atlas Mountains and Sahara Desert)
3 Tunisia (Sahara Desert)
4 Egypt (Sahara Desert)
5 Niger (Sahara Desert)
6 Kenya
7 Tanzania (the Jurassic site is Tendaguru)
8 Madagascar
9 Zimbabwe
10 Lesotho (Stormberg Formation)
11 South Africa (Stormberg and other formations)

233

Dinosaurs from India

Early in the Age of Dinosaurs, the Indian subcontinent formed a crossroads within the southern supercontinent Gondwanaland. Later, it broke away from Africa and Antarctica to form a great island heading for collision with Asia. When that cruise began and ended is a mystery that fossil dinosaurs may help to solve, for island animals tend to evolve unlike their mainland relatives.

Fossil finds suggest that India's great voyage had not started early in the Age of Dinosaurs. This evidence emerged in 1960 when scientists found the great bones of a big, unknown sauropod near Kota in central India. *Barapasaurus*, as the animal was later named, had a strange, primitive type of body and ranks among the earliest sauropods discovered anywhere. Its finding proves that India had not yet broken away before the sauropods appeared, by early in Jurassic times.

A great time gap separates *Barapasaurus* from most dinosaurs that have been found in India. Their bones have come mainly from Late Cretaceous beds of rock buried long ago by the sheets of lava that

Mesozoic India
Three maps show main areas of exposed Mesozoic rocks in the subcontinent. Dinosaurs above a map lived when the rocks it shows were formed. Some rocks that developed under seas hold no fossil bones of dinosaurs. Some rock outcrops are too small to be shown here.
A Triassic Period
B Jurassic Period
a *Barapasaurus*
C Cretaceous Period
a *Antarctosaurus*
b *Indosuchus*
c *Jubbulpuria*

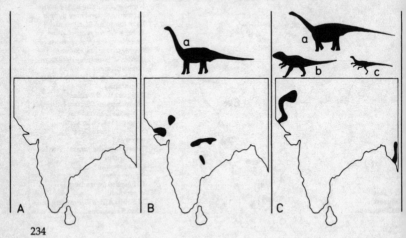

234

now cover much of central India. River valleys cutting through the lava have exposed these older fossil-bearing beds beneath.

Scientists began finding Late Cretaceous fossil dinosaurs as long ago as 1860. By 1920 collectors had unearthed scanty remains of huge carnivorous brutes like *Indosuchus,* nimble coelurosaurs, great sauropods, and an armored dinosaur.

Since 1860, Late Cretaceous dinosaurs have also been discovered in the rocks of southern India. From here come relics of a bulky megalosaurid, massive limb bones of titanosaurid sauropods, and *Dravidosaurus,* a plated dinosaur that survived long after all others of its family had seemingly become extinct. It is possible that reptiles capable of killing off the stegosaurids evolved elsewhere but could not invade island India. Yet this notion seems at odds with finds of almost identical Late Cretaceous sauropods in India and South America. If Late Cretaceous India were still an island, how could these dinosaurs appear in lands so far apart? There seems no easy answer.

Indian sites
The map of the Indian subcontinent (below left) shows selected sites where dinosaurs have been discovered. Symbols show the periods that the sites represent. Some symbols stand for beds of fossil bones, some for isolated finds.
1 Jabalpur (Lameta Formation)
2 Pisdura
3 Kota (Kota Formation)
4 Ariyalur
5 Tiruchirapalli
An enlargement (below) of the area inside the rectangle shows Jurassic sites near Kota, home of the sauropod *Barapasaurus.*

©DIAGRAM

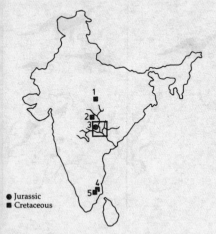

● Jurassic
■ Cretaceous

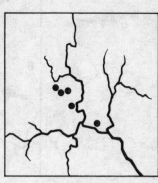

235

Dinosaurs from Australasia

Until recently, Australia had produced few fossil dinosaurs, and New Zealand none. What finds there were had largely been the chance discoveries of stockmen or miners. By the 1980s, though, fossil-hunters were systematically unearthing bones.

Of the early dinosaurs at least one kind of prosauropod reached Australia – migrating overland across Antarctica from South America, Africa, or India, when all these lands were joined. Also, only one Jurassic dinosaur – a sauropod – has been described. But scientists now know that a veritable zoo of dinosaurs inhabited eastern Australia early in Cretaceous times. Many left their bones in what are now Queensland's level grasslands. From that state come the primitive sauropod *Austrosaurus*; the giant Hughenden sauropod; small, armored *Minmi*; and the big ornithischian biped *Muttaburrasaurus*.

Because southeast Australia lay near the South Pole in Cretaceous times, some people thought it must

Mesozoic Australia
Three maps of Australia show the main areas of exposed Mesozoic rocks. Dinosaurs pictured above a map lived when the rocks it shows were being formed. Some rocks that developed under the sea hold no fossil bones of dinosaurs, and some rock outcrops are too small to appear on these maps.
A Triassic Period
a *Thecodontosaurus*
B Jurassic Period
a *Rhoetosaurus*
C Cretaceous Period
a *Austrosaurus*
b *Muttaburrasaurus*
c *Minmi*

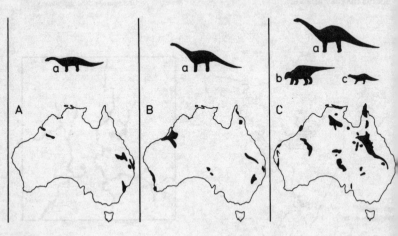

have been too cold for dinosaurs. But by the early 1980s collectors had taken scores of fossil bones from the gray-green sea cliffs of Cape Paterson and nearby tracts of coast. Remains of those dinosaur "gazelles," the hypsilophodontids, proved surprisingly abundant here, and there were traces of a big allosaurid carnosaur. This find suggests some dinosaurs were still migrating to Australia in the Cretaceous Period.

The survival of the old-fashioned sauropod *Austrosaurus* hints at a barrier shutting out those competitors that would have wiped it out. This barrier may have been the three-month polar night that stopped use of the route across Antarctica to Australia before Australia became an island.

A startling clue to more long-lost links between Australia and other lands appeared in 1980. That year Queensland Museum's Ralph Molnar described a tail bone of a theropod – the first dinosaur discovered in New Zealand.

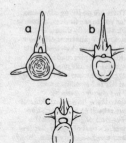

© DIAGRAM

A New Zealand dinosaur (above) Here we show end-on views of tail bones from three animals living in Mesozoic times.
a Mosasaur (a sea lizard)
b Theropod dinosaur
c Late Cretaceous creature from New Zealand's North Island. This resembles (**b**) but not (**a**) or any other Mesozoic bone except perhaps an ornithopod dinosaur's. The bone's owner was probably a theropod (flesh-eating dinosaur) 13ft (4m) long and weighing nearly half a ton. (Illustrations after Molnar.)

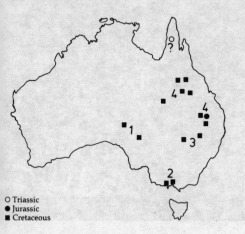

Australian sites (left)
This map pictures sites of finds of fossil dinosaurs. Symbols show the periods they come from. Most symbols stand for isolated finds; a few represent beds of fossils. States where dinosaurs have been discovered are:
1 South Australia
2 Victoria
3 New South Wales
4 Queensland
The location of northern Queensland's important Triassic site is now unknown. Not shown on the map are sites of fossil dinosaur tracks in Queensland and Western Australia.

○ Triassic
● Jurassic
■ Cretaceous

237

CHAPTER 6

DINOSAURS DISPLAYED

There are no living dinosaurs for you to see (unless, of course, birds are really dinosaurs); but dozens of museums can show you dinosaur skeletons, casts (lifesize copies made from molds), lifelike models, fossil eggs, footprints, and paintings of life in Mesozoic times. This chapter starts by describing how fossil skeletons are rebuilt to be put on show. The next pages describe the world's best dinosaur displays, and mention many more. Some are not always open to the public; also many fossils are not shown but kept in store for scientific study. Check access before a visit. Remember that displays may change – and so may the labels as research continues and some dinosaurs are renamed.

These first-ever lifesize restorations of dinosaurs and other prehistoric monsters took shape in 1853 in the studio of British sculptor Benjamin Waterhouse Hawkins. His weird concrete model of an *Iguanodon* (the big beast in the middle) stands in London's Crystal Palace Park. Illustration from *London Illustrated News*, 1853.

238

Cleaning and restoring fossils

One museum displays jumbled, broken fossil bones embedded in a slab of rock. The label simply says: "Dinosaur kit – assembly is required."

Tasks like this take months or even years. First, laboratory technicians may have to soak, saw, and slice away the plaster bandages packed around the rock by the hunter who discovered it. Technicians harden weak areas of exposed bone with special chemical solutions. Then they peck away hard rock with hammer and chisel, first cushioning the slab to stop blows shattering its fossils.

Power tools often speed up the work. Experts may use dental drills armed with fast-revolving diamond cutting wheels, grinding burrs, or wire brushes. Pneumatic "power pens" with vibrating tungsten points eat through rock like cheese, as do jets of gas containing an abrasive powder. Preparators have also freed fossil bones by soaking the rock in dilute acetic acid. And sewing needles are best for

In the museum laboratory
Four laboratory workers here prepare dinosaur remains for exhibition:
A Cutting away a protective plaster jacket surrounding fossil bone
B Cleaning fragile pieces of bone with an electrically powered tool
C Cleaning a mold made by the impression of a fossil skull in glass fiber
D Mounting a *Hypsilophodon* skeleton on slender metal supports

cleaning very fragile skulls.

Once most of a skeleton has been recovered, anatomists can work out how the bones were once joined. Technicians may then rebuild the skeleton in lifelike pose. Hip girdle, skull, ribs, limb bones, breastbone, bones of neck, back, and tail may need fixing in a special order, with missing pieces rebuilt in glass fiber. Big bones are hung by ropes from beams as workers build wooden scaffolding to hold them in position. Next, workers support these jointed bones with metal rods or pipes, bent to fit and fastened to the bones by metal clips. Finally, the scaffolding is taken away. Museum visitors can see almost all parts of the skeleton exposed.

Museums often produce lifesize copies of such skeletons. They make plaster *molds* of the bones and fill these with glass fiber to form *casts.* A museum can exchange such casts with other museums for specimens it lacks.

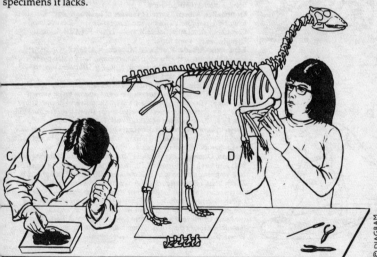

Museum displays 1

Many museums around the world show dinosaur fossils, casts, or models. These six pages name more than 70 museums with exhibits from the Age of Dinosaurs. Many museum directors have kindly sent us information. Museums are listed here in alphabetical order of country and then city.

ARGENTINA
La Plata: Museum of La Plata University   Mostly dinosaurs found in Argentina. Other items include a skull of the horned dinosaur *Centrosaurus* and a cast of *Diplodocus*.
AUSTRALIA
Fortitude Valley, Queensland: Queensland Museum   On show are the remains of the sauropod *Rhoetosaurus*.
AUSTRIA
Vienna: Natural History Museum   Items include remains of the small armored dinosaur *Struthiosaurus*.
BELGIUM

a

Brussels: Royal Institute of Natural Sciences   On show: the world's best and biggest collection of skeletons of *Iguanodon* – 11 mounted, 20 still embedded in rock from a Belgian coalmine.
CANADA
Calgary, Alberta: Zoological Gardens   An outdoor park has 50 lifesize models of dinosaurs.
Drumheller, Alberta: Tyrrell Museum of Palaeontology   On show from 1985: impressive fossils and restorations of Alberta's Late Cretaceous dinosaurs. Some dinosaurs have been displayed in Drumheller for some time.
Edmonton, Alberta: Provincial Museum of Alberta   On show: partial skeleton of the duckbill *Lambeosaurus* (**a**); lifesize models of the duckbill *Corythosaurus*, the ostrich dinosaur *Struthiomimus*, the armored dinosaur *Ankylosaurus*.
Ottawa, Ontario: National Museum of Natural Sciences   On show are Late Cretaceous dinosaurs of western Canada: finest known skeletons of the horned dinosaurs *Styracosaurus* and *Anchiceratops* plus *Leptoceratops*, in stages of restoration; *Triceratops*; the duckbills *Brachylophosaurus*, *Edmontosaurus*, and *Hypacrosaurus*; *Thescelosaurus*; the ostrich dinosaur *Dromiceiomimus*; the carnosaur *Daspletosaurus*; a *Euoplocephalus* tail club; a fine lifesize model of the small theropod *Stenonychosaurus* (**b**).

b

Toronto, Ontario: Royal Ontario Museum   Canada's largest public museum has a three-roomed Dinosaur Gallery displaying mostly free-standing skeletons of 13 dinosaurs with natural backgrounds. Room 1 has a *Camptosaurus*, and two *Allosaurus* attacking a *Stegosaurus* – all from Late Jurassic Utah. Room 2 has a carnosaur (*Albertosaurus*), the duckbills *Parasaurolophus*, *Lambeosaurus*, and *Corythosaurus*, the horned dinosaur *Chasmosaurus*, and the ostrich dinosaur *Ornithomimus* – all from Late Cretaceous Alberta. Room 3 has more Alberta duckbills: *Edmontosaurus* (*Anatosaurus*), *Prosaurolophus*, and *Hadrosaurus* (*Kritosaurus*).

CHINA

Peking: Peking Natural History Museum   On show are five skeletons of Chinese dinosaurs: the prosauropod *Lufengosaurus*, the sauropod *Mamenchisaurus*, the carnosaur *Yangchuanosaurus*, the huge duckbill *Shantungosaurus* (**c**), and the "parrot lizard" *Psittacosaurus*. Some other Chinese museums (notably at Shanghai and Chungking) show dinosaurs.

FRANCE

Paris: National Museum of Natural History   Contains fossil dinosaurs and casts from Europe, Africa, Asia, and North America. On show: fossils of the sauropods *Bothriospondylus* and *Rebbachisaurus*, the iguanodontid *Mochlodon* (*Rhabdodon*), and *Triceratops*; fossil eggs of *Hypselosaurus* and *Protoceratops*; casts of *Allosaurus, Compsognathus, Diplodocus, Iguanodon,* and *Tarbosaurus*. In store: fossils, including some to be displayed.

GERMANY (EAST)

East Berlin: Natural History Museum, Humboldt University   On show: impressive skeletons from Late Jurassic Tanzania – the sauropods *Dicraeosaurus* and *Brachiosaurus* (the world's largest mounted dinosaur skeleton, **d**); the ostrich dinosaur *Elaphrosaurus*; the hypsilophodontid *Dryosaurus* (*Dysalotosaurus*); the plated dinosaur *Kentrosaurus*; the "bird dinosaur" *Archaeopteryx*.

GERMANY (WEST)

Frankfurt am Main: Senckenberg Natural History Museum   Contains fossil dinosaurs from Europe, Africa, Asia, and North America. On show here are: a *Diplodocus*; skeletons of the prosauropod *Plateosaurus*; a mummified duckbill – Europe's only *Edmontosaurus* (*Anatosaurus*); skulls of *Triceratops*; skull casts of *Tyrannosaurus* and *Protoceratops*; skeleton cast of *Iguanodon*. To come: casts of complete skeletons of *Triceratops* and *Stegosaurus*.

Munich: Bavarian State Institute for Paleontology and Historical Geography   Contains the original *Compsognathus* skeleton.

Stuttgart: State Museum for Natural History   On show from 1985: four to six *Plateosaurus* skeletons. In store: important early German dinosaurs (some unique) and Jurassic dinosaurs from Tanzania.

Tübingen: Institute and Museum for Geology and Paleontology   On show: skeletons of the prosauropod *Plateosaurus* and the plated dinosaur *Kentrosaurus*; parts of a *Diplodocus* and *Protoceratops*; complete casts of a *Coelophysis* and *Hypsilophodon*; skull casts of *Tyrannosaurus* and *Iguanodon*.

INDIA

Calcutta: Geology Museum, Indian Statistical Institute   The prize item is the only mounted skeleton of the strange early sauropod *Barapasaurus* (**e**).

ITALY

Bologna: G. Capellini Museum   Includes a cast of *Diplodocus*.

JAPAN

Tokyo: National Science Museum   This has a permanent display of dinosaurs. (In 1981 Tokyo mounted a spectacular show of Chinese dinosaurs including the plated *Tuojiangosaurus*.)

MEXICO

Mexico City: Natural History Museum   Items include a cast of the sauropod *Diplodocus*.

©DIAGRAM

243

Museum displays 2

MONGOLIA
Ulan-Bator: State Central Museum   This museum's Gobi Desert dinosaurs include the carnosaur *Tarbosaurus*.
MOROCCO
Rabat: Museum of Earth Sciences   When completed, this will include the world's largest known *Cetiosaurus* skeleton.
NIGER
Niamey: National Museum   Here is a complete skeleton of the strange, sail-backed iguanodontid *Ouranosaurus*.
POLAND
Warsaw: Paleobiology Institute, Academy of Sciences   Impressive Mongolian dinosaurs are studied here but rarely displayed.
SOUTH AFRICA
Cape Town: South African Museum   This shows remains of important early dinosaurs: a skeleton of the prosauropod *Massospondylus* and a skull of the ornithopod *Heterodontosaurus*.
SPAIN
Madrid: Natural Science Museum   Includes a cast of *Diplodocus*.
SWEDEN
Uppsala: Paleontological Museum, Uppsala University   Chinese dinosaurs collected by Scandinavian fossil hunters include the sauropod *Euhelopus*.
UNITED KINGDOM
Cambridge: Sedgwick Museum, Cambridge University   Contains partial remains of some British dinosaurs.
Elgin, Scotland: Elgin Museum   Includes remains of Scotland's Early Mesozoic reptiles.
Dorchester: Dorchester Museum   Contains numerous dinosaur footprints, not all displayed.
Glasgow, Scotland: Hunterian Museum   Includes dinosaur footprints and a *Triceratops* skull.
Ipswich, Suffolk: Ipswich Museum   Contains a few teeth, bones, and footprints.
Leicester: New Walk Museum   Has four *Cetiosaurus* vertebrae.
London: British Museum (Natural History)   Possesses fossil dinosaurs and/or casts from North America, Europe, and Central Asia. On show: *Iguanodon* and *Hypsilophodon* (a) skeletons from Southern England; fossil skin of a *Euoplocephalus (Scolosaurus)*; casts of *Diplodocus* (b), *Gallimimus*, and *Triceratops*, and of *Protoceratops* eggs. In store: one of the world's greatest collections of fossil dinosaurs, some unique.
London: Crystal Palace Park   Outdoor, lifesize, inaccurate but fascinating models of dinosaurs completed in 1854.
Maidstone: Maidstone Museum   On show: *Iguanodon* bones and a related display.
Oxford: University Museum   Shown or stored: remains of the carnosaurs *Megalosaurus*, *Metriacanthosaurus*, and *Eustreptospondylus* (Europe's most complete theropod); the sauropod *Cetiosaurus*; the only known English *Camptosaurus*; the stegosaur *Dacentrurus* (*Omosaurus*); cast of an *Iguanodon*.
Sandown, Isle of Wight: Museum of Isle of Wight Geology   Houses a partial skull of *Yaverlandia*, the oldest-known boneheaded dinosaur. On show are footprints of *Iguanodon* and of a megalosaurid.

UNITED STATES OF AMERICA

Amherst, Massachusetts: Amherst College   Here is the first described specimen of the prosauropod *Anchisaurus*.

Austin, Texas: Texas Memorial Museum   Includes Mesozoic fossils.

Berkeley, California: University of California Museum of Paleontology   This has Triassic reptiles and *Dilophosaurus*.

Boulder, Colorado: University Natural History Museum   Includes Jurassic dinosaur remains.

Buffalo, New York: Buffalo Museum of Science   Contains: the skeleton of a young *Allosaurus*; casts of a *Triceratops* and *Psittacosaurus*; a *Hypselosaurus* egg; various bones, skin impressions, teeth, tracks, and gastroliths ("gizzard stones").

Cambridge, Massachusetts: Museum of Comparative Zoology, Harvard University   This has North America's best collection of early Mesozoic South American reptiles (including *Staurikosaurus*); a *Scutellosaurus*; Late Cretaceous fossils from Montana.

Canyon, Texas: Panhandle Plains Historical Museum   On view: local Triassic reptiles pre-dating dinosaurs.

Chicago, Illinois: Field Museum of Natural History   Includes: skeletons of an *Albertosaurus* and its *Lambeosaurus* "victim"; an *Apatosaurus* and a *Protoceratops*; skulls of horned dinosaurs, a duckbill, and a *Diplodocus* (cast); also theropod tracks (c).

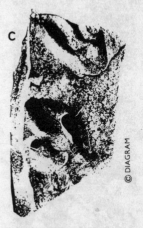

Cincinnati, Ohio: University of Cincinnati   Items include sauropod and stegosaur bones.

Cleveland, Ohio: Natural History Museum   Best known for early fishes, pre-dating dinosaurs. On show: the world's only mounted skeleton of *Haplocanthosaurus*.

Denver, Colorado: Denver Museum of Natural History   Skeletons on show: *Diplodocus*, *Stegosaurus* (one of the best preserved specimens), *Tyrannosaurus* (cast), and *Edmontosaurus* (*Anatosaurus*).

Durham, North Carolina: North Carolina Museum   The collection includes sauropod bones.

East Lansing, Michigan: The Museum, Michigan State University   A big walk-through Hall of Life includes fossils and wall paintings of Mesozoic reptiles.

Flagstaff, Arizona: Museum of Northern Arizona   Items include the early ornithopod *Scutellosaurus*.

Hays, Kansas: Sternberg Memorial Museum   Its local Cretaceous fossils include toothed birds.

Houston, Texas: Houston Museum of Natural Science   Exhibits include much of a *Diplodocus* skeleton.

Jensen, Utah: Dinosaur National Monument   These 206,000 acres of fossil-rich canyons include a covered Quarry Visitor Center where spectators view technicians revealing 2000 dinosaur bones embedded in this former Carnegie Quarry (d). Late Jurassic fossils found here include: the carnosaurs *Allosaurus* and *Ceratosaurus*; the sauropods *Apatosaurus*, *Camarasaurus*, and *Diplodocus*; the ornithopods *Camptosaurus* and *Dryosaurus*; the plated *Stegosaurus*, of which the smallest known specimen is on display.

Laramie, Wyoming: W.H. Reed Museum   Exhibits include part of a sauropod, *Apatosaurus*.

Museum displays 3

Lawrence, Kansas: University of Kansas Museum of Natural History Includes Mesozoic fossils.

Lincoln, Nebraska: University of Nebraska State Museum Exhibits here place the emphasis on mammals.

Los Angeles, California: Los Angeles County Museum of Natural History Displays include skeletons of five kinds of dinosaur: the flesh-eater *Dilophosaurus*; an *Allosaurus* as if attacking a *Camptosaurus*; and the duckbills *Corythosaurus* and *Edmontosaurus (Anatosaurus)*. There are also skulls of *Tyrannosaurus* (finely preserved) and *Parasaurolophus*.

Newark, Delaware: University of Delaware The collection includes sauropod remains.

New Haven, Connecticut: Peabody Museum of Natural History, Yale University Pioneered by Othniel Charles Marsh, this museum features many important type specimens (first of their kind to be described). It includes an *Allosaurus (Antrodemus)* skull; skeletons of the sauropods *Apatosaurus* and *Camarasaurus*; skeletons of the ornithopods *Othnielia (Laosaurus)*, *Tenontosaurus*, *Camptosaurus*, *Claosaurus*, and *Edmontosaurus (Anatosaurus)*; skeletons of *Stegosaurus* and *Monoclonius*; skulls of the horned dinosaurs *Chasmosaurus*, *Torosaurus*, and *Triceratops*; and various casts.

New York City, New York: American Museum of Natural History This has the world's largest dinosaur collection, with a wealth of skeletons and skulls of North American dinosaurs, also fossil tracks, skin impressions, and eggs(**a**). There are complete skeletons of the following dinosaurs: the coelurosaurs *Coelophysis*, *Ornitholestes*, and *Struthiomimus*; the carnosaurs *Albertosaurus*, *Allosaurus*, and *Tyrannosaurus*; the prosauropod *Plateosaurus*; the sauropod *Apatosaurus*; the ornithopods *Camptosaurus*, *Corythosaurus (Procheneosaurus)* (adult and young), *Edmontosaurus (Anatosaurus)* (mummy), "*Edmontosaurus (Anatosaurus) copei*," *Lambeosaurus* (young), and *Saurolophus*; the plated dinosaur *Stegosaurus*; the armored dinosaur *Panoplosaurus*; and the horned dinosaurs *Monoclonius*, *Montanoceratops*, *Protoceratops*, *Psittacosaurus*, *Styracosaurus* (**b**), and *Triceratops*.

a

b

© DIAGRAM

**Norman, Oklahoma: Stovall Museum, University of
Oklahoma**   Fossils include *Acrocanthosaurus* remains.
Peoria, Illinois: Lakeside Museum and Art Center   This includes
sauropod remains.
Philadelphia, Pennsylvania: Academy of Natural Sciences   This
holds remains of some of the first dinosaurs found in North America
and a *Corythosaurus* (**c**).
Pittsburgh, Pennsylvania: Carnegie Museum of Natural History
The Mesozoic Hall has some of the world's best specimens of Late
Jurassic dinosaurs, with 10 skeletons: the carnosaurs *Allosaurus* and
Tyrannosaurus; the sauropods *Apatosaurus*, *Camarasaurus*, and
Diplodocus; the ornithopods *Camptosaurus*, *Corythosaurus*, and
Dryosaurus; the horned dinosaur *Protoceratops*; and the plated
Stegosaurus. There are also five skulls, plaster casts, and scores of
stored bones.

Pittsburgh, Pennsylvania: Duquesne University   Items include
isolated *Apatosaurus* bones.
**Princeton, New Jersey: Museum of Natural History, Princeton
University**   This includes a show of Late Cretaceous dinosaurs and
Triassic footprints.
St Paul, Minnesota: The Science Museum of Minnesota   Local
(non-dinosaur) Cretaceous fossils include those of the prehistoric
reptiles champsosaurs.
Salt Lake City, Utah: Utah Museum of Natural History   Here are
two *Allosaurus* and a *Camptosaurus* from Emery County's Cleveland-
Lloyd Quarry (source of 10,000 dinosaur bones), plus a
Parasaurolophus.
San Francisco, California: California Academy of Science   Items
held include isolated sauropod bones.
San Francisco, California: Junior Museum   Items include isolated
sauropod bones.
Scranton, Pennsylvania: Everart Museum   Exhibits include spinal
bones of a *Camarasaurus*.
Vernal, Utah: Utah Natural History State Museum   This has a
Diplodocus skeleton and cast.
**Washington, DC: National Museum of Natural History, Smithsonian
Institution**   This has a fine collection of displayed skeletons, and
stores many type specimens. The renovated Dinosaur Hall reopened
in 1981. National Museum specimens include the following (all from
North America): the carnosaurs *Albertosaurus*, *Allosaurus*,
Dilophosaurus, and *Tyrannosaurus*; the sauropods *Camarasaurus* and
Diplodocus; the ornithopods *Camptosaurus*, *Corythosaurus*,
Edmontosaurus, *Maiasaura*, and *Thescelosaurus*; also *Stegosaurus* (**d**) and
the horned *Brachyceratops* and *Triceratops*.
USSR
Leningrad: Central Geological and Prospecting Museum   Items
include the duckbill *Mandschurosaurus*. There is also a cast of the
sauropod *Diplodocus*.
Moscow: Paleontological Museum   An impressive show features
five skeletons of the Mongolian carnosaur *Tarbosaurus*.

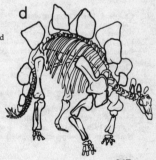

247

FURTHER READING

General

Charig, A.J. *A New Look at the Dinosaurs* Heinemann, 1979
Colbert, E.H. *Dinosaurs: Their Discovery and Their World* Dutton, USA 1962; Hutchinson, UK 1962
Halstead, L.B. *The Evolution and Ecology of the Dinosaurs* Peter Lowe, 1975
Lambert, D. *Dinosaurs* Crown, 1978
Moody, R.T.J. *A Natural History of Dinosaurs* Hamlyn, 1977
Steel, R. and Harvey, A.P. (editors) *The Encyclopaedia of Prehistoric Life* Mitchell Beazley, 1979
Swinton, W.E. *The Dinosaurs* Allen & Unwin, 1970
Tweedie, M. *The World of Dinosaurs* Weidenfeld & Nicolson, 1977
Note: News of major dinosaur discoveries appears in serious newspapers, and in science magazines such as *Nature*, but many finds are published in specialist journals. Special bibliographies list articles from these. Journals and bibliographies can be seen in some science libraries.

Chapter 1: What were the dinosaurs?

Desmond, A.J. *The Hot-blooded Dinosaurs* Blond & Briggs, 1975
Stout, W. *The Dinosaurs* Bantam Books, 1981
Thomas, D.K. and Olson, E.C. (editors) *A Cold Look at the Warm-blooded Dinosaurs* Westview Press, 1980

Chapter 2: Making of the dinosaurs

Colbert, E.H. *Evolution of the Vertebrates* Wiley, 1980
Cox, C.B. *Prehistoric Animals* Hamlyn, 1969
Moody, R. *Prehistoric World* Chartwell Books, 1980
Romer, A.S. *Vertebrate Paleontology* University of Chicago Press, 1966

Chapter 3: Dinosaurs identified

Glut, D.F. *The Dinosaur Dictionary* Citadel Press, 1982
Halstead, L.B. and J. *Dinosaurs* Blandford, 1981
Olshevsky, G. *Mesozoic Meanderings No.1* G & T, 1978 (Updated lists of all dinosaur families, genera, species, plus synonyms. Available by mail from George Olshevsky, PO Box 11021, San Diego, California, USA.)
Steel, R. (ed. O. Kuhn) *Handbuch der Paläoherpetologie, Vols 14, 15* (English edition) Fischer Verlag, 1969
Bibliography of Fossil Vertebrates American Geological Institute and The Society of Vertebrate Paleontology
Bibliography of Vertebrate Paleontology Geosystems, 1973–1978
Bulletin Signalétique, Section 227 Paléontologie Centre Nationale de la Recherche Scientifique

Chapter 4: Their changing world

Calder, N. *The Comet is Coming* BBC Publications, UK 1980; Viking Press, USA 1981
Colbert, E.H. *Wandering Lands and Animals* Dutton, USA 1973; Hutchinson, UK 1974
Kurtén, B. *The Age of Dinosaurs* Weidenfeld & Nicolson, 1968
Russell, D.A. *A Vanished World* National Museums of Canada, 1977

Chapter 5: Discovering dinosaurs

Colbert, E.H. *Men and Dinosaurs: The Search in Field and Laboratory* Dutton, USA 1968; Evans, UK 1968
Kielan-Jaworowska, Z. *Hunting for Dinosaurs* MIT Press, 1969

Chapter 6: Dinosaurs displayed

Rixon, A.E. *Fossil Animal Remains: Their Preparation and Their Conservation* Humanities Press, 1976
Note: Many museums issue booklets about their fossil collections.

248

INDEX

Notes:
1) Bold figures indicate key entries, where terms are defined and subjects described in detail.
2) Dinosaur names that are no longer used by scientists are followed by the sign = and by the name now used instead. (Scientists stop using a name if they find it describes an animal already given another name.)

A
Aachenosaurus 216
Abrictosaurus **142**, 143
Acanthopholis 178, **180**
Acrocanthosaurus 84, **85**
Adasaurus 61, **62**
Aegyptosaurus 124, **125**, 232

Aepisaurus 124, **125**
Aetonyx = Massospondylus
Africa, fossils in 214, **232–233**, 234, 236
  in Mesozoic Era 200–201
  (see also maps in Chapter 3, and national entries in index)
Agathaumas **193**
Agrosaurus = Thecodontosaurus
Alamosaurus 124, **125**
Albertosaurus 72, 86, **87**, 89, 242, 245–247
Alectrosaurus 86, **87**
Algeria, carnosaurs in 76
  coelurosaurs in 56
  fossils in 233
  sauropods in 116
Algoasaurus 124, **125**
Alioramus 86, **87**
Allosaurid (-ae, -s) 32, **80**, 81–82, 205, 237
Allosaurus 76–77, **80**, 81–82, 93, 205, 220–221, 231, 242–243, 245–247
Alocodon 144, **145**
Altispinax 84, **85**
Ameghino, Carlos 230
Ameghino, Florentino 230
Ammosaurus **102**
Amphibians 26–28, 208
Amphicoelias 130, **131**
Amphisaurus = Anchisaurus
Amtosaurus **184**, 185
Amygdalodon 113, **114**, 115
Anapsids 28–29
Anatosaurus = Edmontosaurus
Anchiceratops 189, **192**, 193, 206, 242
Anchisaurid (-ae, -s) 32, **100**, 101–102
Anchisaurus **100**, 101, 203, 222, 245
Andrews, Roy Chapman 226
Ankylosaur (-ia, -s) 33, 37, 171–173, **178–179**, 180–187
Ankylosaurid (-ae, -s) 33, 178–180, **184**, 185–187, 200, 213
Ankylosaurus 15, 178–179, **184**, 185, 242
Anodontosaurus = Euoplocephalus
Anoplosaurus **152**
Antarctica, fossils in 210
  in Mesozoic Era 200–201, 234, 236–237
Antarctosaurus 124, **126**, 234

Anthodon = Paranthodon
Antrodemus = Allosaurus
Apatodon = Allosaurus
Apatosaurus 130, **131**, 221, 245–247
Aralosaurus 156–157, **160**
Archaeopterygid (-ae, -s) 32, 39–40, **52**, 53
Archaeopteryx 39, 49, 51, **52**, 53, 224, 243
Archaeornis = Archeopteryx
Archaeornithomimus 54, **56**
Archosaur (-ia, s) **29**, 31–32, 203
Arctic Circle, ornithopods in 92, 152, 159
Arctosaurus **92**
Argentina, carnosaurs in 81, 93
  coelurosaurs in 48
  fossils in 230–231
  museums in 125, 242
  ornithopods in 143, 146, 162–163
  prosauropods in 99, 102, 104–105
  sauropods in 114–115, 126, 128, 134–135
Argyrosaurus 124, **126**
Aristosaurus **102**
Aristosuchus 44, **45**
Armored dinosaurs 37, 172, **178–179**, 207, 225, 227, 231, 235, 242, 246
  (see also Ankylosaurs)
Arrhinoceratops 189, **192**, 193
Asia, fossils in 223, **226–227**, 228–229, 234, 243–244
  in Mesozoic Era 200–201
  (see also maps in Chapter 3, and national entries in index)
Asiamerica 200–201
Asiatosaurus **121**, 228
Astrodon **116**, 119
Atlantic Ocean 200–201
Atlantosaurus **134**
Aublysodon = Albertosaurus
Australia, carnosaurs in 81, 93
  coelurosaurs in 46
  fossils in **236–237**
  four-legged ornithischians 181
  in Mesozoic Era 200–201
  museums in 242
  ornithopods in 145, 154
  prosauropods in 100–101
  sauropods in 114–115, 118

251